121
110 Imipramine

All about Drugs

179 Cocane chemical name

Everyday Handbooks

All about Drugs

Franz Bergel
and D. R. A. Davies

with the collaboration of
Peter Ford

BARNES & NOBLE, INC. • NEW YORK
Publishers • Booksellers • Since 1873

First published 1970
By Thomas Nelson and Sons, Ltd.

Copyright ©1970 by Franz Bergel and D. R. A. Davies

Reprinted, 1972 by
Barnes & Noble, Inc. by special
arrangement with Thomas Nelson and Sons, Ltd.

L. C. Catalog Card Number: 71-149829

SBN 389 00324 7

Printed in the United States of America

Contents

PREFACE   ix
1. Introductory   1
2. Alcohol: the Products of Fermentation   22
3. Cannabis: the Hemp Resins from the East   41
4. Opium, the Opiates, and the Mild Analgesics   63
5. Cocaine and the Coca Leaf   88
6. The Mental Stimulants: Amphetamines and
   Anti-Depressants   99
7. The Sedatives: Tranquillizers and Barbiturates   112
8. The Hallucinogens: LSD and the Products of
   the Sacred Cactus   130
9. Further Enjoyments and Hazards   141
MAIN TEXT REFERENCES   159
APPENDICES   172
INDEX   200

Acknowledgements

We would first like to acknowledge our gratitude to our wives, for their infinite patience; to Senator Cyril Le Marquand, President of the Finance and Economics Committee of the States of Jersey, for permission to publish; as well as to the Medical Officer of Health for Jersey, Dr W. Williams; to the Chief Pharmacist of Jersey General Hospital, Mr Charles W. Harwood; to members of the Jersey States Police; to the staff of the Official Analyst's Laboratory, in particular to Mr S. A. Castledine, Assistant Official Analyst, for invaluable help given during the preparation of this book. We are also indebted to our secretaries for their untiring typing of the early manuscripts, and to the Home Office, H.M. Stationery Office, the Scout Association, and the office of Health Education for assistance with references and literature.

Our task has been greatly eased by practical support from the Bureau of Narcotics and Dangerous Drugs, U.S. Department of Justice, and its Divisional Chief, Mr J. W. Gunn Jr, and the Division of Narcotic Drugs, under S. P. Sotiroff, at the United Nations Office in Geneva, as well as by the ready co-operation of the Librarians of the Royal Society, the Royal Society of Medicine, the Science Library, the Chemical Society, and the Institute of Cancer Research (the Chester Beatty Research Institute), all in London, and the Countway Library, Harvard Medical School, Boston, Mass.

Finally, we would like to acknowledge the encouragement and

wise counsel that has been freely given by Mr A. Lawrence Abel, F.R.C.S., former Chairman of the National Association on Drug Addiction, and an indebtedness to Dr Sidney Farber, Director of the Children's Cancer Research Foundation, Boston, Mass., and his associate, Dr E. J. Modest, for hospitality and practical help as well as various introductions which helped to widen our understanding of the American drug situation, as did conversations with Dr McGary of the State Legislature of the Commonwealth of Massachusetts and personnel of the Boston Branch of the Bureau of Narcotics.

Preface

The problem of drug abuse is hardly exclusive to the twentieth century, and in fact it seems likely that man's experience of drugs in one guise or another may go back almost as far as his earliest beginnings. In its present form, however, it can be seen specifically as a contemporary phenomenon on a world-wide scale: almost a fact of life, closely involved with changing social patterns and the relationship between generations, with the stresses imposed by modern urban conditions, and with the enormous advances in medical science which have created new problems at the same time as they have solved old ones.

In this field it has become increasingly important to recognize that a prejudiced or ignorant opinion helps no one, and there is no doubt whatever that the private obsessions of partisans (pro-drug and anti-drug) have already obscured many of the central issues. The aim of this book is therefore to present as objectively and concisely as possible all the major facts concerning drugs and their different origins and effects in accordance with our current state of knowledge, and to look at the present emphasis of and justification for legislation as it stands in Europe, Britain and the United States.

Inevitably there must be gaps in the account. A fully comprehensive coverage would grow to encyclopedic length, while each individual group of drugs deserves a full-length book in its own right. But today even the specialist is hard-pressed to keep up with the proliferation of papers, pamphlets and authoritative books, and the layman can hardly begin to develop a comprehensively informed view. It is hoped that *All about Drugs* will help to bridge the gap that exists between often highly specialized material and the urgent need for an informed public.

Education is the first priority, freedom and responsibility the ideal, while legislation remains at the best of times only a tool – though unfortunately one upon which society has had to depend more and more in recent times. The present account has been kept concise so as to be readily accessible as much to the concerned parent and teenager as to the layman generally, to those who feel baffled and alarmed by the situation as much as to those who already have an awareness but who would like to extend their area of knowledge. Teachers and educators and members of the medical and legal professions should also find most of the facts they need digested here in a form that will not make too extensive a demand on their already fully occupied time.

To avoid a great many footnotes appearing within the text, the main references have been grouped together at the end of the book, and to avoid creating breaks in the narrative, material that has a strictly technical emphasis has on the whole been collected together in the appendices, where the more technically minded reader may follow it through should he wish. Meanwhile our first objective has remained to do everything possible to clarify a subject that often seems to have as many facets as there are people to look at them.

F.B.
D.R.A.D.
P.F.

Chapter One

Introductory

This book is about a special group of drugs: namely, those which, from a variety of initially attractive psychological and physiological effects, can, and all too often do, lead to the states we know as habituation, addiction, and dependence, and from these to illness, depredation, and even death. Some of them are in active pharmacological use and have a great value to medical practice under controlled conditions. Others, like the barbiturates, remain in wide medical use but have often created special problems through the medical profession's failure to recognize their potential in time. There are also those whose only application is for the 'kicks' they can offer, the sense of a lift from anxiety into euphoria or of hallucination or of a 'new reality' which they produce. The different ways in which these are known to act on the central nervous system, the social and psychological factors involved, will all be discussed fully in the following pages. For the moment it is simply enough to say that what they have in common is the fact that they present society on both local and international levels with problems of great and ever-increasing dimensions.

It has unfortunately become difficult, if not actually impossible, to discuss the problems raised by drug abuse rationally and objectively. The reasons for this are no doubt highly varied. We might indicate, for instance, the often conflicting views of the experts on exactly how undesirable 'soft' as opposed to 'hard' drugs are, to the fact that our knowledge of the way in which these substances work on the brain is still at an early stage, to the inevitable fear within a society of anything that is not understood and which seems to imply a contempt for the *status quo*, and to the persuasive arguments of those who see in drugs a conscious gesture of rejection of a violent, disillusioned world.

The debate in the British House of Commons in 1969 on what has become known as the Wootton Report on cannabis[1] provided a striking example of how the general atmosphere surrounding any discussion of drugs seems to descend almost inevitably into a highly emotional atmosphere, in this case with the Home Secretary himself as well as his opposite number on the opposition benches playing prominent roles. (A more detailed discussion of this whole affair comes in the chapter on cannabis on pp. 56–62.) The authors of this book believe that while legislation has its part to play in the control of drugs and the need to protect vulnerable individuals, legislation on its own can achieve very little in the long run. The real front in the battle against every kind of drug abuse must be at an educational level, involving doctors, teachers, parents, and everyone who comes into contact with the young (perhaps even politicians!). A full understanding and knowledge of what is involved in the multifarious problems of drug abuse is a first essential for anyone who has any connexion with or responsibility in these problems. If we are against the taking of drugs, whether they are 'hard' or 'soft', we must know exactly *why* we are. The phenomenon of drug taking is a reality in Western society today, and often a very damaging one. But the kind of emotively loaded argument based on fear and a highly partial knowledge which we meet with all too often can itself only do harm. It is to be hoped that this book will, in its own way, make a positive contribution towards emphasizing the facts of drug abuse, as opposed to the folklore of which the 'pro' and 'anti' lobbies are equally guilty.

A recent editorial of the *Journal of the American Medical Association*,[2] commenting on the recommendations of a number of highly placed bodies on marijuana or cannabis resin, said that 'like the Vietnam question and the new morality, marijuana is one of the issues in the credibility gap between youth and their elders'. While drugs are by no means a prerogative of the younger generation, as we shall see, the place they occupy in dissension between the generations is an important factor. It is essential that we should develop a full awareness of the underlying features in present-day trends; to both the personal and the more general strains and stresses, the loneliness and alienations under which many people live in our society (and which not every individual is equally equipped to cope with, for whatever reasons). A moral, essentially paternalist standpoint does not seem to be a great deal of help when condemning drug abuse. Simply to tell adolescents that drug-taking is 'wrong' will merely confirm their impression that here is another example of their elders' intolerance of open-mindedness and insensitivity to youthful patterns of thought. They can at the same time, perhaps, point to a mother's dependence on barbiturates or even aspirin, to a father's on alcohol, and hence to a fundamental hypocrisy. Maybe the real answer to the controversy involving alcohol and cannabis is that controls similar to those at present applying to cannabis should also apply to alcohol. It won't happen, of course, and anyway the American experience with Prohibition in the 1930s has shown how banning a drug on which a society has a general dependence can create an even greater disaster. But if it did, it is tempting to imagine how some of the voices raised loudest in protest would belong to those expressing greatest horror at any suggestion that lighter penalties be applied in cases where people were merely smoking as against selling or distributing cannabis. Unfortunately the Wootton Report did not make any differentiation between traffickers and first offenders.

As will be clear, it is essential to define personal attitudes to drug-taking and to be as fully informed as possible on every aspect involved. Until we do this, we cannot claim to be properly equipped to inform and educate young people concerning the very real risks and dangers to psychological and physical health thrown up by the 'drug syndrome', or to demonstrate the false values in fashionable temptations where these exist.

Historically speaking, there is nothing new about mankind's yearning to 'get away from it all', to evade or transform reality. Few can achieve this by mental and spiritual strength alone. From earliest times, men have searched in their environment for natural materials that, when ingested, offer pleasurable and often seemingly magical effects (not to mention dire consequences). Sugar and starch-carrying materials were fermented to give alcoholic beverages; the secretions of poppies and hemp were found to produce agreeable states; alkaloids, present in certain leaves, fruits, and roots, removed pain. Man, looking for food in the first place, stumbled upon new sources of pleasure in the non-lethal but intoxicating products evolved in nature, and used them to relieve the discomfort of his condition as well as props to create hallucinatory visions in the rituals of primitive religious cults. Priests and magicians had for centuries taught their followers and neophytes what the writers and poets of the nineteenth century reported about re-discovered products which, apparently, could take them beyond normal states of mind into new spheres of experience. In 1822 Thomas de Quincey published his *Confessions of an English Opium Eater*,[3] and in 1860 the French poet Baudelaire published *Les Paradis artificiels*.[4] These two books, more than any others, introduced the public of their time to the ethos of drug-taking. Some of the drugs concerned had been known to physicians as remedies against pain and illness for a long while, and as sources of pleasure and escape in many lands for even longer. Was the wave of interest at that time only an aberration on the part of 'degenerate literary bohemians', or was it an actual revival of the kind of drug cult that had been practised over the world through the ages? It is curious how the present interest in drugs and intensification of drug-taking seems to have begun in the

1950s with the publication of Aldous Huxley's two books, *The Doors of Perception* and *Heaven and Hell*.[5]

It seems probable that preoccupation with drugs goes in waves which can be related to prevailing social conditions, reaching heights during periods of upheaval, distress, or change in the cultural and/or political structure of a civilization. In such a situation the individual is subject consciously or subconsciously to a multitude of stresses, and certain people may feel driven to replace or bypass reality through dreams and illusions or by inducing tranquillity or euphoric or psychedelic states. Drugs of abuse will always be likely to find a ready market in these circumstances. Dr James Hemming, however, has expressed the dilemma created by drug experience in these terms:

> The positive incentive to take drugs is to create or recapture . . . heightened states of awareness, but the flaw here is that this particular road to perception is artificially induced – not arising from the personality but imposed upon it – so that the drug-taker may be left with a devastating habit while the perception fades into unrecapturable remoteness.[6]

WHAT IS A DRUG?

The word 'drug'* is popularly associated with two meanings: first, with medicines applied in the treatment of illnesses; secondly, with preparations which, because of the mental states they produce, are consumed occasionally or regularly by numbers of people. These individuals can, after a while, become drug habituates, addicts or dependants. They do not need the drugs for medical reasons, but because they have come to depend on the 'lift' they get from taking them or because the drug has become necessary to stave off withdrawal symptoms. Normally a drug is a substance (not necessarily chemically pure) or compound (analytically pure) which can be introduced into the body by oral, anal, subcutaneous, or intravenous routes, or in the form of an aerosol (smoke or powder) through the mouth or nose; it may be of natural or synthetic origin, and sometimes of a relatively simple, sometimes a complex, chemical structure.

Whether of natural or synthetic origin, all those materials

* It is ironical that the French word, *drogue*, also means 'rubbish' or 'trash'.

which have a biological (physiological or pharmacological) effect either stimulate a normal function in a tissue or organ, or depress or even paralyse such a function. In the hands of doctors or psychiatrists, their therapeutic effects are controlled by carefully calculated doses, though these medicines can become toxic administered in larger doses or taken over long periods. It is not always fully enough appreciated that taking several drugs simultaneously may re-enforce their action, the mixture thus becoming more effective or dangerous than the single constituents. Table 1 shows the main classes of drugs, or, as they are known, 'pharmacotherapeutic agents'.

TABLE 1

THE MAIN TYPES OF PHARMACOTHERAPEUTIC AGENTS OR
DRUGS, AND THEIR PRINCIPAL ACTIONS

Symptomatic	Chemotherapeutic	Restitutional
C.N.S. depressing or stimulating: e.g. opium, morphine, and the other opiates; synthetic analgesics (synopiates); amphetamines and congeners; cocaine.	Used against helminths (worms), protozoa, bacteria. Used against fungi; viruses (including interferons); tumours and leukaemias. Used as anti-hormones; immuno-suppressors.	The proteins; amino-acids, nucleosides, and nucleic acids, etc. The vitamins; minerals, holo- and/or co-enzymes: hormones, immunological products (i.e. vaccines, sera, etc.).
Used to treat mental disorders: tranquillizers, anti-depressants, stimulators, hallucinogens, and euphorics.	Used against fertility (as oral contraceptives).	

Nearly all of the drugs in this book belong to the first column. Symptomatic drugs do not affect the cause of a disease, in contrast to chemotherapeutic agents (column 2), which neutralize or destroy (e.g. bacteriological) invaders. The former only influence the *symptoms* of an illness, such as pain, excitement, depression, faulty blood circulation, and so on. Among them there are those which act on the central nervous system

(C.N.S.), which consists of the brain with its important divisions such as cortex, cerebellum, thalamus and hypothalamus, pons, medulla oblongata, and upper parts of the spinal cord. This fact has, over many years, been established by the physiologist and pharmacologist. Drugs can act on the central nervous system in two main ways: either (1) by depressing, that is, slowing down certain brain functions, or (2) by stimulating them. Also, by a more complex and not yet entirely understood action, they can produce either euphoria (a sense of well-being) and wakefulness, or sleep, anaesthesia, or hallucination. These interactions do not necessarily involve all parts of the nervous system, certain drugs acting selectively on specific parts of the brain and its appendices like the thalamus and hypothalamus (see Fig. 1, page 8).

In recent years, the drugs of dependence which have a traditional medical application have been joined by the new compounds which have revolutionized the treatment of mental disorders. A good number of these (see Table 1, column 1) have also developed into drugs of misuse, and so have expanded widely the possibilities open to the potential and established addict.

While medical scientists have by no means completely explained the biological mechanism behind the action of each single drug, it can be said fairly certainly that some drug-induced depression is caused by a reduction in the supply of oxygen to parts of the brain and the release of biogenic amines, such as noradrenaline, this occurring as a counteraction and consequently leading to an increase in the blood supply in certain areas.

This is an over-simplified picture, meant only to illustrate the kind of effect that drugs have on brain function, since there can and do exist several interesting direct and indirect processes going on side by side. The latter may also involve the 'autonomic nervous system'. This, as its name conveys, controls certain organ and body functions by nerve structures which originate in the spinal cord and by-pass the central controlling forces of the brain. They are thus not registered by the 'thinking' segment. Consequently drugs of dependence, which, with a few

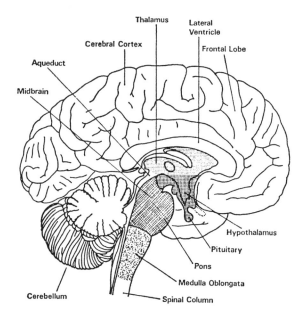

FIG. 1. Diagram of the brain showing the principal areas of the central nervous system on which drugs are thought to act

exceptions, may possess valuable therapeutic properties under medical supervision, can become a scourge and a curse. The disagreeable toxic side-effects may at first obliterate or diminish the effects the drug addict is seeking. He loses the initial enjoyable sensations and acquires instead, especially with hard drugs, something corresponding to the phenomenon of bacterial resistance to antibiotics – tolerance. Also, as he tries to stop taking the drug, he may experience the often horrifying phenomena of abstinence or withdrawal. These are caused by deep-set changes in the biochemistry of body and brain functions, and occur mainly with opiates and amphetamines (see Chapters Four and Six). With these, overdosing up to lethal amounts can occur as the addict adjusts his dose levels. Table 2 illustrates the progression.

TABLE 2

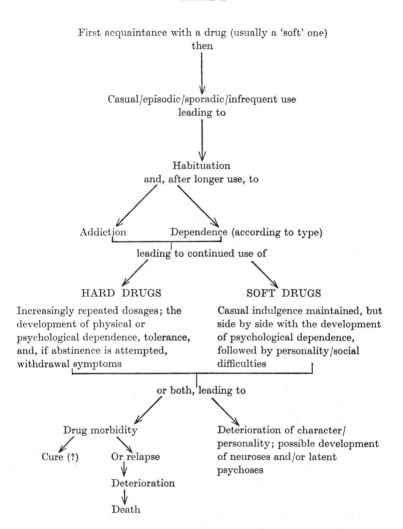

First acquaintance with a drug (usually a 'soft' one)
then

Casual/episodic/sporadic/infrequent use
leading to

Habituation
and, after longer use, to

Addiction   Dependence (according to type)

leading to continued use of

HARD DRUGS   SOFT DRUGS

Increasingly repeated dosages; the   Casual indulgence maintained, but
development of physical or   side by side with the development
psychological dependence, tolerance,   of psychological dependence,
and, if abstinence is attempted,   followed by personality/social
withdrawal symptoms   difficulties

or both, leading to

Drug morbidity   Deterioration of character/
                                  personality; possible development
Cure (?)   Or relapse   of neuroses and/or latent
                                  psychoses
            Deterioration

            Death

This may be thought to give a pessimistic picture, but once
an addict has left the experimental episodic stages behind and
has entered his world of dependence, it is difficult to avoid taking
a sombre view.

HABITUATION, TOLERANCE, ADDICTION AND DEPENDENCE

These terms, so often met with in connexion with drugs, are not easily defined. The World Health Organization has been greatly concerned with the terminology, and in 1955 the Expert Committee on Addiction-Producing Drugs attempted the following definitions:[7]

Drug habituation (*habit*) is a condition resulting from the repeated consumption of a drug. Its characteristics include:
   (1) A desire – but not a compulsion – to continue taking the drug for the sense of improved well-being which it engenders.
   (2) Little or no tendency to increase the dose.
   (3) Some degree of psychic dependence on the effect of the drug, but absence of physical dependence and hence of an abstinence syndrome (withdrawal symptoms).
   (4) Detrimental effects, if any, primarily on the individual.
Drug addiction is a state of periodic or chronic intoxication produced by the repeated consumption of a drug (natural or synthetic). Its characteristics include:
   (1) An overpowering desire or need (compulsion) to continue taking the drug and to obtain it by any means.
   (2) A tendency to increase the dose.
   (3) A psychic (psychological) and generally a physical dependence on the effects of the drug.
   (4) A detrimental effect on the individual and society.

This has not, however, satisfied either experts or laymen.[8] It did not completely rule out confusion, and the two definitions fail to explain completely the terms *tolerance* (defined as a necessity to achieve the same effect by increasing the dose), *withdrawal and abstinence symptoms* (or *syndrome*), *dependence*, and *hard* and *soft* drugs.

By 1964 the Expert Committee,[9] 'after much thought and discussion', produced 'a term covering all kinds of drug abuse'. Although still not a full answer, the phrase *drug dependence* combined with the qualifying expression *of such and such type* (for instance, *drug dependence of the cannabis resin type* or *of the cocaine type*) was introduced. While this nomenclative method is far from ideal, it does cover the narcotics (practically identical with hard drugs and representing in the main opium, morphine, heroin, cocaine) and the soft drugs.

DRUGS AND THE LAW

Any legislation[10] attempting to regulate the practices of
minority groups finds critics and adversaries. As has been said,
the subject of drugs has tended to become a platform in the
rebellion of the younger generation against that of their parents,
and in the demands of the libertarians against the imposition of
authority. In the context of the 'ethics of protest', there are
many voices which still often mistakenly but sincerely attack
measures that, in their view, reduce freedom and threaten
liberty. They are motivated by the conviction, idealistic in
itself, that individuals should exercise responsibility for their
own behaviour and personal destiny. Nevertheless, nothing is
more difficult than to argue a case for legislation by trying in the
first instance to define the social gifts of freedom and liberty,
since it is also necessary to fix precisely at which point these
become transformed into a licence and danger. This is particularly the case with drugs of dependence. People conditioned by
such acceptable social habits as the consumption of alcohol in
the West and cannabis in the East will fervently defend
their 'right' to enjoy them. Their argument loses sight of the fact
(see Chapters Two and Three) that large areas of the world have
heavy restrictions imposed on alcohol consumers, and that
hashish consumption is outlawed internationally, except in
certain regions of India and a small number of other countries.

There are two legal aspects which need to be clarified.[11] First,
there *is* a link between the criminal underworld and the excessive consumption of drugs. (See, for example, page 15.) This is a
quite distinct problem from public and legislative attitudes
towards the obtaining, possession, and consumption of drugs by
an individual. Obtaining and possession at least are considered
to be offences of a criminal nature, but there is no doubt that
some confusion exists about both these main aspects, and it is
one intention of this book to try to put this into perspective
wherever it seems appropriate.

The growth of modern legislation can be considered under
three main headings:

(a) *International*

Until just before the First World War, relatively little international control was exercised over the traffic, sale, and consumption of drugs. However, that the manufacture, especially of opiates, should be limited, was recommended in The Hague in 1912. After 1918 serious discussions led eventually, via the Geneva Conventions of 1925 and 1931, to the United Nations' Single Convention of Narcotic Drugs of 1961.[12] This historic convention tried to tackle the problem on a world scale. Under international supervision, the groups of drugs represented by opium, morphine, and diamorphine (=heroin), cocaine (=ecgonine), and extracts and tinctures of Indian hemp (=cannabis), were to be declared illegal and subject to penalties. Representatives of seventy-three States, together with a number of observers, attended, and a considerable percentage (including the United Kingdom) subscribed to the recommendations. Some countries, India, for example, put forward reservations on cannabis resin. Nevertheless, the convention now deals practically with all aspects of drug control – from production to consumption. Obviously this must rest on legal measures put into force by the signatories, provision for medical and scientific use being duly allowed.

(b) *Britain and the U.S.A.*

In some instances legislation on a national level preceded international recommendations, and in others followed it. In Britain, the control of *narcotic* drugs was initiated in 1920. Recommendations by the Rollestone Report, six years later, produced some improvements. Most importantly, however, the Rollestone Report created the typically British approach to the whole problem of the addict. According to this, a drug addict is first and foremost a *sick* person who should have the right to consult a doctor about his trouble and to submit himself for treatment. This should consist of being allowed drugs, 'while he is capable of leading a useful and relatively normal life, when a certain minimum dose is regularly administered until he is in such a state that further treatment by persuasion (not force) must consist of a withdrawal cure'.

In 1961,[13] the first Report of the Interdepartmental Committee on Drug Addiction[14] appeared, more or less coinciding with an upward trend in the number of narcotics addicts (according to Home Office figures, from 454 in 1959 to 927 in 1965). This report was followed by the 'Brain Report',[15] and by two legal control measures, the Dangerous Drugs Acts 1965, 1967,[16] and the Drugs (Prevention of Misuse) Act 1964[17] – covering amphetamine and similar drugs, two later modifications adding LSD, tryptamine derivatives, and mescaline. These strengthened the executive power to search, confiscate, and prosecute where people were dealing illegally in drugs, the most severe attitudes being shown towards illegal importation and the possession of hard or soft drugs. The 1964 Act follows international recommendations. The problem confronting the nation, and certainly its law-makers, remains to find the right balance between preventing a drug black market as it exists in America and preserving the British system of keeping medical help available for the co-operative or even not so co-operative addict. The original idea of individuals visiting their physicians is now discouraged; instead, special centres are being formed to provide efficient treatment, so avoiding the danger of over-prescribing. In future a number of in-patient centres will also be provided. Thus the Acts visualize a combination of medical approach to the individual with severe penalties for the professional or amateur smuggler, 'trafficker', and distributor. Reasons and counter-reasons will be discussed later (Chapter Four). Meanwhile, it should be pointed out that these legal adjustments reflect dramatically, not only the international scene, but also a changing social and cultural structure, which shows, here at any rate, a significant narrowing of the gap between America and Britain.

In America itself, as with so many other aspects of that large country, the drug problems are certainly far more spectacular than in any other country of the West, especially so since the drug traffic, once its profitability was recognized by the underworld, and in particular by the Mafia, was treated like an oil rush. On the other hand, its legislators were not slow to establish countermeasures,[18] starting with the Harrison Act (1914), which covered illicit traffic in narcotics. Laws enacted in subsequent years were less liberal than those of Britain and some other countries and the penalties stiff (fines of several thousand dollars and imprisonment for five to twenty years). But this was measure for measure, since the methods of the organized drug peddlars were often ruthless in the extreme. In 1937 the Marijuana Tax Act was placed under the control of the Federal Bureau of Narcotics, which was joined later by the Bureau of the Drug Abuse Control under the Food and Drug Administration (also responsible for the introduction of new and experimental remedies). This bureau is now called the Bureau of Narcotics and Dangerous Drugs (Department of Justice). A number of amendments were added to the basic legislation, such as Drug Abuse Control Amendments (1965) of the Federal Food, Drug and Cosmetic Act, covering depressant and stimulant drugs (e.g. amphetamines), similar to the British law passed during the same period; more recently, hallucinogens, LSD, and other psychotropic drugs and barbiturates have, at least in some states, been placed under the same law. It is important to remember that a number of states have special regulations governing the inter-state traffic and sale of certain drugs.

(c) *Other Countries*

There are, of course, other countries with special internal legislation, adjusted, as far as possible, to traditional and climatic circumstances. India has proposed, for instance, that cannabis preparations should be retained in some of its pharmacies for locally well-established therapeutic uses. During the meeting of the Commission on Narcotic Drugs in 1961,[19] the Yugoslav representative stated that there was no problem of addiction in his country. Although France has for years had strict narcotics legislation, in 1953 it introduced a special decree providing for the compulsory treatment of drug addicts in special institutions.[20] In 1961,[21] it reported to the U.N. Commission that the addiction problem was not important there. A similar situation with the addiction problem under severe control, mainly governing heroin and cannabis, prevails in Japan.[22]

In comparison with Switzerland, which reports specifically on barbiturates, tranquillizers, amphetamines, and hallucinogens,[23] it is rather difficult to assess the legal side of the abuse situation with drugs other than narcotics in Eastern and a number of other countries.[24]

*

To sum up, it could be said that while all the drugs discussed here should be kept under some control, the practical application of the law must be carried through with common sense and in the context of local circumstances. The degree of severity in penalties, for instance, should be considered side by side with the danger to which the drug consumer, and the society in which he lives, is exposed. Ideally one may hope that the present crisis in drugs may dwindle away of its own volition, as people find a fuller purpose in life. But it would be complacent to think this is likely to happen in the immediate future. It is meanwhile obviously essential for the distinction to be clearly emphasized between the drug ring, the pusher and tempter, and the victims of human greed.

THE PUSHERS AND THEIR VICTIMS

Many of us enjoy being entertained by mystery stories and television plays which describe the existence of international drug rings as well as the individual addict who is willing to peddle his surplus wares to anyone, including school-children. Unfortunately, both of these exist in ordinary life and are not always among those for whom crime does not pay.

There would be no drug problem if there were no suppliers of any kind. There has to be a first source. In the case of purified and synthetic products, this must be a manufacturer. Besides the reputable manufacturer, from whose factories a certain amount of material may leak through theft, there also exist back-street laboratories which have no great difficulty in equipping themselves with the necessary chemical apparatus and materials, and which deliver direct to the middle man. If the drug is of natural origin – opiates, hashish, coca leaves – then the grower of the commodity is the first man in the chain. How far growers of the plant materials from which drugs are made may ever be induced to co-operate is difficult to say, particularly where the growing is done in places with difficult access and where the grower lives constantly on the brink of poverty or economic disaster.[25] But once the merchandise is in the pipeline, the 'organizations' take over, whether they are branches of the Mafia or other international syndicates or only hooked consumers. This may appear an over-dramatization, but the situation should not be underestimated. Particularly in recent years, the rough arrogance of the bootleggers of the 1920s and 1930s has given way to an outward appearance of legitimate business. There can be no doubt that the high-placed or low-placed pushers, especially of heroin, whatever their other activities, are pursuing one of the dirtiest professions.*

The other player in this drama, however, is the victim.[27] How he looks depends very much on who is looking at him – the public, the law-maker, the law executive officer, the peddler, or the addict himself – and from what vantage point. On the whole, the attitude of the public at large is mainly negative. 'The addict is for them a person to be scorned, derided and socially ostracized. If he transgresses the law, he must be punished.'[28] In the same article the author comments that the social conscience regards addiction as a vice which is degrading, destructive, and a reflection of weakness and depravity. This may in part be true; but to put it in these terms reflects an unhelpful hostility. The man in the street usually adopts a fierce if not actually brutal attitude to delinquency, behind which, not infrequently, there are hidden aggressive sadistic impulses and an unconscious wish to cover up his own psychological shortcomings. Luckily there are also those who do have a deep understanding of the victim and his problems, quite apart from the fact that it may have been the victim's own failing that made him start on his journey to nowhere.[29]

Unfortunately the present younger generation's reaction

---

* Any reader interested in the drug underworld, its sub-culture and 'trade', can be recommended to read *Drug Traffic*,[26] a vividly written account.

against any form of authority places an obstacle in the way of the drug addict himself entering into a mutually useful relationship with those who can best help him. It is not only with the drug problem that there arises this lack of communication between generations. And anyway this may be one factor which in the first place contributes towards driving those with basic personality problems, either to the company of marijuana habituates or towards the often desperate, unimaginable loneliness of the hard drug abusers.

In *The British Drug Scene*[30] the authors state that future studies will need to concentrate more on relationships between the adolescent sub-culture and drug sub-culture. Since the drug problem today centres upon youngsters, the authors give biographical sketches of individual cases. Among them are those who belonged to the world of jazz and rock and roll in the 1950s, or the pop world of the early 1960s. These had 'fun' with amphetamines and progressed from purple hearts (see Chapter Six) to cocaine and heroin, or to cannabis smoking, and represented big problems for themselves and their surroundings. Among ninety young male addicts treated,[31] the average age for starting on amphetamine was 16·5 years, on cannabis 16·9 years, and on heroin and cocaine 18·6 years.

In the excellent American booklet, *Drug Abuse: Escape to Nowhere*,[32] the symptoms of drug abuse are described as warning signals which can be observed by teachers. Sudden changes in the personality and performance may indicate that the young person has started to 'sniff glue' (see pp. 157–8), to take barbiturates or tranquillizers (the symptoms are similar to those of alcohol intoxication), has graduated to swallowing amphetamines or hallucinogenic drugs like LSD, to smoking marijuana, or is even on to opiates. The victims themselves can consist of individuals and groups from all walks of life. They may be adventurous or timid, frightened and lonely, weak or strong. Some are hedonists, some ritualists or seekers of orgastic experiences,[33] who, in the absence of traditional rituals, try to create their own. Some are bored with their jobs, or with narrow surroundings. Instead of taking refuge in neurosis or a curable

psychosis, they turn to a kind of 'self-medication' with amphetamine, barbiturate, or related depressants. Certainly many of
them do genuinely detest the evils behind so many contemporary
events – the national upheavals, political hypocrisies, social and
military bungling for which older generations cannot evade
responsibility. Some have adopted the protest garb of faded
denims and pullovers, some have joined the flower children –
anything that leads away from city suits or umbrellas (not that
this uniform has protected all its wearers from becoming drug
addicts!). Some have their hair long and flowing, some have it
curly or short, but most are prepared to pay a high price for
feeling not only 'good', but for the illusion that the world is
again complete and wholesome. Sooner or later, however, they
must discover that their flight from reality is, after all, a dream
which can in fact produce the opposite: a reinforced vision of
alienation and despair.

Is a complete cure from addiction to hard drugs possible? It is
necessary to look now at all the positive forms of help which
society can offer the drug-taker who wishes to shed his compulsion.

THE FIGHT AGAINST DRUGS

There are two avenues: (1) prevention, and (2) treatment
and cure. It is an open question as to how far severe penalties as
such have a real deterrent effect, and the world-wide measures
based on legal control and punishment have already been
discussed (see pp. 11–15). But these could only be completely
effective if they were able to create a total embargo on specific
drugs. This would mean blocking the growing of plants concerned
at their source and the synthetic manufacture of chemicals at
factories. (Controls of this kind already exist for cancer-producing substances.) But such an ideal situation might interfere
severely with those drugs used in legitimate medicine. America
and some other countries have completely banned the preparation and import of heroin, and in 1968 the Island States of
Jersey, in the Channel Islands, did the same, in contrast to
the U.K., which has so far refused to impose a complete ban,

mainly for medical reasons. Yet cannabis resin, in any form, has long ceased to be of therapeutic value (except in India), and in 1932 was removed from the *British Pharmacopoeia*,[34] the official list of accepted remedies.

Since it is impossible to expect that these substances will cease to be distributed in society, we obviously need to develop a much clearer idea of the type of personality particularly at risk. This is more easily said than done. Our knowledge on the whole psychology of drug addiction is still only fragmentary, just as our understanding of the way any drug operates on the brain remains far from complete. For the adolescent, the problems raised by the necessity to rebel against their parents' generation and to come to terms with themselves are universal. It would seem natural to assume that it is the individual who, for one reason or another, fails to work through this phase of development who is most vulnerable.

Here we can only hope that the medical profession will in the future find ways of working far more closely with teachers, parents, probation officers, and welfare workers in educating young people in the full implications of drug-taking and the nature and properties of the drugs themselves, hard and soft.[35] As with sex, a full, responsible knowledge is the greatest safeguard against trouble. And like sex, education should ideally begin in the home as soon as the child asks for information. It is half-knowledge and information given evasively which are the real menace: partial knowledge can indeed be a dangerous thing. Besides which, the propaganda from the other side is often highly persuasive and attractive and must be countered with great subtlety and honesty.

If the young, or not so young citizen, has the misfortune to become involved, what are his or her chances? What kinds of treatment are available to the psychologically or physically dependent, the willing or even the 'unwilling'?

With soft drugs he can break his dependence relatively easily, since he has started on substances which carry no severe withdrawal symptoms, while discussion with doctors may be a help with any personal difficulties. But the hard drugs are a different

matter: the opiates (heroin especially) and, possibly, combinations with other drugs. Here, for those who wish to escape,
long periods of rehabilitation are inevitable, involving close
co-operation between the victim and doctors or the personnel of
addiction clinics in hospitals and special treatment centres. The
various techniques for treating addiction to opiates and synthetic analogues have been worked out in Britain, America, and
other countries over many years. Some believe in enforced treatment, often made necessary by antagonism, some in voluntary
approaches. It is interesting here to look at the term 'after-care',
deliberately chosen to indicate the British attitude of seeing the
addict as a sick person, not as a criminal; in the U.S.A. in 1966
the Narcotic Addict Rehabilitation Act gave a rather belated
recognition to addicts as sick people with provision for their
commitment for treatment and rehabilitation.[36] From personal
observation by one of the present authors, a new emphasis on
education, understanding, and a sense of proportion seems to
be genuinely in the air.*

Unfortunately, the percentage of 'cured' addicts returning to
drugs again and again remains relatively high, and the mortality
rate for British male heroin addicts[37] is nearly twenty times as
high as the mortality rate which can be expected in a male population of similar age composition. It is therefore essential to
improve and explore every kind of rehabilitation procedure. In
the long run, however, encouraging actual self-help may be
found the most effective method of all, either in the variation of
the Alcoholics Anonymous principle called 'Narcotics Anonymous', or in youth groups, like that in New Rochelle called
'Renaissance' founded by former drug addicts.[38] Anything
should be considered that prevents the pattern of 'going down
to the old crowd merely for a chit-chat with the boys and before you know where you are you have a "fix" '.[39]

Like the alcoholic, the addict on hard drugs is capable of

* Drug abuse at the university or college level in the U.S.A. has actually
diminished in recent years, but at high schools (ages 11 to 17) it has increased
alarmingly. A similar trend has been noted amongst elderly people. These
seem to be the most vulnerable groups, since they are the ones who, for different reasons, have most difficulty coming to terms with their times.

building an astonishingly complex fabric of deception and self-deception about his own needs and motifs as well as the intentions of those trying to contribute to his recovery. The ingrained human reaction of fighting shy of bringing personal problems into the open, as is so often the case with alcoholism, hardly helps. There even seems to be a social taboo against helping those who fall in with this type of misfortune. For the future, the emphasis must be firmly on the value of human contact – the original failure of which, after all, has created the situation. A way must be found of bringing these individuals back to reality without undermining their love of liberty, their desire to see the world a better place, and their right to constructive criticism of society (which should, of course, also include an element of self-criticism). These are after all ideals in which the whole of society has a stake.

Chapter Two

Alcohol:
The Products
of Fermentation

Alcohol (ethanol) is well known to all civilized countries,
especially those of the West. It is traditionally accepted by
society, and in some circles is connected with masculinity and
the social graces. Its production is linked to large industries, its
sales not only bringing riches to some but, through taxes and
customs duty, also to governments. It has been attacked by
teetotallers, preached against by abstinence movements, restricted and abolished, cursed and praised in literature and
poetry, but it is still there, possibly representing a discreet
safety valve for social pressures and mankind's eternal desires. As
we shall see (Chapter Three), it shares many properties with cannabis.* Nevertheless, as recently as 1967, the Committee on Mental
Health of the World Health Organization published a pamphlet
which described the 'Services for the Prevention and Treatment
of Dependence of Alcohol and Other Drugs'.[1] This must be read
in connexion with the following formulation by the same committee: 'Although there are many aspects in common to the

* Though simulated driving tests have shown wide differences.

problems of both alcoholism and other forms of drug addiction, there are also significant differences.'

Consequently two sub-committees were formed, one on alcoholism and one on drug addiction. In 1953,[2] it was decided that alcohol should be placed in a category of its own, intermediate between the addiction-producing and habit-forming drugs. This is therefore how we shall try to approach the problems arising from its excessive consumption and misuse. While alcohol dependence from a medical and social point of view contributes the majority of cases of drug misuse, it also gives a picture of what might be expected to happen if people were exposed to a corresponding situation of personal responsibility towards other drugs.

When we talk about 'alcohol', usually ethyl alcohol or ethanol is meant. The word is derived from the Arabic *al kuhl* or *al kohl*, a very fine powder. Gradually the term acquired the meaning of essence, and in the sixteenth century Paracelsus described it as 'the most subtle part of anything'. He refers to alcohol vini as the most subtle part of wine. Wine, as the fermented juice of the grape, is certainly one of the oldest forms in which alcohol was consumed. Noah, of course, is the first inebriated figure to appear in ancient literature. In the Mediterranean area, Greece and Italy knew both the good and bad sides to fermented grape juice and the Greeks even considered it riotous to imbibe it without mixing it first with water. Horace sang the praise of Falernian wine, and the year 42 B.C. was reported as a vintage year. However, the full maturing of wine was not practicable until bottles and corks were in general use. The Romans planted vines wherever the soil and climate were suitable, and viticulture spread to North Africa, Spain, Germany, France, and even to Britain.

Because of the use of wine in the communion service, viticulture became an ecclesiastical occupation. However, the British tradition was lost in time, though a revival has taken place in recent years in Hampshire and Pembrokeshire. Of course, wherever conditions are favourable vines are planted, and so there are today flourishing vineyards in North and South America, Australia, and South Africa.

Whether it was the fermented grape which inspired the Chinese poet Li-po (A.D. 701–62) to compose his hymns of praise of the wine is not certain, but we know the fermentation product of rice, called *sake* in Japan, plays an important part in the hospitality in that country and is as potent as wine. The traditional alcoholic fruit products, among them cider, have their greatest admirers among farming and gardening communities. Animal materials can also be fermented: mead from bees' honey and kumiss and kefir from mare's milk have been known for centuries.

Two technical changes can be rung with a great number of agricultural and horticultural products. One is to submit selected wines to a second fermentation – like the first, resulting from the transformation of sugars, glucose and fructose, in the presence of yeast with its ferments, or enzymes, to alcohol and carbon dioxide. The latter, being a gas, produces the sparkle in Champagne, Asti Spumante, and the German Sekts. The other variation springs from another discovery mankind must have made in antiquity, namely that alcohol has a lower boiling-point than water and so can be partially separated from it. This is done by carefully heating the mixture, the subsequent condensation forming a liquid of greater alcoholic strength. This process of distillation has given a great variety of spirits, the quality of which depends on the nature of the raw material, usually submitted to a fermentation process prior to the distillation. Distilled wine, for instance, gives Cognac or brandy in France; a mash of cereal grains gives whisky in Scotland (or whiskey in Ireland), and rye and bourbon in North America; other materials produce gin, rum, vodka, and so forth.

The spirit industry and the beer brewing industry, using malted barley and oats, represent a considerable capital investment for certain countries or regions. Leaving aside specific restrictions by governments in the production, import and export, and sale of alcoholic liquids, these same governments have for many centuries obtained income from all these industries. The consumers' money taken by the British government in the form of duty, excise, and tax amounted to £698·2 million for the year 1966–7, the U.S. figure for the corresponding period, covering state as well as federal revenue and excise duty, standing at $9,193 million.[3]

CONSUMPTION

Alcohol, in contrast to the other drugs in this book, is invariably consumed as a potable liquid admixed with water. From the customs and excise viewpoint, a beverage is considered alcoholic if it contains more than 2 per cent of proof spirit. However, at least in Britain, most public analysts in administering the Food and Drugs Act 1955 prefer to observe a lower limit, since labelling a beverage as non-alcoholic merely because it contains less than 2 per cent proof spirit could cause danger to young children susceptible to small quantities of alcohol. Even the small amounts present in liqueur chocolates can do harm to minors.

Beer is perhaps the most widely drunk of all alcoholic beverages. This is illustrated by the comparative expenditures on alcohol in the United Kingdom during 1965: beer, £837 million, as against wines and spirits, with cider, £580 million. (Between 1965 and 1967 each American citizen consumed annually on average 25·5 gallons of beer as against 3·7 gallons of wines and spirits.)[4] Beer may be defined as a beverage obtained by the fermentation of malted cereal, usually barley malt, with or without other starchy material, and to which hops have been added. The use of hops, which dates from the ninth century, and their resinous product represents an interesting link with the subject of Chapter Three – *Cannabis sativa* – as both plants are usually classified as belonging to the same botanical family *Urticaceae* (the nettle family), or *Moraceae*. A distinction must be drawn between the 'lager' type of beer, most popular in Europe and the United States, and the ale, stout, and porter usually consumed in Britain. The word 'lager' derives from the German word for storage and is used for the light-coloured beer produced by bottom fermentation, where the yeast sinks to the bottom of the tank after fermentation carried out at a relatively low temperature; the end product is then kept near the freezing-point of

water for a month or two in large storage tanks. During storage
the liquid becomes saturated with carbon dioxide and mellows
in flavour. In the preparation of ale, the yeast used rises to the
top (top fermentation) and forms a thick foam. The annual
production of beer in Britain amounts to about half a barrel per
person, as compared to over three fifths of a barrel per person in
the U.S.A.

Beer has had a more chequered history than many people
realize. During the first half of the nineteenth century the
adulteration of beer by unprincipled brewers in Britain reached
amazing proportions.[5] Among the substances commonly used
were *cocculus indicus*, a dangerous poison, and sulphuric acid,
both to give 'strength' and flavour to diluted beer, and also
sulphate of iron to put a good head on it. No doubt it all helped
to bring a stupefying relief to the miseries of those living under
the heavy shadow of the Industrial Revolution, but the Adulteration of Food, Drink and Drugs Act 1872 and the Sale of
Food and Drugs Act 1875 put an effective stop to the worst
abuses. We may well imagine veteran drinkers of the day lament-
ing the fact that their beer no longer had its old kick.

Cider or *cidre*, is particularly popular in the western counties
of England, and in Brittany in France or wherever an abun-
dance of apples is grown. Cider in Britain, coloured brown with
caramel or small legally permitted amounts of brown dye, is not
liable for duty, unless it is fortified to a strength of over 15 per
cent proof spirit. However, its alcohol content often exceeds
that of many popular beers. In its roughest form (popularly
called 'scrumpy') it serves as a cheap drink for habitual drinkers.
The beverage in which pears are used instead of apples is known
as *perry*.

As mentioned earlier, wine is the fermented juice of the grape,
the fruit of *Vitis vinifera*. It is classified according to its place of
origin, method of manufacture, alcoholic strength, and other
characteristics. France and Italy head the list of wine-producing
countries, where the quantity reaches over a billion gallons a
year. Connoisseurs of wine are interested in the flavour and
aroma, the vintage, and the subtle pleasure given to the palate.

From their point of view such a thing as alcoholism or habitual heavy drinking hardly exists.

The alcohol content enables a customs officer to distinguish a light from a heavy wine, the dividing-line being 25 per cent proof spirit. For wine we can draw up three main divisions:

(1) Still or natural wines, also known as table wines.
(2) Fortified wines, such as sherry, port, madeira, and vermouth, which contain more alcohol than that produced by natural fermentation due to the addition of spirit, e.g. brandy.
(3) Sparkling wines, which, as mentioned before, undergo a process of double fermentation, the second fermentation taking place in a strong bottle (i.e. the champagne bottle with its specially wired cork).

Red wines are pressed from black grapes, the skins being left in contact with the must until the colour is attained. White wines are sometimes made from black grapes, but then the skins are separated from the must. There are sweet or medium sweet wines, and those which contain less than about 0·15 per cent of sugar are known as dry wines.

Spirits are the manufactured produce of distillation processes. Their alcohol content in Britain is above 70 per cent proof, although the Food and Drugs Act 1955 allows a spirit to be sold at 65 per cent. If the alcohol content drops below this figure, the liquid has to be labelled as diluted spirit. The initial product of distillation is colourless. The colours many spirits have when offered for sale may result from storage in wooden barrels or the addition of a permitted colouring agent or caramel. Rum, often transported from the West Indies at a strength of about 145 per cent proof, is diluted to 70 per cent before being retailed, the dilution with water often being accompanied by adding caramel.

Liqueurs are normally prepared from spirits by introducing various fruit or other flavours. Their alcoholic strength varies greatly as may be seen in Table 3. These values should also serve as an illustration of the conversion of proof spirit into a percentage of alcohol based on volume.

TABLE 3

THE ALCOHOL CONTENT OF LIQUEURS

(*as examined at the Official Analyst's Laboratory, Jersey*)

Name	Strength % P.S.	Alcohol % V/V
Advockaat	24·8–35·5	14·2–20·3
Anisette	40·7–79·4	23·3–45·3
Apricot Brandy	39·8–67·7	22·8–38·7
Bitters	41·0–87·1	23·5–49·7
Crème de Cacao	41·5–62·3	23·8–35·6
Crème de Cassis (Blackcurrant)	27·8–44·1	15·9–25·3
Cherry Brandy	29·8–79·1	17·1–45·2
Chartreuse Jaune	75·1–77·4	42·9–44·2
Cocktails	27·0–61·1	15·5–34·9
Curaçao	47·1–73·4	27·0–42·0
Half on Half	54·0–55·3	30·9–31·7
Kümmel	52·4–86·6	30·0–49·4
Mandarine	41·2–71·5	23·6–40·9
Maraschino	47·4–62·2	27·2–35·6
Crème de Menthe	29·7–64·9	17·0–37·1
Mocca	45·7–60·8	26·2–34·8
Orange	53·7–69·8	30·8–39·9
Peach Brandy	42·2–65·2	23·0–37·3
Pimms	60·0–62·7	34·3–35·8
Sloe Gin	45·6–50·2	26·3–28·8
Van der Hum	48·2–55·5	27·6–31·8
Tia Maria	54·5–55·6	31·2–31·9
Drambuie	69·6–71·9	39·7–41·1
Benedictine	75·1–6	43·0–43·2

As a general indication, we can list alcoholic beverages according to their content as follows:

Certain liqueurs, brandy or cognac, gin, rum, whisky, or bourbon: 40–50 per cent alcohol;

Fortified wines, sherry, port, madeira: about 20 per cent alcohol;

Table wines such as Burgundy, Claret, Moselle, Hock, Champagne: 10–15 per cent alcohol;

Ale, porter, beer, lager, cider: 2–8 per cent alcohol;
Ginger beer: 1–3 per cent alcohol.

We should not omit to mention home-made wines. It may
seem tactless to discuss them in this particular book, considering
their associations with the peaceful atmosphere of sleepy vil-
lages, maiden aunts, and church fêtes. But these can, as easily
as any others, lead to secret drinking sessions and subsequently
to alcoholism. Their alcoholic strength is roughly those of grape
wines, but it can also be increased by fortification.

THE EFFECTS OF ALCOHOL

This section is important, since it attempts to resume briefly
all the evidence for alcohol being a drug of dependence and the
grounds that exist for treating it – in spite of large vested
interests – as something the abuse of which should be publicized
and prevented by education and reasonable restriction.

The physiological effects[6] of alcohol in small doses sound
innocent enough. It can act as a food and, if taken in small,
repeated amounts not sufficient to produce high alcohol levels in
the blood stream, can supply up to 40 per cent of the body's
daily requirement in calories. Again in small doses, it will
increase the flow of gastric juices and stimulate the heart beat.
But with larger, particularly concentrated, doses, acute and
later chronic toxic levels are reached.[7] The sense of appetite may
be inhibited and the emptying of the stomach retarded, but
the secretion of mucus by the mucosa (lining) of the gastro-
intestinal tract may increase to a point where acute inflammation sets in.

The main pharmacological effect, however, is on the central
nervous system, and, to a lesser extent, on the heart and blood
vessels, kidneys, and body temperature. Its main action is
definitely depressant, even though in small amounts it may act
as a stimulant. As this depression also involves the inhibitory
functions of the cerebral cortex (see Figure 1, page 8), the initial
impression is of fatigue being postponed, talk becoming easier,
ideas springing more freely, and work becoming easier to carry
out. About 16 to 25 grams circulating in the system will produce

toxic symptoms, although the concentration in the blood may be below 0·1 per cent; if, with increasing consumption, the blood concentration (in an average case) approaches 0·2 per cent, drunkenness sets in. This involves a large number of psychological symptoms deviating from the normal, memory, concentration, and the power of self-criticism becoming dulled. Excited speech and irresponsible actions follow and self-confidence increases, while a loss of body balance may hardly be noticed by the inebriate himself. Mental and physical abilities are not in fact increased, nor is sexual prowess, although desire is provoked and inhibitions may drop away.

All these signs are anyway well known. But other events occurring within the body are not always generally realized. Alcohol widens the blood vessels, especially those of the skin. This produces a sensation of warmth, but also leads to a loss of heat reserves with a consequent lowering of body temperature. There is an increase in the flow of urine, owing to indirect inhibition of an anti-diuretic hormone. Large quantities of alcohol may damage the inner lining of the kidneys. All these are fundamental symptoms connected with acute alcoholism, and the degree of their manifestation depends very much on the individual's tolerance to drink and his psychological make-up. In other words, his personality and surroundings, how conducive these are to excitement and social contacts, play an important part in the type of drunkenness shown.

Alcohol taken over long periods leads to the illness called chronic alcoholism. The individual has by that stage left behind his or her period as simply a drinker and has become a compulsive drinker. First he will be a restricted alcoholic, perhaps observing longish periods of sobriety between bouts. Finally, the continued consumption of alcohol and a lack of proper food and vitamins will produce a painful neuritis, and he becomes the classic alcoholic experiencing a damaged central nervous system (*delirium tremens*) and a possibly fatal disease of the liver (cirrhosis). This physical deterioration may be expected to be accompanied by social deterioration, loss of income or even job, and so to the destruction of his or her personal life.

During this process of self-destruction the concentration of alcohol in the blood stream will go through many stages. The alcohol content in the blood increases from 50 mg/100 ml to about 450 mg/100 ml in acute poisoning. Examining one set of analyses of post-mortem samples over a period of seventeen years, the frequency is impressive with which the cause of death in such cases has been given as 'death from acute alcohol poisoning' when the concentration is of the order of 450 milligrams. Only one case of survival was observed where the alcohol content was slightly above this figure; this patient received hospital treatment that narrowly averted death. With high blood alcohol concentrations, the danger of death from the regurgitation of vomit is a reality, the reflexes being dulled to such an extent that the patient literally drowns in his own body fluids. The same can happen with even lower alcohol concentrations if barbiturates have also been taken (see page 121).

Alcohol is rapidly absorbed through the stomach and small intestine, particularly if there is not much food present in the digestive system. After absorption, the diffusion into the tissue fluids is rapid, and its appearance in the blood rises steeply and reaches a peak about thirty minutes to two hours after being taken, the exact time depending mainly on the dose.

When a peak concentration is reached, the rates of absorption and elimination are equal; from then on, the concentration falls. The removal can occur by two routes – either by oxidation (an average man can combust biochemically 10 cc. of alcohol an hour), or by excretion. The oxidation occurs with the help of an enzyme called alcohol dehydrogenase, the process taking place in the liver and, according to recent work,[8] in the brain, where, as in other tissues, so-called acetyl-coenzyme A is formed. The body uses this and similar ancillary factors for the biosynthesis of fats, carbohydrates, and other body constituents. In a manner suggested by the biochemist Krebs in 1967,[9] it is the upsetting of these processes which is a major factor in the pathogenesis of cirrhosis. Collins and Cohen[10] have recently put forward a hypothesis connecting the interaction of compounds in the brain with the formation of hallucinogenic agents.

In excretion, alcohol is removed by way of the breath (less than 0·5 per cent), the urine, the saliva, or perspiration and tears. The last four account for about 2–10 per cent of the alcohol that has been consumed. Opinions differ to some extent over how quickly final traces of alcohol disappear from the body, since this may depend on the initial amount that has been ingested and the peak of concentration which exists in the blood.

Although there is no cast-iron proof as yet, it is not improbable that people who cannot 'carry their liquor well' may suffer congenital enzyme deficiencies. Research into this phenomenon could throw new light on the whole problem of alcoholism. Whether the compulsive drinker, the 'born dipsomaniac', is a sick person in a chemical and physical and not only a psychological sense has been the subject of many studies. However, the question has not yet been completely answered because of the complex psychosomatic causes underlying the development of alcoholism and the difficult techniques involved in characterizing biochemical aberrations.

For medical and forensic determinations, breath testing has advantages. Breath is obtainable with minimum inconvenience to the patient or suspect. The concentration of alcohol in the urine, like that in breath, depends on the concentration in the blood. But as alcohol, after absorption, is evenly distributed in the aqueous parts of the body (that is, it enters tissues according to their water content), urine consisting of more water than blood will carry more alcohol than plasma. Thus, while the kidneys do not increase the alcohol concentration in the urine, the ratio between blood and urine varies, and it has been established that a peak of alcohol concentration in urine occurs about twenty to twenty-five minutes later than in the blood.[11] This fact plays an important part in cases where a driver is suspected of having been in charge of a car while under the influence of alcohol or drugs.

Methyl alcohol shows some important differences from ethanol, and in our big cities the 'meths drinker' is increasingly in evidence. As it is not immediately oxidized, and its excretion through the breath and urine is not as rapid as that of ethanol, the methanol can remain in the body for several days. Some of its toxic effects do not appear until twelve hours after intake, and may consist of severe abdominal pain and disturbance of vision, but can be, it is claimed, counteracted by consuming ethanol. Eye disorders may develop into blindness from damage done to the optic nerve. Severe acidosis may progress to coma and even death. Other symptoms resemble those of acute ethanol poisoning, except that after recovery from coma, lasting twenty-four hours, the patient can become drunk again upon drinking water or any other liquid. This strange phenomenon has been observed in people who drank a mixture known in London and Glasgow as 'Red Biddie or Lizzie'. This is apparently a concoction of red wine and methylated spirit which has all the properties of a very dangerous drug.

MISUSE AND PREVENTION

As discussed in Chapter One, the prevention of misuse of any drug of dependence rests on recognizing potential candidates, on proper education in the home and at school, on friends or social contacts, and on the effectiveness of the law. With alcohol being an 'accepted drug', its toxic consequences being on the whole easily forgivable, it naturally becomes doubly difficult to create effective controls. Social and cultural attitudes towards the consumption of alcohol and other drugs appear to have a bearing on the development of dependence. In France, where children are brought up on *vin ordinaire*, the incidence of alcoholism was among the highest in the world in 1951.[12] That this figure is now evidently lower is probably due to a vigorous drive by French governments against alcoholic drinks and a general growing fashion for milk bars. Although the unlimited drinking hours in force on the Continent may be observed with envy by the citizens of other countries, restrictions imposed through licensing hours do produce a kind of preventive measure, though their full effectiveness is not easily assessed, especially as taxation usually also plays a part. On the other hand, where regulations limit licensing hours excessively, as in certain states of Australia, for example, this can lead to acute intoxication as a result of the exaggerated hurry in which many pints of beer are consumed, possibly on an empty stomach.

Alcohol and the Motorist

Perhaps motoring is the most urgent area where excess of alcohol consumption must be controlled and prevented. Drunken driving causes more than 25,000 traffic deaths each year in the United States,[13] while in England and Wales alone, in 1966 and 1967, in *each* year, about 70,000 offences for drunkenness were committed.[14] It is simply common sense to introduce legislation that attempts to prevent motoring accidents arising from misuse of alcohol.

A considerable argument took place about the introduction of the Road Safety Act 1967 in Britain. This specified as an offence driving or being in charge of a motor vehicle with a concentration of alcohol in the blood above a prescribed limit. The resistance of the average citizen to new regulations, even though they may have existed for many years in comparable form elsewhere, can create an outcry in most countries against precious areas of personal freedom being eroded. In this case the freedom defended was one to drive a vehicle in a condition of impaired judgement and reduced responsibility, possibly to injure or kill someone else as well as oneself as an end result.

It has to be emphasized that great care was taken in framing the British Act, numerous expert reports and investigations being translated into legislation. The regulations in other countries provide an interesting comparison (see Appendix C, pp. 188–9). It empowers a constable in uniform to require a suspect to undergo a screening breath test under three conditions: (1) suspicion of consumption of alcohol, (2) involvement in a traffic offence, or (3) of being party to an accident. If the screening breath test* indicates that the concentration of alcohol in the blood exceeds the prescribed level, then the constable may arrest

---

* It rests on an interaction of alcohol breathed on to silica gel impregnated with a solution of potassium bichromate in sulphuric acid solution. In a positive reaction the colour changes to green. Contrary to popular belief, it is not the 'breathalyser' test that is used in the United Kingdom, but the 'alcotest', which has been in use in Germany for over ten years.

the motorist with a warrant. If the motorist refuses to take a
breath test, then the constable is empowered to arrest without
warrant, provided he has reasonable cause for suspicion. However, if the suspect has been taken to a hospital, this does not
apply if the medical officer in charge raises an objection on
medical grounds. A person arrested must be given an opportunity to undergo a *further* breath test at a police station before
he is obliged to provide a sample of blood or urine. This is a
safeguard against the first breath test being misleading from the
possible presence of residual alcohol in the oral cavity. The
offence does only start after a certain level in the blood is reached
sufficiently high to indicate decisively that a person is unfit to
drive.

If the motorist refuses to provide a blood sample, he is invited
to deliver two samples of urine within the hour. If this condition
is not fulfilled, he is given another opportunity to provide a
sample of blood. Only after a further refusal is he regarded as
having failed to give a sample. The constable, when requesting a
motorist to give a sample, must warn the driver that failure to
provide this will render him liable to imprisonment, fine, and
disqualification. On the provision of the sample, the constable
must offer to supply the suspect with part of the sample in a
suitable container or, in the case of a blood sample, which is
insufficient for sharing, another sample that the suspect may
consent to have taken. These samples, so the law provides, are
to be taken by the police doctor, even if the suspect is a patient
in hospital. As blood is an unstable medium, it is advisable to
have these samples analysed without delay and stored in a
refrigerator whilst awaiting analysis. Such delays, coupled with
unsatisfactory storage in the intervening period, may well
account for reports of disagreement between analysts acting for
prosecution and defence.

The Act is drafted in such a way that many of the sometimes
spurious defences under the old Act are unavailable for defence.
Medical evidence of fitness to drive is of no help to the accused.
As the urine level is defined, theoretical arguments with regard
to the conversion factor of urine concentration to blood values

are irrelevant, and this also applies to arguments based on changes in blood alcohol concentration during the period between the suspect's detention and the time a sample is taken, as the Act makes it clear that the blood alcohol concentration is that at the time the sample is taken. If there should be conflicting results between two analysts, this may be due to errors arising through inefficient sampling, bad sealing, or careless storage – all factors outside the analyst's control.*

Two points deserve some attention: how successful has the new regulation been, and how do other car-crowded countries manage their traffic–alcohol problem? Between October 1967 and the end of the year, the United Kingdom experienced a sharp drop in car accidents after closing hours. In the London area alone, this was over 40 per cent lower than in the corresponding period in 1966. However, there are signs that the first impact of the Act is wearing off and accidents at night, during May and June 1968, were down by only 9 per cent. In August 1968 they exceeded those of the previous August. Without trying to explain this phenomenon, it should be mentioned that in other countries which have similar alcohol–traffic laws a similar pattern has emerged.

The situation in the United States is complicated by the fact that regulations vary between states. Here is a country which has continued to have a major alcohol problem on its hands since the days of prohibition, and which has perhaps twelve million alcoholics (about 6 per cent of the total population), of whom maybe half remain undetected. To take Massachusetts as an example, its population of between 200,000 and 300,000 alcoholics can be expected to have regular social contact with two million other people, either family and children, business contacts, or neighbours. As a passenger in an alcoholic's car,

* One solution to such an *impasse* could be to divide the samples into *three* parts, the third being sealed and stored in a refrigerator pending the hearing of the case. This would go far to eliminate any potential miscarriage of justice arising from differing analytical results. A court would then be able to request that the third portion be forwarded to a referee analyst. This has been standard procedure for many years with samples taken by local authorities in the U.K. administering the Food and Drugs Act and the Fertilizer and Feeding Stuffs Act 1926.

any one of these can be placed at very high risk at any time.

It seems surprising that until now this most car-conscious of nations has continued to tend to place a greater emphasis on speed regulations than on laws governing driving under the influence of drink or drugs.* However, the 1968 Drinking and Driving Laws are now in force in about forty states,† though not all of them have simultaneously introduced the Implied Consent Laws, which allow that a person operating a vehicle on the highway shall be deemed to have given consent to a breath or blood test where there are reasonable grounds for believing him to be intoxicated. The lack of uniformity between states thus creates a major anomaly, astonishing in the face of statistics which indicate clearly that out of a total of drivers killed on America's roads, over fifty per cent showed a blood alcohol content reaching levels of intoxication. (A similar fatality ratio exists for intoxicated as against sober pedestrians.)

THE TREATMENT AND CURE OF ALCOHOLISM

Firstly we must distinguish between acute and chronic poisoning. Even the tyro in the drinking game can fall foul of the first condition during or following a bout. Usually in these circumstances it is simple enough to let the victim 'sleep it off', though if he can be watched a tepid bath may help him, and otherwise he must be kept warm. A hangover will be one inevitable result, with throbbing headache, weakness in limbs and joints, nausea, and general debility. Complete rest and light, mainly liquid food is the answer here. Some, however, seek temporary relief by repeating a small intake of alcohol and so taking 'the hair of the dog'. If coma should become pronounced, however, prompt medical attention is advisable. Intoxication is

---

* In 1967 in Massachusetts, 7,264 speeding offences were recorded, against 5,468 for 'operating under the influence of intoxicating liquor'—*Commonwealth of Massachusetts Registry of Motor Vehicles*, Statistician's Office, Boston, Mass.

† In most states the blood level at which a person is presumed to be intoxicated stands at 0·15 per cent (150 mg/100 ml blood), while in others it is 0·08 per cent (as in the U.K.) and 0·1 per cent (see Appendix C, pp. 188–9).

actually accentuated by an atmosphere deficient in air and the application of oxygen can often aid recovery.

If there are underlying psychological or metabolic factors, a few experiences of drunkenness can become chronic and lead from daily tippling to severe alcoholism.

The most effective treatment then includes prolonged hospitalization in a special institution, especially if periods of mental upheaval (*delirium tremens*) make the use of sedatives and tranquillizers imperative. Drugs which produce severe vomiting if alcohol is taken at the same time, or which make life thoroughly miserable if the alcoholic continues drinking, may be of some use. When withdrawal treatment is carried out, the W.H.O. Report recommends that this should only be a start to treatment and that withdrawal should be abrupt and complete, particularly for such drugs as cannabis and the hallucinogens as well as alcohol. It should be followed by rehabilitation which, apart from direct medical care, can be successfully carried out by groups and teams, not necessarily medically trained. On the contrary, the presence of a considerable number of former alcoholics such as those available through organizations like 'Alcoholics Anonymous' can lead to complete rehabilitation (a success rate of 50 to 70 per cent of cases being recorded in various circumstances). This is a remarkable example of the 'amateurs' outstripping the 'experts' by offering moral and social support not available under clinical conditions, and perhaps demonstrating how centrally important the social aspects are to the whole problem.

In the case of alcoholics with neurological symptoms, intensive treatment with Vitamin B_1 injections may relieve pain and afterwards cure most of the underlying degenerative processes in peripheral nerves. However, other degenerative changes in the body, such as fatty degeneration or cirrhosis of the liver, and pathological changes in blood vessels cannot be repaired short of a complete return to sobriety. Even then the damage may be too far advanced, the deterioration of mind and body having progressed too far to save the alcoholic from premature senility and death.

The size of the problem that alcoholism presents in Western society is one conveniently and consistently ignored on the whole. In the U.K. in 1967 there were calculated to be at least 200,000 alcoholics, with the corresponding figure for known hard drug addicts standing at 1,729. The fact that it is a 'socially acceptable' drug has a lot to do with this, and the horror with which society views the more exotic drug scene in contrast to its passive regard of common or garden alcoholism reflects a basic ambivalence. All drug problems interconnect so closely that it is impossible to see how alcohol can be left out of account, though many writers do leave it on one side in view of its special position.

In the words of an analytical psychologist:

> Whether or not alcohol is a drug would seem . . . to depend on the motive for which it is taken. In his paperback on drugs Peter Laurie excludes alcohol on the grounds that our society itself is dependent on it and that prohibition has done more harm than its legal presence. I do not think that the issue can be settled in this way. But it is certainly true that if alcohol is a drug then it is the only one in our civilization which also has a mythology and an established ritual.[15]

The conventional attitude is that a society needs to have at least one drug at its disposal, though more than one may well be undesirable. The waste of human potential and the wreckage of so many individual lives as a consequence of alcoholism may on the other hand seem a heavy price, but we know that prohibition can create even vaster evils. The line of moderation is probably the only one possible.

As with other drugs, there are as we have seen certain individuals who for unknown reasons are particularly vulnerable to the dangers of alcohol. This, as always, is the aspect which above all others cries out for intensive research and knowledge beyond what is at present available. The field of psychology can offer us one further clue here. In 1938 Karl Manninger termed alcoholism a form of chronic suicide, and, in the words of the psychologist already quoted, 'we must remain mindful of the frequency with which acute suicidal attempts supervene in compulsive drinkers'.[16] Possibly those who drink themselves to death have literally succeeded in what they set out to do, albeit evading any direct responsibility for their action. A therapy which aims to revive a fundamental belief in the value of living and human contact is therefore the one we would most expect to be successful.

Chapter Three

Cannabis: The Hemp Resins from the East

Whether we like it or not, and in spite of the existing drug laws, the use of cannabis in Western society is steadily increasing. A United Nations report published early in 1969 in association with Interpol showed that illicit traffic has grown to considerable proportions, becoming in the United States 'a source of grave concern since it was taken over by criminal elements with virtually inexhaustible sources of supply'.[1] The drug is in effect freely available to any young people who may wish to risk the law in experimenting with it and who distribute it among themselves. It remains, however, essential to keep a firm sense of proportion. Cannabis is not a drug that suits everyone's psychology. Many will try it once or a few times and never again. The hard-core of individuals who come to take it regularly, or who become to some degree dependent on it, are possibly a minority. Should the availability of cannabis broaden, however, statistically we can expect their number to increase. Those who take it occasionally are often literate, creative people who feel they can thereby expand their perceptions.

With no other drug in modern use has controversy created

quite so much heat at the same time as so little enlightenment. In this chapter we shall try to present all the main lines of argument involved and give a fair résumé of the present state of knowledge.

ORIGIN AND HISTORY

Cannabis drugs are everywhere topical news these days. Over thirty-five years ago one of the present authors[2] went for several months to work on cannabis resin in the laboratories of University College, Colombo. There, in Ceylon's capital, at a time when opium was still seen as a mystery drug of the East, a lively trade took place along the sea front. America's marijuana problem and Europe's 'pot' parties lay well within the future.

Even today there still exists considerable confusion about the origin, name, and true nature of the dried, compressed, or resinous products of the hemp plant and its extracts. Hemp was given the botanical name *Cannabis sativa* by Linnaeus, and is also sometimes called *Cannabis indica*, according to its place of growth. It is said to have originated from Western and Central Asia and to have spread from there via the Himalayan region into India, possibly by about 800 B.C., then to North Africa and other parts of the world. Rope has been made from its fibres from at least as far back as 2800 B.C. Whether South America produced its own wild variety is not certain (many aspects of its history are of a legendary character), but it has been known for a long time in Brazil and Mexico. One of the oldest reports apparently originates from China, where the Emperor Shen-nung wrote a book on medicinal plants in about 2700 B.C., in which he mentions hemp, its botanical properties, and its cultivation for euphoric effects. Even then the emperor seems to have felt disapproval for a plant which offered facile happiness, labelling it 'Liberator of Sin'.

The most widely known legend connected with hashish, and one which seems to have something of a basis in fact, is the one which gave the word 'assassin' to the English and French languages. The *hashashi* (hashashan = herb-eaters) were members of a fanatic sect originating in Ismailia and later settling in Persia whose leader became known as the Old Man of the Mountains to the first Crusaders. They pursued a deliberate policy of training specially chosen squads to infiltrate the ranks of their enemies and to kill enemy leaders who offended them. Initially they struck against their rivals in the Moslem world, but, with the coming of the Crusades, played their part in fighting the invading infidel, accounting among others for Conrad of

Fig. 2. The leaves and flowers of *Cannabis sativa*

Montferrat. Henry of Champagne and Navarre is said to have
paid their fortress a friendly visit when he was King of Jerusalem
(c. 1195), and to have witnessed an astonishing display of
devotion.[3] One after another, as their leader beckoned, his
young men launched themselves from the parapets into the
abyss below, until the tough Crusader could no longer bear it
and begged him to stop. Afterwards the Old Man of the Mountains invited Henry to call on the Assassins' services any time he
should need them!

The trained bands of the Old Man of the Mountains were, of
course, in effect suicide squads, and so that they should have a
foretaste of the bliss awaiting them once their missions were
completed, the Old Man of the Mountains (there was a whole line
of 'Old Men' over the two centuries or so of their existence) fed
his élite with hashish to give them dreams of the paradise to
come. Marco Polo, however, states in his account that it was
opium which was used, and this might possibly fit the reported
effects better than hashish, and would, of course, have given the
leader an increasingly powerful hold over his protégées as their
dependence deepened. At this stage of history we can only
speculate – perhaps they used opium for their dreams and
hashish to fortify themselves to carry through their terrible
missions. Both drugs were certainly widely used throughout the
Arab world at the time. The Assassins were themselves eventually eliminated by one of the Mongol hordes.

Closer to modern times, hashish was brought to Paris in the
nineteenth century and experiments on the drug were carried
out by members of Le Club des Hachachins, whose founders
included Gauthier and Baudelaire. Baudelaire's *Les Paradis
artificiels* contains the classic account of the drug's effects on a
sensitive, imaginative mind:

Here is the drug before yo r eyes; a morsel of green jam. . . .
Here, then, is your happiness!

But, he goes on to warn,

I presume that you have chosen the right moment for this expedi-
tion. . . . You must have no duties to accomplish that require punc-

tuality or exactitude, no pangs of love, no domestic preoccupations, griefs, anxieties. The memories of duty will sound a death-knell through your intoxication and poison your pleasure. Anxiety will change to anguish, grief to torture.[5]

The Hasheesh Eater by the American Fitz Hugh Ludlow belongs to roughly the same period,[6] and similarly testifies to the fact that his 'voyages' were as likely to take him down into hell as to lift him heavenwards. Ludlow discovered, in fact, that as he continued to take the drug the downward trips came to predominate.

Depending on climate, location, and other factors, the quality, quantity, and composition of cannabis resins change. This is of considerable importance, and will be discussed later. The proliferation of names for one or the other variety of cannabis products arises from the fact that, while knowledge of their euphoric properties has been passed down from mouth to mouth, each valley, each district where hemp plants grow, has given its own name to this or the other type and preparation, a state of affairs that may (and often does) even confuse a High Court judge. A review of the extant literature produces this breakdown:[7]

(a) The botanical names, *Cannabis sativa L.* or *indica*, hemp, and Indian Hemp (*Urticaceae, Moraceae, Cannabinaceae,* or *Cannaboideae*).

(b) *Ganja* (Hindustani): is derived from the unfertilized resinous flowering shoots (female) grown in the plains. The resin diminishes rapidly after being fertilized by pollen from the separate but proximate male flowers.

(c) *Charas*: the name of the cannabis resin itself, which exudes from the leaves, stems, and fruit of plants growing in the mountain at 6,000 to 8,000 feet.

(d) *Bangh*: comes from plants grown on the lower hills of the Punjab, consisting of dried, crushed, mature leaves and the cut tops of female plants. From it comes hashish (see (h)). On the whole it is of poorer quality than *ganja*.

(e) *Kif* (Arabic): the North African form of dried cannabis leaves, from the tip of the female plant (consumed, in the main, in Algeria, Morocco, and Egypt).

(f) *Maconha*: the Brazilian equivalent of the above drugs, mainly in the form of dried leaves, stalks, flowering stems, and fruits. It is sometimes mixed with earth.

(g) There are further local names and many slang terms: *Ganga* (West Indies), *Dagga* (South Africa), *Kabak* (Turkey); *grass, pot, hash, tea, weed, locoweed, griefo, hay, hemp, jive, Mary Jane, mezz, mor-a-grifa, rope, Texas tea*, and others.

(h) There are two names, one from India or the Middle East, the other from South or Latin America, which are widely used in speech and in print often to refer to all forms of cannabis products: *hashish* (mainly in Britain, Europe, and the East), and *marihuana* or *marijuana* (on the North and South American continents).

The American-Spanish-Portuguese expression 'marijuana' (however it is spelt) could stem from *maraguango*, meaning 'intoxicant'. This indicates that the effects of the native or imported hemp plant must have been known to at least some of the American Indian nations or their colonizers. The name was used originally for a low-grade tobacco, but was later transferred to materials containing some components of *Cannabis sativa*. Like bhang in India, it now represents a smoking mixture mainly, but the American preparations, as with other hemp products, are also chewed, drunk, and eaten as sweetmeats (called in India majoom or majun).

In spite of the nineteenth century's intellectual vogue for drugs, by the 1920s cannabis was hardly known in the West and its consumption remained small. Hashish and marijuana were mainly brought in by travellers from countries with a cannabis 'tradition' in the Near and Middle East, parts of Africa, and perhaps the West Indies. Medical scientists at the time actually stated that the euphoric principle of the hashish family did not suit the Western psychological taste;[8] that only the Oriental mind could obtain its full effect. It was beer from the hop plant (strangely enough a botanical relative of *Cannabis sativa*, see page 25) which provided the main pleasure or consolation for the average Western citizen. But at that time marijuana was making its increasingly forceful entry, particularly in the Americas, into the underworld as well as into fashionable hedonistic circles. Negro society began to give it preference over tobacco, and so did white youth in the big cities, although it must be emphasized that marijuana cigarettes ('reefers', 'joints', 'sticks') were on the whole weaker than most of the forms in which hashish is consumed in Eastern countries.

The marijuana habit spread so rapidly that, by the mid 1930s, a committee under Mayor La Guardia of New York was called to study the problem and report on its dangers,[9] which many then believed to be similar in seriousness to that of alcoholism, to have a close link with criminal acts, or, even worse, possibly to be as bad as the hard drugs – opium, morphine, and heroin. Since those days there has been a tremendous increase, especially among the younger generation, of people taking hashish or marijuana either occasionally or regularly. A protracted social battle is now joined between those who propose that cannabis preparations, their purchase and consumption should be legalized in a way comparable with alcohol, and those who are against any form of liberalization whatever. Before the end of this chapter we shall have made our own contribution to the argument.

Botanically, as we have seen, cannabis belongs to the family *Urticaceae* (nettle plants) or *Moraceae* (mulberry plants), of which the hop (*Humulus lupulus*) is also a member. The cannabis plant is a shrub-like herb which grows to between twelve or twenty feet, the male plant being the taller and the female the shorter. They are grown separately but in close proximity so that fertilization can take place. It is the male plant which produces the hemp fibres and the female one which produces in its flowering tops the resin containing the physiologically active compounds. A recent report from Brazil,[10] however, has announced the discovery of active principles in the male plant as well.

THE PROBLEMS OF ANALYSIS AND THE LEGAL SITUATION

It took many years of research before the active principle in cannabis and its related but inactive compounds were isolated and characterized chemically and biologically. For chemical reasons it was difficult to prepare the compounds as crystallized derivatives: heat damaged the product and new methods of distillation under greatly reduced pressure had to be applied. Even when they were, in the 1930s and 1940s,[11] it was still difficult to separate the really complex mixtures.

Once again it has to be emphasized that cannabis resin, mixed with whatever plant materials may also be present, represents a great number of possible variations. So much depends on the way the hemp has been planted and cultivated, upon climatic conditions (whether sub-tropic or tropic – even European for recent experimental purposes), upon the height above sea-level and the air's oxygen content, upon the stage at which the plants were harvested. These are only some of the factors involved. However, the analytical chemist now has at his disposal a number of techniques for analysing with a high degree of accuracy the content of any samples given to him. (The reader interested in following through the technical details may turn to pp. 174–6 of the Appendices.) This means that the legal profession today should have no fears that samples placed before them have been inadequately analysed.

The tetrahydrocannabinols, the active ingredients, are identifiable in whatever form the material may come. The percentage ratio of active compound to other ingredients is not in itself important, since heating the mixture may transform one type into another, and exposure to air in hot climates may change the composition of the mixture before it reaches the consumer. It must remain the responsibility of the forensic scientist and analytical chemist to identify any material presented for analysis by the police or legal authorities, and since cannabis is legally classified within the group of 'dangerous drugs', it is obviously essential for such tests to be carried out on suspected samples by skilled analysts if the course of justice is to be safeguarded.

CONSUMPTION

Cannabis resin can be eaten as sweetmeats (majoom) or mixed with dates into a paste. It can be drunk, like a milk shake: bhang is rubbed to a powder, mixed with equal parts of black pepper, dried rose petals, *khuskus* (poppy seeds), almonds, cardamoms, cucumber, and melon seeds, to which sugar, milk, and water are added.[12] There is also a tradition that cannabis leaves make a good snuff. The most frequent method, however, is by inhaling the smoke from any one of the many preparations, either in Eastern or South American style with hookah or narghile-like contraptions, the kif-pipe, in frequent use in North Africa, or even clay pipes among the sailing fraternity. But the most frequent guise is that of cigarettes, which often contain a mixture of tobacco and marijuana. For every method the load is prepared from the leaves and flowering tops, stems, seeds and fruit pods, derived from the dry or resinous hemp plant. In Ceylon hashish (*ganja*) is peddled as cubes of the compressed resinous flower tops, wrapped in paper, which is removed before the contents are pressed against the glowing tip of a cigarette. Slabs or pieces of extract residue can be used in pipes instead of botanical specimens or mixtures. A recent report from Mexico describes marihuana being fortified with an extract from hashish resin to form tar-like pellets known as *smash*.

In animals, as well as in humans, a remarkably high degree of individualized responses has been observed. These variations could be due, biologically speaking, to the differences in mixtures already mentioned, to different chemical forms of the active compounds, to variations in the metabolites which the body produces from the material introduced, to the low water- but high fat-solubility of certain components. All this will greatly influence the course and absorption of the substances in various organs and tissues.

Any drug taken up through inhalation must expose the absorption system in the mouth and lungs to varying mixtures of the aerosol carrying the finely dispersed particles. The best comparison is with tobacco, where different portions of nicotine and similar poisons, and possibly different ratios of cancer-producing agents, reach different parts of the organism. From the point of view of its concentration of effects on the nervous system, alcohol also may show some similarities to cannabis. Here again the distribution in the body may give very little indication as to the strength of concentration in the receptive parts of the brain. This may be relatively small in comparison with the total concentration in the blood or other parts of the body, and yet be enough for an individual to behave abnormally and show intoxication symptoms.

Some interesting, if tentative, conclusions have been drawn recently by a group of doctors working on a project in the Boston University School of Medicine, to study the effects of marijuana.[13] They found that under laboratory conditions subjects who had not smoked marijuana previously did not have strong subjective experiences even with high doses, but that their performance on simple psychological tests was impaired. Regular users, however, did not have their performance in tests affected. The implications are that the potential user may have to 'learn' how to smoke cannabis, either through physical adaption to it or in a psychological sense.

THE EFFECTS OF CANNABIS

The biological activities of cannabis in its many forms are of great general fascination because of their variability, but this complexity is at the same time a source of frustration to the pharmacologist. Its long history, while it can show relatively little use as a true medical remedy over the centuries (despite recommendations in Oriental medical treatises and herbal cures), is full of contradictions which are only slowly giving way to rational analysis. It long preceded modern knowledge of the so-called psychotropic drugs (see Chapters Seven and Eight), with which it shares a number of properties and whose development taught new methods of evaluation. Although cannabis was consumed, like some of the psychiatric medicines, for euphoric effects, the consumption differed from that of tranquillizers and anti-depressants since these consist mainly of synthetically pure drugs. Today cannabis resin is still consumed in a variety of crude mixtures rarely representing purified substances.

In spite of a general agreement that the physiological effects of the hemp principles (especially in man) is in the main on the central nervous system, the symptoms produced are not straightforwardly either stimulant or depressant. They may range, in man, from a form of manic drunkenness to a partly withdrawn apathy. It is clear that, as with some other drugs, we must distinguish between *subjective* effects, particularly in man, and of *objective* phenomena, which can be evaluated by scientific research, usually through observing animals under experiment.

One of the first comprehensive reports on the pharmacology and toxicology of the active principles of cannabis was published in 1950 by one of the contributors to the La Guardia Report.[14] Since then, a number of other results have helped us to see more clearly what the connexion is between actions in animals and the effects in man. Two tests were introduced some years ago: the first being with rabbits (the Gayer Test), named 'corneal areflexia' test. Cannabis extracts or purified fractions, when administered to an animal, abolish the eyelid's winking or closing reflex, so that it is possible to touch the centre of the eye with a calibrated horse hair. This test helped to distinguish between active and inactive fractions and compounds. Far more significant, though, was the other test, this time on dogs, rats, and mice to produce ataxia. This was more selective and more reasonably correlated with psychic effects in man, although ataxia in humans can only be produced with very large toxic doses.*

The pharmacologist was, of course, looking for other measurable symptoms, and found some: like other sedative drugs, cannabis products create a drop in body temperature (hypothermia) and make the blood sugar level fluctuate. An original suspicion that they have a bloodsugar-lowering action has not been confirmed, though both man and animal show an increased

* Ataxia is an inco-ordination of muscular action which becomes noticeable in the animal, its walking movements being disturbed and a kind of paralysis appearing to overtake its hind legs.

appetite and a strong craving for sugar and sweets while under the drug's influence.[15] (The Boston doctors were able to confirm that marijuana increases the heart-rate slightly, but could detect no effect on pupil size or on the blood sugar level.)[16]

In man, the subjective effects include among outward signs of psychic sensations, hilarity without motivation, carelessness, loquacious euphoria with a wish for increased social contacts (gregariousness), distortion of sensation and perception, particularly of space and time, and impairment of judgement and memory.[17] The effects produced depend very much on the psychic make-up of the person who takes the drug, as Baudelaire himself warned, and it is obvious that any mental events occurring are individually coloured. One description, however, which does seem to be consistent is that which likens the hashish consumer to a person who is deeply in love without having the 'bother' of an actual sexual partner.

One of the most comprehensive clinical researches was undertaken as part of the study by the La Guardia Committee.[18] Between seventy and eighty subjects participated, including volunteers with no previous experience of cannabis in any form. This went in two phases, corresponding to a medical and a psychological study, and these comments are taken from the Chairman's summary:

> The effect of smoking appeared immediately and lasted from one to three or four hours. Those who had been given the cannabis extract experienced a much slower onset which lasted up to twenty-four hours. With increased dosage the effects were usually more marked and of longer duration but the action of any measured dose varied with the individual patient.

> Restlessness and loquaciousness accompanied mental experiences, 'such as a sense of well-being, relaxation, unawareness of surroundings, followed by drowsiness'.

It is important to note that the observers reported that pleasurable effects were frequently replaced by a state of apprehension. Physical symptoms consisted of tremor, ataxia, dizziness, a sensation of floating in space, dilation of pupils, dryness of throat, nausea and vomiting, an urge to urinate, hunger, and a desire for sweets. A small, but significant, number of patients showed mental confusion and delirious excitement with alternating periods of anxiety and laughter. The participants were in large part inmates of a penitentiary, serving sentences of between three months and three years, mostly for minor criminal offences, and included some emotionally unstable persons. It is therefore not surprising that there should have been a small percentage who reacted somewhat unfavourably.

Nearly all the physical symptoms can be explained as actions on the central nervous system and to some extent on the autonomic nervous system. The psychological study investigated psychomotor effects and concluded that static equilibrium and hand steadiness were affected while intellectual functions were in general impaired. However, there was no indication that the drug could change the basic personality of the individual. This is significant:

. . . the drug lessens inhibition and this brings out what is latent in his thoughts and emotions but it does not evoke responses which would otherwise be totally alien to him. It induces a feeling of self-confidence, but this is expressed in thought rather than in performance. There is, in fact, evidence of a diminution in physical activity.[19]

Although the drug in its various forms may produce sexual desires or phantasies and a kind of 'aphrodisiac' effect, there is, on the whole, no proof that sexual aggressiveness and performance is augmented – another of its aspects by which it might be likened to alcohol.

How far the removal of inhibitions and repressions may lead a habituate to crime is, of course, important in any argument for or against present legislation. Taking into account the available objective social research, one is inclined to say that no causal relationship between indulgence in cannabis and major crime can be demonstrated. It is hard to gather any satisfactory evidence to support those cases reported from the Far East of 'running amok' put down to long-standing hashish abuse. The only available authenticated account is one from India which supports, but at the same time somehow contradicts, these tales.[20]

Little has been said so far about the chronic pathological effects of the cannabis principles. There appears to be, at least among the majority of those who take it, no tolerance reaction, which means they do not find it necessary to increase their dose to maintain its effects. Likewise, the great majority of users have no trouble in stopping episodic or long-term dependence abruptly: no withdrawal symptoms, or only few of a physical nature, are experienced. (A number of American experts, however, have objected to this as a relatively simplified finding (see below).) In general, it could be said that it is the individual's underlying psychology, what happens to his friends and contacts, what his attitude is to life in general, his personal stability and genetic make-up which will determine how he reacts to prolonged habituation to marijuana or hashish.

In an unstable, disorganized personality prolonged abuse may bring on a psychosis. Acute forms of intoxication can resemble those precipitated by LSD or mescaline (see pp. 135–8). If physical or psychic symptoms become pronounced, respiration grows laboured and pallor and perspiration occur, other disturbing symptoms leading eventually to a state similar to *delirium tremens* (see page 30).

As with other drugs of dependence, the cannabis products, natural as well as (more recently) synthetic, have attracted medical attention for whatever potential therapeutic values they might offer. The hypnotic properties of certain preparations, and the anti-bacterial activity discovered in cannabidiolic acid, must have justified their early use in folk medicine, but their euphoria-producing qualities mainly attracted the psychiatrists, particularly in the days before the modern 'drug revolution' (see pp. 114–15). The synthetic preparation 'Synhexyl' was used in one important experiment in treating patients suffering from a type of depressive illness,[21] when an alleviation of symptoms was claimed in fifty-nine cases out of seventy. Unfortunately for its future, this treatment was made difficult by the drug's insolubility and slow, erratic action. Then, a little later, Wrigley and Parker[22] reported results which indicated no difference in the responses of patients suffering from similar depressive states to placebos or the synthetic derivative. While there have been other experiments, particularly to treat depersonalization as well as alcoholism and withdrawal symptoms, these have tended to be isolated, and in modern times the products of *Cannabis sativa* have not regained the role which they could claim to have held in the medicine of ancient China.

TREATMENT AND CURE

It is certainly a cliché and probably an over-simplification to say that most cannabis users are unstable persons who suffer from personality defects. A leader in the magazine *Science* (1968)[23] stated that between 30 and 35 per cent of the students at leading universities on the East and West Coasts of the U.S.A. had tried marijuana at least once – and added even more emphatically, 'today some of our finest youth are engaged in experiments that could have very damaging long-term effects'.

It is hard to say exactly what influence education and law enforcement can exert at this point in time and given present circumstances. As we know, withdrawal presents no difficulty, abstinence effects, if they exist, are light. It is the period following voluntary or enforced renouncement that needs special attention. Breaking with old 'pot party' friends is not always easy. Some contact with volunteers who have had training in countering drug habits generally will, of course, be helpful. Ex-habituates with actual personality defects should be treated in any case. Where the habit can be linked with socio-economic factors, then ensuring security and improving prospects may be a first condition to curing dependence, but, ironically, in the West the problem often occurs among those in a society whose sometimes hollow standards of affluence they reject. Symptoms of a serious nature – lethargy, inertia, self-neglect, false feelings of an increased capability and the resulting failure as well as the precipitation of psychoses – need special medical, social, and educational care which is not always immediately available. In many cases the simple processes of growing-up and managing to cope with the challenges that life presents will mean the cannabis user simply leaves the habit behind him.

Problems arising from cannabis are basically the same as those connected with other drug habits and concern soft drugs, as no tolerance and withdrawal difficulties occur. However, the introduction of ritualistic features, the link with a 'fight for individual liberty and self-responsibility', could carry greater dangers and difficulties than the actual drugs themselves, since ideological dreams developed under these conditions may be expected to be misunderstood, misapplied, and misleading.

THE CANNABIS CONTROVERSY

The whole atmosphere of controversy surrounding the use of cannabis in Western society looks like being with us for some time to come. In this area, as much as in the field of drug abuse generally, we must look at all the facts and implications available to us and define our attitudes accordingly. The partisans are joined in argument, but the arguments they rely on and the emotively loaded overtones they often adopt do not always contribute a great deal of basic value or encourage confidence in their statements. During the 1960s, cannabis in particular has come to symbolize the generation gap, especially in the minds of the young. It partly symbolizes their emancipation from parental control in the same way that smoking symbolized the spirit of female emancipation for many young women earlier in the century. But more than this, it also carries implications of rebellion against and rejection of the parental society. Society can and does prosecute (some would read 'persecute') those who commit the misdemeanour, including those who belong to the hierarchy of youthful culture, 'pop' idols and others in the public eye. We can take it that many who sympathize with this viewpoint are themselves young people who have never had any intention or wish to take cannabis in any form. The exasperation of the older generation can be explained easily by simply turning the situation on its head. As Professor Zinberg, one of the contributors to the Boston doctors' report, has been quoted as saying:

There is a definite reason why there is such a hysterical reaction from the public either for or against pot smokers. If we could understand that, we could understand a great deal more about our society.[34]

Clear minds have reached exaggerated conclusions, whether for or against the legalization of cannabis or the relaxing of existing laws. It is not easy to sort out fact from folklore, as the Wootton Committee has discovered for itself (see below). At our present stage of knowledge, even the most objective approach cannot disperse the difficulties. It is often as hard for the serious investigator to point out positive dangers as it is for those arguing that cannabis is harmless to support their case. The atmosphere of the hashish dream seems to have the power to spread beyond its actual boundaries. Only with LSD and other hallucinogens have such violent arguments and areas of disagreement been thrown into prominence.

We must re-emphasize that even the most stringent clinical experiments have shown an extraordinary variability of observation. Pharmacologists have been puzzled by the indecisiveness of experiments in animals. In humans, the present mental attitude or the individual psychology of a subject seem to govern the effects gained. It may be that the effects themselves often correspond to what is expected consciously or unconsciously from the drug – a respect in which it can again be considered in the same light as alcohol. Artists, poets, and writers who have tried it have found it a source of great disappointment as well as one of high enjoyment.

The case for the legalization of cannabis has been based on these assertions: that it has no short or long-term adverse effects so long as it is used in moderation, and used in this way may even be less harmful than tobacco or alcohol. That, like the psychedelic or 'consciousness-expanding' drugs, it can produce hallucination or mental states which are of positive value to the consumer; that it may, for instance, actually help to hold off a psychosis for someone in a precarious mental condition.

The famous (or infamous) advertisement in *The Times* of London, signed by a group of well-known scientists and artists,

appeared during 1967.[25] More recently the Executive Committee
of the British Humanist Association recommended that cannabis
resin should be removed from within the scope of the Dangerous
Drugs Act and the heavy penalties now imposed for possessing
the drug be replaced by small fines.[26] The final vote, however,
rejected any move to commit the association to demanding the
immediate legalization of cannabis subject to controls similar to
those applied to alcohol.

'Marijuana goes to College' was the title of an article in a
journal of the New York Academy of Sciences,[27] and it came to
the conclusion

... that marijuana will eventually be legalized, that the major
tobacco companies will market it. Whether educational reforms,
improvements in international and domestic relations, and a de-
emphasis on material wealth and success in America will reduce the
number of student marijuana smokers is debatable. The simple fact
is that the pleasure of smoking has convinced many that marijuana
is superior to alcohol and pills.

It cannot by any stretch of the imagination be said that all
those who favour legalization are irresponsible individuals. But
having considered their view briefly, it is essential to look at the
other side of the coin.

The permissive standpoint is based on the argument that
cannabis should at least be as available as alcohol, if subject to
similar controls. There is no evidence to suggest, however, that
cannabis is any less dangerous than alcohol: both alcohol and
tobacco present major problems and health hazards in our
society, and it may well be thought a major folly to add a third
potential factor. It is not perhaps unreasonable to speculate that
cannabis may produce its 'alcoholics', a proportion of users who
become obsessively dependent upon it for deep-set reasons and
who are eventually destroyed by their addiction. The widespread use of cannabis is a recent development and we can in
fact know very little about long-term effects without a great
deal more long-term research. What will the cumulative effects
be, for instance, in the individual who starts smoking marijuana
at eighteen and continues regularly for twenty or thirty years?

And what of the 'mind-enhancing' qualities? These are a highly subjective phenomena. What seems profound or exquisitely comic under the influence of hashish is often simply banal in the cold light of day. As Professor W. D. M. Paton has expressed it:

> There is no evidence whatever that these drugs 'enhance' the mind. . . . This [claim] may prove to be one of the frauds of the age. It is true that detachment from reality by one means or another . . . can be associated with fascinating sensory distortions, even with feelings of 'insight', of being near to ultimate reality. . . . But the actual insights brought back from these 'voyages' have always proved trivial.[28]

On the basis of the inadequacy of the present evidence and the general facts that we have presented in this chapter as a whole, we can only conclude that any society which made cannabis readily available to its members would be courting a potential tragedy. While, in time, views may be changed by increased knowledge, it is hard to see how the dubious benefits obtained or the equivocal motives for taking the drug can begin to justify the possible risks of such a course. To consider whether or not the law as it stands is unfairly harsh on the individual consumer is another question.

*

The publication in 1968 of *Cannabis*, the Report of the Advisory Committee on Drug Dependence (now, of course, popularly known as the 'Wootton Report', the Baroness Wootton having been the committee's chairman), had a more than parochial importance. Any proposal for changing the drug laws or for reconsidering their basis inevitably involves not only the country concerned, but also, if the country is a subscriber to the Geneva Single Convention of 1961, all the other signatories. The fundamental question in our context here remains should any of the preparations containing the active principle of the hemp plant be exempted from the necessity of being labelled as Dangerous Drugs and have their legal status revised? So far the only major leads have originated in the U.S.A. and the U.K.

From the U.S.A. an important statement appeared recently in

the *Journal of the American Medical Association*,[29] issued by the Committee on the Problems of Drug Dependence of the National Research Council, the National Academy of Sciences and the Council on Mental Health, and the Committee on Alcoholism and Drug Dependence of the American Medical Association. It is carefully worded and comes down decisively in favour of retaining the Marijuana Laws:

Cannabis is a dangerous drug and as such is a public health concern. . . . Legalization of marijuana would create a serious abuse problem in the United States.

Nevertheless, at the same time, it points out that the penalties for violating these laws seem in certain circumstances to be harsh and unrealistic:

Laws should provide for penalties in such a fashion that the courts would have sufficient discretion to enable them to deal flexibly with violaters. There are various degrees of possession and sale. . . . While persons should not be allowed to become involved with marijuana with impunity, legislators, law enforcement officials, and the courts should differentiate in the handling of the occasional user, the frequent user, the person sharing his drug with another, and the dealer who sells for a profit. . . .

This, on the face of it, eminently sane and well-reasoned proposal is more or less in harmony with the recommendations made by the Wootton Report,[30] which forms, however, a far more extensive document. The reaction accorded to the Wootton Report in the British House of Commons has already been commented on briefly (page 2), and one would never have guessed from the terms of that debate that,[31] besides being an advisory report open for discussion, it is also a document bristling with facts and data, bringing wisdom and compassion to bear on the central social and cultural problems involved – qualities that seem to evaporate only too readily in the political arena.

The sub-committee's recommendations amounted to this: hashish, in all its forms, should remain for the time being under restriction, though further research into all aspects of cannabis abuse should be encouraged and supported. The penal code regarding cannabis should be reviewed, retaining 'the principle of a single offence namely unlawful possession, sale or supply of cannabis or its derivatives'. The offence would carry 'a low range of penalties on *summary* conviction but a substantially higher range on *indictment*' (author's italics).*

If such legislation were brought in we would anticipate that the police would proceed on indictment only in those cases in which they believed there was organized large-scale trafficking. Offences involving simple possession and small-scale trafficking would, we hope, be dealt with summarily.

. . . In considering the scale of penalties our main aim, having regard to our view of the known effects of cannabis, is to remove for practical purposes, the prospect for imprisonment for possession of a small amount and to demonstrate that taking the drug in moderation is a relatively minor offence.

The failure of the sub-committee to face up to the difficult but vitally important distinction between the pusher and the merely casual consumer can be seen as the central flaw in the Report, and it seems possible that had they done so they would have put themselves in a stronger position. Be that as it may, the British Home Secretary, and, indirectly, his opposite number in the Shadow Cabinet, in effect rejected the Report, in itself an astonishing reaction. The motivations at the back of this were no doubt complex enough, involving political pressures as well as the ever-present latent fear of the older generations that any liberal humanizing of the law as it effects the young may herald an opening of the floodgates of depravity. Lady Wootton's subsequent protests at the emotive vocabulary used by the Home Secretary and her description of it as being offensive to her colleagues[32] appear by no means out of place in the circumstances.

It can only be seen as a profoundly retrograde development that a subject of this importance should have been treated so arbitrarily at the level concerned. A high standard of dialogue between legislators, educationists, and the generations themselves is not simply something to be hoped for, but an

---

* A summary offence is one that is dealt with in a magistrate's court, the magistrate deciding the verdict, while a trial on indictment takes place before a jury at a court of assize or quarter sessions.

urgent necessity. For reasons that have been indicated earlier in this chapter, it seems impossible to accept any body of opinion that advocates removing cannabis from within the scope of the Dangerous Drugs laws as reflecting a socially responsible viewpoint. Meanwhile the problem is not going to disappear overnight from the fabric of Western society. In the end it is probably up to us as individual citizens to exercise our right to demand from our governments and politicians that they should, at the very least, devote as much time and energy towards promoting or making possible long-term research as at the moment they seem to expend on often heated and ill-informed debates whenever the subject forces itself upon their attention.

Chapter Four

Opium, the Opiates, and the Mild Analgesics

1. The Opiates

ORIGIN AND HISTORY

Opium, the product of the juice of the poppy *Papaver somniferum* (so named by Linnaeus in 1753), is a drug that has a venerable place in history and which has been in medical use as a pain-killer at least for 2,000 years, possibly for very much longer. Dioscorides has left us the first full account of how it is derived, written in the first century A.D. Some have suggested it is Homer's *nepenthe*, which Helen gave to Telemachus and Menelaus at Sparta to bring oblivion of grief, and Theophrastus recorded its presence in the botanic garden in Athens in about 300 B.C. The word 'opium' is the latinized form of the Greek ὄπιον or ὀπός meaning vegetable juice. The opium poppy is a native of Asia Minor which rapidly spread over the whole of the Mediterranean area and then to Persia, India, and China, Arab traders acting as go-betweens.

In Western medicine its standard use was probably handed down as part of the classical tradition. References to it occur in Chaucer and Shakespeare. The fact of its enormous benefits

carrying the counterpart of an unimaginable curse, however,
and the need for caution, seems to have always been recognized
at least in part, even if the real extent of its potential power to
devastate a human personality did not become common knowledge before the early nineteenth century. Both Dioscorides and
von Hohenheim (known as Paracelsus), the man who has been
credited with inventing laudanum in the 1500s, left dire warn-
ings to posterity. Pomet, on the other hand, in his *Compleat*

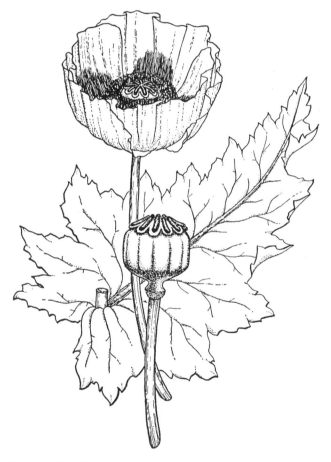

Fɪɢ. 3. The flower and seed head of the opium poppy,
Papaver somniferum

History of Druggs,[1] offers no hint of menace as he recounts the virtues of various opium preparations:

Opium is narcotick, hypnotick and anodyne; it composes the Hurry of the Spirits, causes Rest and Insensibility, is comfortable and refreshing in great Watches and strong Pains; provokes Sweat powerfully – helps most Diseases of the Breast and Lungs; as Coughs, Colds, Catarrhs, and Hoarseness – prevents or allays spitting of Blood, vomiting, and all Lasks of the Bowels; is specifical in Colick, Pleurisies and hysterick Cases. . . .

[It] procures Rest, by its viscous and sulphureous Particles, which being convey'd into the Chanels of the Brain, by the volatile Parts, agglutinates and fixes the animal Spirits, in such a Manner, that it stops, for some Time, their Circulation, from the Swiftness of their former Motion; so that during that Obstruction, or Tye upon the Spirits, Sleep ensues; for the Senses are, as it were, fettered or lock'd up by the viscous or agglutinating Property of the *Opium*.

Until de Quincey's *Confessions of an English Opium Eater* was published in 1822,[2] tinctures of opium were continued to be regarded as simple remedies for the family medicine chest. Among the eminent of their day, Byron, Shelley, Keats, Moore, Lamb, and Scott are all on record as having taken opium at one time or another for various ailments, though apparently without becoming dependent on it. Those who were not so lucky, on the other hand, found themselves bound by what de Quincey called 'the accursed chain which fettered me'. De Quincey himself, in spite of the claims he made in his book, never broke with the habit until the day of his death; neither did Clive of India – who died of an overdose – William Wilberforce, Crabbe, Coleridge, nor Wilkie Collins, to name only some of the more well known. In more recent times, the great French writer and artist Jean Cocteau did undertake successfully to cure himself of a craving for smoking opium, and the diary he kept during his days in the clinic is a remarkable artistic document.[3]

This is not the place however to consider the literary value of whatever the tormented poets and writers involved may have brought back from their strange journeys: their visions of grandeur progressing to black horror and sometimes to the disintegration of their talents. It has been shown that Coleridge's opium dreams in fact contributed practically nothing of value to his verse.[4] Passages in Crabbe's poetry often have a strange and sinister beauty – what the English poet and critic Geoffrey Grigson has called, in one instance, a 'piercing, thrilling desolation'[5] – but while Crabbe made art of this experience, it is hard to see that opium as such in any way added to the value of his art. It is important to consider this aspect carefully since many still tend to claim some basis of justification for drugs at this point. As with cannabis (see page 51), opium can add nothing to existing insight, sensitivity, or talent, and the illusion that it does has been a major deception that none of the above writers would for one moment have endorsed.*

In glancing at the literary scene, however, we are ignoring the plight of many hundreds or thousands of ordinary people who at the same time were dependent on their regular supplies of laudanum or pills from local chemists. Their fates have gone largely unrecorded, and they have left few statistics. De Quincey has given us a small indication of the problem's extent:[6]

Three respectable London druggists, in widely remote quarters of London, . . . assured me that the number of . . . opium-eaters was at this time immense; and that the difficulty of distinguishing these persons, to whom habit had rendered opium necessary, from such as were purchasing it with a view to suicide, occasioned them daily trouble and disputes. . . . But, . . . some years ago, on passing through Manchester, I was informed by several cotton manufacturers that their work-people were rapidly getting into the practice of opium-eating; so much so, that on a Saturday afternoon the counters of the druggists were strewed with pills . . . in preparation for the known demand in the evening.

As we have already seen, the use of opium started within the precincts of early medical science. It was used mainly to counter traumatic pain, overactivity of the gut (dysentery, diarrhoea), and inflammation of the respiratory tract (coughing). The application of opium simply to achieve pleasurable effects does not seem to have taken root before the end of the

---

* As Baudelaire rounded off *Les Paradis artificiels*: 'he who makes use of a poison in order to think may soon not be able to think without the poison. Think of the frightful state of a man whose paralysed imagination can no longer work without the help of hashish or opium.'

eighteenth century in China, when first Portugal, and later Britain, encouraged the import of opium into the Orient for hardly reputable reasons. China lost the war which she waged against Britain in 1840, following the destruction of the British merchant ships which had taken opium to the Chinese mainland. Had the Chinese government won, we might speculate that our present-day problem would have never developed on such a worrying scale. At least the plant's growing and harvesting would never have reached its present dimensions.

The black or white seeds, which contain only an inactive oil, are used in Central and Eastern Europe to flavour local dishes. They are also sprinkled on the outside of many Continental breads. Poppy straw,[7] on the other hand, has become an additional source for the active principles, and, with every other form of opium, has been controlled since 1925, and placed under international restrictions following the Single Convention of 1961.[8] The pure opium alkaloids were originally isolated from the brown, bitter crude opium that came in the form of granulated powder or cake as well as from its medicinal forms, still in use into the twentieth century: paregoric (camphorated tincture), laudanum (alcoholic tincture), and other mixtures. The pure alkaloids include morphine and codeine among others (see Table 5, page 177). The derivation of the names of some of these powerful natural drugs is interesting, reflecting as they do the inclination of the early nineteenth century towards the classics: *morphine*, also *morphia*, comes from Morpheus, the Greek god of dreams, son of Somnus, god of sleep and brother of Death (perhaps not irrelevant to the drug problem); codeine comes from the Greek word for 'poppy head'. Medicine, in its old and new forms, has used these alkaloids intensively, either as such or in mixtures, or as relatively simple derivatives. Morphine seems to have first been used on an extensive scale during the American Civil War. Later remedies, like dihydromorphinone (Dilaudid), diacetylmorphine (heroin), and methyldihydromorphinone (metopon), came to be developed and manufactured by a young pharmaceutical industry.

The pain-killing (analgesic) action of opiates in the treatment of war wounds, accident injuries, and, in more modern times, post-operative discomfort and the intractable pain of incurable diseases, has been of incalculable value to medicine. Their wide use, on the other hand, has at the same time made them available for purposes of misuse (medical people and nurses not being exempt from the temptation). The hope that the analgesic element might be separated from the euphoric one has prompted chemists to experiment with the natural products and to synthesize many of the molecules which are mostly akin to parts of morphine structure.*

Yet, with only a few exceptions, none of these compounds has helped to diminish or remove the dilemma. Through some of them the gate to physical and psychological dependence, with tolerance thrown in as a special Pandora's gift of misfortune, has been opened even wider.

A systematic, sustained attempt to prepare an ideal morphine substitute was carried out over a period of ten years during the 1930s. But while a considerable body of knowledge about the relationship between its chemistry and its physiological effects accumulated,[9] no totally synthesized active compounds had been made in the laboratory at that time. Dramatically an active product was discovered by chance in Germany just before the Second World War[10] in a series of piperidine derivatives, designed to produce remedies against spasms. Medical men, at about that time, only had the natural products atropine and papaverine at their disposal for treating painful spasms in patients. Some of these piperidine derivatives, to everyone's surprise, showed genuine analgesic activity but no particularly pronounced euphoric effects. One of the present authors[11] recommended with a group of colleagues at the beginning of the war that the production of pethidine, as one of the members of the series was called, should be undertaken in Britain to counteract a possible shortage of opium imports. While the hope continued to exist that the disadvantageous properties of the opium alkaloids would diminish or even be eliminated, this hope was

---

* These we propose to call the 'syn-opiates', in America the term 'opioids' being used fo r the whole family.

not fulfilled in pethidine. A small number of more recent synthetic products, however, have shown signs of some success
in this direction, two or three of them being of potential assistance in the treatment of addicts, and one, pentazocine, which is
an analgesic with low dependence liability and a drug outside
narcotics control.

At the present time therefore the medical profession has at its
disposal a considerable number of effective and valuable drugs
to be used to fight deep-set, intractable pain, none of which is
completely satisfactory in this respect. In cases involving the
later stages of terminal cancer, the question of repeating large
doses of a substance like heroin and creating dependence does
not arise, but in other instances, where a fatal illness may not be
involved, the physician has to tread with care. Only a partial
solution to the problem of separating these drugs' effectiveness in
combating physical pain from their addiction-forming properties
has so far been achieved.[12]

CONSUMPTION

The opiates and related compounds are the first group of
drugs we have so far looked at which in some instances may be
taken by injection (in slang terms 'pop', 'bang', 'shot', 'fix'),
three ways being employed:

(a) under the skin (subcutaneously or s.c., 'skin popping');
(b) into a large muscle (intramuscularly); and
(c) into a vein (intravenously or i.v., 'main line').

The last method needs a certain degree of skill, especially as
the veins do not swell up sufficiently after a series of injections,
even after a tourniquet has been applied. Also scarring makes
the walls tougher and more difficult to puncture. It takes only a
minimal knowledge of hygiene to realize that syringe, needles,
and water should be made sterile before use. But the addict on
hard drugs, owing to his general low state of health, is more
susceptible to infection to an above average extent, besides the
fact that his concern for hygiene as such may fade out alto-
gather. (Doctors and nurses who have fallen victim to addiction

are less exposed to these dangers.) Death from sepsis and liver damage is relatively high among the opiate dependants, and the other major risk for the active drug population, apart from over-dosing ('o.d.'), is embolism from an air bubble being introduced into a vein by the clumsy handling of a syringe's plunger, which may in extreme cases result in death without the addict even having had his 'high'. There are two books, William Burroughs's *Junkie*[13] and Larner and Tefferteller's *The Addict in the Street*,[14] which contain vivid descriptions of these methods based on first-hand experiences. Books like these are valuable, but are really only a substitute for the real confrontation with the 'junkie's' world which is necessary to reach a wholly realistic and objective impression.

One aspect which demands serious consideration is the psychological background and its various overtones. It often happens that when an opiate or its surrogates has lost the power to produce feelings of well-being and security – the addict using the drug mostly to avoid the worst of the withdrawal syndrome – the ritual connected with the injections seems to gain enormously in importance: the sterilization of paraphernalia, the prepara-tion of the solution, the search for and finding the right spot in the vein, the slow pushing of the plunger and the drug's entry into the system. . . . It looks almost as if the dependent person under these circumstances is hooked on the process of applica-tion itself.[15] Others, on the other hand, seem to dislike the ritual and the needle, and prefer an oral intake, swallowing tablets or anything equivalent.[16] Such a preparation may additionally carry inert dilution material to give it bulk – 'lactose' powder, for instance. Any mixture like this which has not been provided legally through a doctor's office or a reputable pharmacist may often contain less drug than claimed by the pusher. This is, in one sense, to the disadvantage of the addict as buyer, but in another is also to his advantage since there almost certainly exists a relationship between the total dose and the steepness of the tolerance curve and the severity of with-drawal symptoms, and it looks as if a stringency of dosage and supply can keep the overall problem within certain limits.[17] The pusher also obviously comes out of the deal well, but then he usually does, unless he fails to avoid prosecution.

Opium, although sometimes taken orally in its natural state, is traditionally smoked in a special type of pipe. Heroin can be added to cigarette tobacco and smoked like reefers ('chasing the dragon').[18] It can also be inhaled or snuffed like cocaine (see page 93). Whatever country the addicted population may live in, the reasons for the different forms of consumption remain the addict's desire to produce either slow or speedy biological and toxicological actions, according to personal taste, while avoiding detection by the law. When a doctor or surgeon uses any of the opiates or syn-opiates for legitimate purposes, he has to make a discretionary choice, as we have seen, according to the clinical circumstances.

THE EFFECTS OF THE OPIATES

This section will, as far as possible, deal with the straightforward, objective pharmacological, therapeutic, and toxicological facts and leave the more problematical fields of psychology and sociology on one side for the moment. Such phenomena as tolerance, dependence, and withdrawal, however, as yet have no clear-cut scientific explanations, and compulsion towards recurrent lapses, after apparent cures in some addicts, may be caused by a combination of physiological, biochemical, and psychic phenomena. People outside the medico-scientific world may attribute this absence of satisfactory theories to vaccillation and even ignorance on the part of medical specialists. To lay people, scientists often appear to change their theories and hypotheses like soiled shirts whenever new facts come to light that do not fit with provisional explanations. As a *New Scientist* editorial has asked,[19] however, 'Do non-scientists really understand the nature of this kind of activity?' Each small step forward leads to greater understanding, and in this case all the complex events which happen as a drug meets a living organism or any of its parts and cells results in a highly intricate and complex pattern of effects.

These biological effects can, as we know, often be utilized for therapeutic use. With the opiates and syn-opiates, however, safe dose levels are narrow and, if raised, can easily lead to acute toxic symptoms or even prove lethal. The same thing happens, of course, with a great number of drugs and substances which no one would usually consider toxic and which are consumed in the course of everyday events. It all depends on the size of a dose and its safety limits. But effects can also be produced which may be called pathological or chronically toxic, this referring specifically to dependence and all its consequences.

Besides recognizing the blessings which opium and all its derivatives have bestowed on mankind, we must develop a more exact impression of their pharmacological actions. The most pronounced examples are depression of the central nervous system and through it relief of deep-set pain, a fair degree of sedation, and, in some cases, sleep.[20] A few individuals respond to opiates with excitement, often accompanied by nausea and vomiting, while with larger doses convulsions can occur and administration to anyone susceptible to these undesirable side-effects should be avoided. One of the most undeniable depressing effects exerted by most opiates and syn-opiates is that on the respiration, though it is claimed that this central action is less pronounced with a number of synthetic products. While a depressed respiration is naturally never a good thing, the under-lying mechanism is at least partly responsible for the anti-tussive (anti-cough) action of morphine, codeine, and related compounds which occur mainly in cough mixtures. In Britain no prescription is necessary for a cough mixture that contains less than 1·5 per cent of an opiate or syn-opiate, especially if it is codeine, though in most states of the U.S.A. any codeine-containing compound is subject to special restrictions.

Another important physiological effect is a relaxing action on the stomach and intestinal muscles. Most opiates can calm down any strong movements of the small and large intestine, which may relieve sufferers with non-specific diarrhoeas and intestinal infections but in addicts will lead to chronic constipation. Mixtures of opiates, particularly morphine, with kaolin and antibiotics are often prescribed for intestinal infections, but prolonged consumption must be avoided because of the dependence danger. This also applies to any other low-potency preparation like chlorodyne, liquorice-lozenges, as well as other preparations like paregoric.

The chances of taking an overdose of opiates or syn-opiates under medical supervision are very slight, unless the patient gets hold of a number of dosages surreptitiously and attempts suicide with his accumulated supply. The addict, on the other hand, may poison himself inadvertently or by gross error, paying the supreme penalty or becoming very sick. The seriousness of such acute toxicity depends on the dose level.* It is difficult to state with certainty an exact acute toxic dose because of the varied responses to opiates in different individuals, especially in the young and elderly, who are very vulnerable. On average, 20 to 30 milligrams ($\frac{1}{3}$ to $\frac{1}{2}$ grain) will produce mild symptoms; 100 milligrams ($1\frac{2}{3}$ grains) cause serious symptoms. In a fatality it looks much as if the person had died of slow suffocation, mainly from a respiration collapse. Like the alcohol-barbiturate combination (see page 121), other drug mixtures like the 'MAO inhibitors' (see page 110) combined with opiates can reinforce each other with disastrous results.

Before moving on to the intriguing subject of the mechanisms of analgesia, tolerance, and dependence, we should look at several questions which are commonly raised in the public mind: Why should there be all this fuss concerning narcotic drugs? And why such a wild-goose chase, costing many countries a fortune just to aid the minority, small at that, represented by the 1968 figures of 2,000 known heroin addicts in U.K. and 62,000 (1967) in the U.S.A. (risen from 45,000 in 1960)? Apart from any moral obligation for the luckier portion of a nation towards its hapless fellow men – an ethical philosophy still not

* Pharmacologists express a medium lethal dose as LD_{50}, when it kills half out of a sufficiently large group of experimental animals in a toxicity test. Morphine, when injected into mice subcutaneously, has an LD_{50} of 531 milligrams per kilogram, which compares with its analgesic dose, 0·75 mg/kg (i.m.) in cats, or ED_{50} (effective dose s.c.) of 2·1 mg/kg in mice quite favourably with respect to its therapeutic safety. This corresponds to a total dose of 10 milligrams in an average man.

fully accepted even in some of the most 'Christian' parts of the
world – anyone who has the misfortune to suffer severe pain
through an accident, serious illness, or post-operative discomfort
as well as medical and para-medical personnel merit protection
against the dangers of becoming dependent. To take one comparison, the number of citizens in England and Wales who have
died of various forms of leukaemia amount, perhaps to everybody's surprise, to a similar number of the opiate addicts
registered with the Home Office. It is true that the latest figures
for people dead of lung cancer in the U.K., principally caused by
the tobacco habit (see page 146), is fourteen times that without
anybody taking much notice. But hardly anyone would grudge
money spent on research into the causes and treatment of
leukaemia. The attitude of the general public tends to be
unfriendly and hostile towards the person dependent on opiates
and syn-opiates, even in countries where the law treats him as
essentially a sick person. We do not on the whole today consider
neurotic or mentally disturbed states as despicable, but when it
comes to a drug addict or an alcoholic, the dominant attitude
still seems to be symbolized by the question, 'Why doesn't he
pull himself together?' As everyone working in this area has
reason to lament, if only it was as simple as that.

THE BIOLOGICAL MECHANISMS

If we could produce a complete answer to the question of how
analgesic action works, it would represent an enormous step
forward in resolving the phenomena of tolerance, dependence,
and withdrawal. The known facts indicate that the nervous
system is involved, but this is not all; some experimental results
point to the participation of hormonal substances,[21] and another
contributing factor is the breakdown of opiates and related
drugs in the body. Anyone who wishes to follow through
exhaustively all the available information on this subject could
not do better than to turn to *The Addictive States*,[22] published
recently by the Association for Research in Nervous and Mental
Diseases, an excellently produced book which presents most of
the problems and their possible solutions. The overall impression

is as follows: out of hundreds of observations no all-embracing theory is as yet available. But there exist a host of hypotheses which, while not giving final answers, confirm the complexity of the events which lead to analgesia and the various facets of chronic toxicity. Very many changes take place within a human body under the influence of opiates and syn-opiates, both grossly physiological or subtly biochemical. It is therefore extremely difficult to pick out those which are actually involved in the cause and effect of any particular process. Scientists face here a considerable challenge, but one day we shall have a complete answer.

Meanwhile, it has been found that the acute administration of morphine, for example, diminishes the excretion from the brain and adrenal glands of adrenaline and nor-adrenaline (epinephrine in the American terminology).[23] More recently, the situations connected with acute administration, tolerance, and abstinence has been reviewed and the conclusion reached that, particularly during withdrawal, the response of the sympathetic nervous system (adrenaline or epinephrine) was the same as that which occurs during stress and strain.[24] In fact, during a state of chronic intoxication – identical with a period of dependence and tolerance – an increase in these hormone-like amines was observed. The one helpful aspect of these investigations is that these changes are long-lasting, and this may in turn reveal a more profound damage to vital centres of the brain than the 'optimists' have hopefully anticipated.

It would take up too much space to give a full description of all the difficulties and complexities involved. Laurie has already pointed out the number of 'myths' created by cautious scientists withholding as yet incomplete answers,[25] and we have no wish to add to them. Scientific truth is, in any case, more often than not a 'non-news' item, since it only comes in bits and pieces and only after many tedious sifting processes.

Here, for the reader's convenience, are a few of the main hypotheses summarized:

1. *Pain and analgesia*: no nerve cells of the brain exist

specifically for pain sensation; there is increasing evidence that parts of the thalamus act as relays for pain, and consequently Descartes's idea of a specific pathway is probably incorrect.[26] Whether there is such a thing as 'psychic' pain is a matter for conjecture and depends very much on whether the effects of opiates on physical and 'psychic' pain go in parallel.

2. *Development of physical dependence and other manifestations of chronic toxicity*: interplay between depressing and exciting effects has a part in this development; in contrast to Laurie's[27] presentation of ideas about withdrawal, some research workers consider it unlikely that excitatory symptoms represent those of abstinence after the depressive effects have disappeared. Another hypothesis, which seems plausible, is that a prolonged intake of opiate destroys a biological balance (called homeostasis). This leads to delay in a process of adjustment as the drug is withdrawn. Fitting in with this is the possibility that, in contrast to the excitatory reactions mentioned above, withdrawal symptoms result from a rebound, or 'overshoot hyperexcitability', and that, in addition, certain nervous pathways have fallen into disuse. In other words, when the normal nervous system is exposed for any length of time to drugs which, by their depressing action, reduce nerve activity, the nerve cell in its altered environment attempts adaptation which one could rightly call 'chemogenic' (caused by chemicals).

Considering the tolerance phenomenon in particular, it has been proposed that three part-mechanisms could be responsible for this feature of chronic toxicity, not only with the opiates, but also with such other drugs as barbiturates:[28]

1. Animals and human addicts made tolerant by repeated doses may have a reduced sensitivity of drug receptors (mainly in the central nervous system – the site where agents interact with tissues).

2. They may have lost, or been depleted of, physiologically active neuro-hormones.

3. They have an increased production of enzymes which are responsible for drug metabolism, i.e. increased removal of drugs

(see also Chapter Seven). Such enzymic activities, among others, might be responsible for the loss of methyl from the nitrogen of opiates. In fact an opiate antagonist such as nalorphine inhibits nitrogen demethylation, an action which supports the proposal. (See Table 6, page 178.)

The fact that animals, mice, rats, dogs, react to narcotics in a way very similar to man may represent evidence against the conviction of some writers and members of the public that all potential addicts suffer from personality problems and therefore belong to the considerable number of schizoid and paranoid persons. The voluntary self-injection by rats to maintain their dependence on morphine, and by monkeys with heroin and cocaine, illustrates that the behavioural aspect and physical dependence are not a specific human characteristic.[29] On the contrary, these rats and monkeys have exhibited all the symptoms of tolerance, dependence, and withdrawal so often described in man.

The opiate antagonists have a role to play in the treatment of chronic intoxication by acting as precipitators of withdrawal symptoms and as replacements for heroin and morphine, since their own abstinence symptoms are milder. Most importantly for future development, some are examples of drugs that possess a high analgesic activity, but which, dose for dose, show less tolerance effect and sometimes have no euphoric, or even have dysphoric,* properties.[30] This, at any rate, is a hopeful signpost for the future (see comments on pentazocine, p. 69).

MISUSE AND THE PSYCHOLOGICAL AND SOCIAL ASPECTS

'How can we best characterize, in psychological or psychiatric terms, those persons who have become addicted to opioid drugs?' This question is asked by Chein et al.,[31] and the following answers are given:

Addicts are not intrinsically psychiatrically or psychologically discriminable from many other psychiatric patients. . . . There is no specific psychodynamic determination of addiction . . . there are no psychological traits which can be uniformly applied to addicts. Some

* The opposite to pleasurable effects.

are more sociopathic, more inadequate, more hysterical, more depressive, more lower class, more uneducated, more anxious, more exploitative, more sadomasochistic and more infantile than other addicts, or than comparison control groups.

This seems to be a clear-cut condensation of the psychiatrist's viewpoint. But, the reader may ask, 'How does it all begin? Do people, whatever the history of their becoming acquainted with hard drugs, either through therapy, professional opportunities, or social contacts, maybe by way of the soft drugs, have a recognizable psychological make-up that makes them candidates for dependence?' This has been partly answered, but there are also many who insist that psychic deviation from the 'normal' is a spring-board from which to begin intake of opiates and to become dependent on them. It is perhaps more rational to assume a *multiple* causation, especially considering the 'normal' rats and monkeys mentioned above.

Significantly, addicts themselves do not seem to differentiate between reasons for initial use and reasons for dependence.[32] We must mistrust any over-simplified assumption that addicts have a specific personality.[33] A. M. Freedman also points out that 'narcotic addiction (or as we would call it nowadays, dependence of the opiate type) is a disorder, the aetiology of which is based upon a multitude of factors with variable contributions from each factor. . . .'

These factors are psychology, biology, perhaps an inherited bio-chemistry which includes metabolic deficiencies; social and economic backgrounds, pressing housing problems, employment, living conditions in cities, difficulty in adolescent adjustment to a rapidly changing world; insecurity, loneliness, revolt against authority.

Is there, then, a *social* type who can avoid becoming a victim? Freedman says no! There is at least one type of addict who manages to live a conventional life, holding regular jobs, remaining devoted to his family, and so on.

Is it true that the opiate dependent person who has undergone treatment, achieved a cure, but relapsed, possesses a certain character trend? (This may still be asked in spite of the evidence for complex causations at the start and continuation of taking drugs.) There is a possibility that people who have gone through a state of physical dependence and the trauma of abstinence are predisposed to relapse: something in their metabolic or physiological make-up may have changed permanently, and some animal experimental results support this idea. Is it correct, then, that addicts can spontaneously 'mature' out of their habit, as Winnick claims[34] and Laurie emphasizes?[35] It is obviously important to obtain firm confirmation if it should be so. There are indications that strong religious belief, engendered by something like 'conversion', as well as altered attitudes produced by changes in environment may ease escape from the closed circle, and it is well known that addicts belonging to the medical profession achieve rapid and total cures more readily than members of the general population.

Do addicts suffer bad mental and physical health and die early? As already mentioned, there is no single type of opiate dependant. It would therefore be unscientific to jump to generalized conclusions about deterioration in health, the development of personal and mental sufferings, and social degeneration. Some do come very close to the worst picture the layman has of the drug-takers. Others, on the other hand, over long periods look like anyone else.

It is a great mistake to be either over-pessimistic or over-optimistic, and it is understandable that those connected with narcotics control should take a pessimistic view, because they see the worst that the underworld and the drug-traffickers can achieve. Even if soft drugs were to become socially acceptable, it would not alter the basic situation: that drugs are a hazard to anyone who takes them.

TREATMENT AND CURE

If the abuse of a drug is its consumption in such a way that its use involves a harmful effect on an individual or the society he lives in and so requires control, then, obviously, prevention is the best 'cure'. Educational as much as legal measures must remain the foremost weapons in the fight. This battle is essentially a preventative one, and as such it represents an even vaster challenge than that presented by the need for cure. The reason is quite simple: the size of the most exposed and vulnerable part of the population is naturally far larger than the final number of victims, although there is a definite upward trend in the number of known addicts in the U.K. and U.S.A., particularly of heroin users. As at August 1969, the 1968 figure of 2,000 for the U.K. had risen to 2,782. The expectations are that this could reach 10,000 by 1972,[36] and it is hard to see anything happening to prevent this increase, short of the discovery of an ideal analgesic. Only this event (see page 69) could lead to an embargo on opiates and syn-opiates and the cultivation of poppies. Meanwhile the decision taken by the government of Iran in 1969 to lift its thirteen-year prohibition on the cultivation of opium (previously Iran had been among the world's major suppliers) has caused considerable disquiet to all those engaged in combating illegal traffic at the international level.[37]

Where treatment is concerned, the incidence of cure and the possibility of an individual maturing out of his addiction has to be set against the high relapse rate.

As we have seen, the public at large, as well as certain authors writing in this field, and even a few medical people, seem to look on the addict's personality defects as a sort of manifestation of sin, easily to be redeemed by a simple act of will. For them the addict is a wilful social outcast who must be brought back to conformity, and who, perhaps on an unconscious level, represents for them a scapegoat manifesting society's defects. It would be more helpful if we could all bring ourselves to view the addict in the same light as we do anyone suffering a comparable physical or mental disability. While lack of courage and self-discipline may be one element which needs to be overcome, it is hardly practical to make this aspect the main one to be treated, or to demand that any individual should 'opt back' into society if he has no wish to. We have seen that drugs have come to be a symbol of social rejection or rebellion, but to look at the plight of the heroin or morphine addict in this light is absurd. (In any case, one would think that strength of character is essential in any successful revolutionary, using that term in a very generalized sense.) The main difficulty with the addict's defects of personality is that he tends to seek the company of those having similar defects, perhaps because 'normal' society offers him so little real support. This in itself increases his difficulty in ever finally breaking the chain.

It becomes clear that just as important as education and the weight of the law is knowledge of any personality trends that may lead to drug abuse. Thus, the educator and the law administrator must be prepared to work in close conjunction with the psychiatrist and the psychologist at every level presented by the problem.

Once dependence has developed with the drugs we are discussing, the following techniques are available:

1. Stabilization and withdrawal in centres and hospitals (preferably under voluntary conditions, but in some cases by enforced procedure).

2. Rehabilitation in work and social environment, especially if, under the law of his country, the patient has served a term in prison.

3. In some cases, chemotherapy by opiate antagonists may succeed.

Any future developments, fresh from the medical or social scientist's working bench, must be given cautious but progressive trial. Continuous research, as recommended by addiction committees and almost all authors, should be actively encouraged at a governmental level if we are ever to see a virtually complete eradication of this complex physical and social illness.

Considering this problem in the world at large, it must be remembered that a multiaetiological disease requires a multidirectional therapy, many causations and contributory factors coming together to 'give birth' to the fully fledged addict. On the whole, there is no great difference between one or another country in their treatments. The countries of the Eastern bloc (including Yugoslavia), in addition to Japan, either claim to have no dependence problem or else publish such low figures that one wonders how accurate or realistic they really are.[38] The following selection of areas will help to show up the leading differences.

United Kingdom: The main recommendations upon which medical and legal procedures rest in the United Kingdom are laid down in *Drug Addiction*, the Second Report of the Interdepartmental Committee (see also page 13).[39] As far as treatment is concerned, the establishment of treatment centres, especially in the London area, has been recommended. The most important change it made concerned its proposal to introduce powers for the compulsory detention of addicts by the staff of those centres. At the same time, only the medical people there have the right to prescribe heroin or cocaine to addicts; doctors outside these centres can no longer prescribe for a patient. While these suggestions represent a move away from the more liberal attitudes of the past, known as the 'British system', they should in course of time, we may hope, improve the situation at least where treatment and cure is concerned. Its main effect, of cutting back on over-prescribing and the problems created here by well-meaning as well as certain dubious medical practitioners, is one clear advantage. We must regard this as an experiment in an early stage, though from early reports the main impression is one of cautious optimism coupled with a certain feeling of limitation.

U.S.A.: Some of the legal aspects of addiction and its treatment in the United States have already been mentioned (see page 14). As the authors of *Drug Abuse: Escape to Nowhere*[40] point out, the public (specifically here the American public) has regarded addicts as incurable. The American attitude to law enforcement has been far harsher than the corresponding British one, with the therapeutic side correspondingly more rigid. Only over the last few years have matters changed, particularly since the enactment of the Narcotic Addict Rehabilitation Act of 1966.[41] A number of treatment centres,[42] such as the one in the Federal Hospital at Lexington, Kentucky, have started experimental programmes, and others, like Daytop Lodge, on Staten Island, New York, and at Boston State Hospital, have been opened to treat opiate dependants. It looks as though the U.S.A. and the U.K. are drawing closer together in therapeutic attitudes.

Canada: This country has created a Narcotic Addiction Clinical Investigation Unit in Toronto and, since 1963, treated day and out patients by chemotherapy (the use of antagonists), withdrawal, occupational therapy, psychotherapy, and milieu-therapy.[43] The whole work is based on this principle: that narcotic addiction is a public health problem which involves the patient's whole person, including his physical, psychological, social, and economic make-up and well-being.

Europe: Countries like Sweden, Switzerland, and France,[44] to take only a few examples, apply similar measures to those mentioned above, though there may be differences in the extent to which compulsion to accept treatment in a special institution is applied. France has provided for this kind of 'involuntary therapy' since 1963. For those concerned mainly in the field of prevention, it may seem puzzling that, in those countries where draconic methods exist, the incidence of serious addiction seems surprisingly low. As with the Communist countries, we would not wish to imply that the statistics are inadequate or 'cooked'. But mankind is mankind, and rebellious youth, youth, the world over, so that it will be interesting to follow the statistics published by the United Nations over the next few years to see how those from these countries correspond with the predictions of steady increases made in countries which acknowledge a serious problem.

Far East: Thailand and Hong Kong[45] both have traditional and longstanding opium consumption problems. In 1966, there were still about 62,500 addicts among the Crown Colony's population of 3,800,000 (1 in 60). Both countries run treatment centres; the Thai one was capable of taking 7,000 addicts during the first year, and the voluntary one in Hong Kong closed down in 1965 to be re-opened on an island away from the mainland.

One of the most intriguing reports comes from Japan,[46] where the abuse of heroin has been a problem only since 1955. The treatment, in so-called rehabilitation centres, is compulsory, and the appointment of addiction counsellors by local councils has led to a very remarkable diminution in the number of narcotic addicts. On the other hand, there exist no less than 900 addict centres in mental hospitals throughout Japan, which raises one important question: is coercion the most successful way to treat this physical and social illness?

In the opinion of the World Health Organization's Expert Committee on Dependence-Producing Drugs,[47] the emphasis must be on early diagnosis and possible prevention. They point out the differences that exist between individuals, not only with those more at risk than others, but also when it comes to success in curing by hospital treatment, group therapy, individual psychotherapy, or actual failure, and so on. 'Crisis' organizations, like Narcotics Anonymous, deserve all the support we can give them. The co-operation of the addict population, especially those belonging to certain categories, is essential, though unfortunately this may exclude the 'derelicts', for whom the chance of a cure is very poor indeed.

It may be appropriate to end this section on the opiates with a quotation by an ex-drug addict, taken from *The Addict in the Streets*;[48] not one of the intellectuals or 'philosophers' of the drug scene, but an ordinary individual reflecting the vicious circle that he found himself caught up in:

Times I wish I could do much more. I'd talk to all kinds of people and scream and just tell'em, show'em that they are being misled. . . Of course there is some who will never be off drugs. Definitely. Even when they say they want to stop, you might mean it, but they know. . . . I want my marriage to be successful more than anything in the world. I want children, my wife wants children. That's one thing, though, we will not have. As long as I am shooting dope, I don't want to bring any children in to this world. If I'm clean we've agreed that I have to stay clean for two years before we try for any kids. . . .

2. The Mild Analgesics

Before we leave the analgesics behind, this would seem the place to take a quick look at those varieties of mild pain-killer and sedative which are not derived from opium but which are openly available for self-medication and of which the most well-known is aspirin. Usually regarded as innocuous, these do in fact often have their hazardous side.

Since the pharmaceutical industry's flying start during the later nineteenth century, it has produced a number of preparations which do not lead to physical dependence but which may produce dependence of a psychological kind. After other drugs such as amidopyrine have gone out of fashion, aspirin still remains the favourite after seventy years. Aspirin (acetyl-salicylic acid) was evolved in Germany in 1899. It represented the crowning achievement to a search over many years for a safe derivative of salicylic acid, derived in turn from salicin, an ingredient isolated from the leaves of certain species of willow. Dioscorides, the Greek physician, recorded the use of a decoction of willow leaves to treat gout, and for centuries in Europe infusions of willow were a standard folk remedy for rheumatism, toothache, and ear-ache, among other discomforts. Apart from its antipyretic (anti-fever) effects, aspirin has analgesic and (more recently confirmed) anti-rheumatic activities. Various combinations of aspirin, codeine, and phenacetin, sometimes also with caffeine, are obtainable over the counter in Britain. (In most states of the U.S.A., a prescription is necessary for any codeine preparation.) There are also some other derivatives of salicylic acid, including salicylic acid itself, which are in use as weak pain-killers, called by Fourneau, in France, 'antalgics'. It is certain that quite a number of people are dependent on a regular supply of these preparations, sometimes using them to an extent that may more correctly be called misuse. Several thousand million tablets of aspirin alone are consumed annually in Britain, and over eight million pounds of aspirin were sold in the U.S. in

1966. The 'antalgics' are usually swallowed with a sip of water. The rather irritant action that salicylates have on the stomach's wall, however, has prompted manufacturers to produce tablets which, while still not dissolving in a true sense, disintegrate in a glass of water into a more or less fine suspension with calcium carbonate and citric acid. The danger of sudden gastric haemorrhages from misuse of aspirin is not thus completely avoided, however. Caution remains necessary. Aspirin is only non-toxic so long as it is taken occasionally and in small doses.

Psychological dependence develops for several reasons: the availability of the substance without a prescription, its undeserved reputation for non-toxicity, and, as people say, the need to swallow something from time to time to do the nerves good or to combat sleeplessness. When people become psychically dependent on aspirin, for example, they do not usually realize it. The man or woman who takes aspirin often for frequent headaches may get the headaches so that they can take aspirin. It can become, as it were, a miniature version of the true addict's treadmill.

Overdoses may produce nausea, dizziness, confusion, singing sounds in the ears (tinnitus), cardiovascular collapse, and respiratory failure. Among pathological symptoms produced by large or sudden doses of aspirin and the salicylates, are intense irritation of the gastric mucose membranes, leading to haematemesis (vomiting of blood), and a blood loss into the stomach leading to its contents acquiring the state resembling 'coffee grounds'. Some people, especially asthmatics, are hypersensitive to aspirin. Recent reports of experiments with mice have indicated that the salicylates may not only produce foetal damage early during pregnancies,[49] but also cause premature birth during the latter stages of pregnancy. This indicates that quite a number of what one usually considered 'harmless' drugs carry with them potential embryopathic (malformation) dangers. It appears that thalidomide, though perhaps one of the most powerful, and certainly the most notorious, is only one of many agents which represent embryo-toxic hazards.

Concerning its mechanism of action, aspirin seems to act

mainly centrally, but has its side-effects, which can be called peripheral. Phenacetin is frequently used in aspirin mixtures, and it must be pointed out strongly that anyone taking these tablets frequently may run a risk of severe kidney damage.

The abuse of the mild analgesics is particularly widespread in Australia, and the high incidence of kidney disorder there has led to a call for a warning label to be carried on all aspirin preparations. Phenacetin may be the main culprit, but all the analgesics must be regarded as being under suspicion in this respect until we know more about them.

Cocaine and the Coca Leaf

ORIGIN AND HISTORY

In Chapter Two we remarked how alcohol provides a major revenue source in the West. The tale of one man's profit providing misfortune for many others is echoed here in the cultivation of coca leaves, a matter of considerable economic importance for a number of South American countries, principally Peru and Bolivia, and to a lesser extent Colombia. In these countries, beside being the traditional 'pick-me-up' of the masses, coca has even been used as a medium of currency and a means of exchange – a custom persisting to this day. It also shares with alcohol a reputation for being a sexual stimulant, possibly with slightly more justification.

The coca plant is a shrub resembling a blackthorn bush which grows to about six feet. Botanically it belongs to the dicotyledoneus family *Erythroxylaceae*, the Bolivian variety (*Erythroxylon coca*) being known as 'tuanoco leaf', and the Peruvian (*E. truxillense*) as 'truxillo leaf'. Its place of origin is not definitely established, but it is likely it was cultivated on the eastern slopes of the Andes long before the time of the Incas, since

sacks and baskets full of coca leaves have been found in many
ancient tombs in South America. The habit of chewing coca
leaves therefore existed in ancient Peru, as is confirmed by
works of art and artefacts which depict human faces with one
cheek distended. When the conquistadores arrived from Spain
they found it established among the native Indians, whose lives
were closely regulated by the Inca system of government. They

FIG. 4. Leaves of *Erythroxylon coca*

brewed a beer called *chicha* from maize and cultivated coca among their other crops. Then, as now, coca leaves were mixed with powdered lime, which helped to extract the active content. Naturally coca had a special significance in their religious belief and ritual. In the ancient American myth it was Manco Capac, the Royal Son of the Sun-God, who had sent coca as a gift 'to satisfy the hungry, fortify the weary, and make the unfortunate forget their sorrows'. A *cocada* in the Andes is still used as a unit of measurement, and is the distance a porter can travel on foot with a full load while he chews one cud of coca leaves.

The dried uncurled coca leaf can be recognized by its tea-like odour and by two longitudinal indentations on each side of the midrib. These are more conspicuous on the grey-green underside than on the dark green upper side. Knowledge of the coca plant was first brought to Europe in 1580 by a Dr Monardes of Seville. The chief alkaloid in the leaves, cocaine, was isolated in 1860 by Niemann and was introduced into medicine in about 1884. Its possibilities as an anaesthetic agent were apparently first seen by Sigmund Freud, when he was still working at the General Hospital in Vienna. However, it was Carl Koller who actually exploited these ideas in practical terms in minor operations for eye diseases, and incidentally precipitated one of the classic dissensions in the history of medical science when he later tried to deny that Freud's ideas had antedated his own.[1]

It is estimated that 90 per cent of the coca produced in Bolivia is consumed by the indigenous population, the remaining 10 per cent being exported. An increase in the production and consumption of coca started with the Spanish conquest and had reached the annual figure of more than 8,500 tons in Peru by the early 1950s, equivalent to well over 40,000 kg of cocaine. The increase was mainly due in the first place to a decline in the production of foodstuffs, the collapse of the Inca state and the stability it offered, the institution of forced labour, the large profits derived from the trade, and the feeling of contentment and artificial well-being which the chewing of the coca leaf produces and which helped to relieve the hardships created by subjugation.

The powerful lobbies which defend the use of coca, and also benefit from the lucrative trade, have emphasized its importance as an economic, social, and political factor, quite aside from whatever harmful effects it may have. Greater coca consumption, they claim, means greater wealth for the community as a whole, besides which it is rich in vitamins, and its use is essential for those working at high altitudes. It is, they say, responsible for the traditional sobriety and endurance of the Andean labourer. But this is all a carefully fostered myth (see also page 95). The Bolivian Indian suffers from advanced malnutrition, either because he cannot afford to eat enough or because, when he can, cocaine has debilitated his digestive organs. During his few short years of drug dependence, he makes an effort out of all proportion to his actual physical powers and becomes a human derelict before his early death.[2] The benefits to any society of such a pattern are highly dubious both in a moral and practical sense, to say the least. The report of the United Nations Commission which visited Bolivia in 1949 clearly demonstrated how harmful coca-chewing was, as well as the case for its suppression. Meanwhile, by way of contrast, it has been claimed that in Ecuador the Indians have completely abandoned the habit and have as a result made considerable physical and social progress.[3]

Coca addicts in Peru and Bolivia begin to form the habit after leaving school, between the ages of 12 and 14. There may be a relation between the extent of cocaine dependence and dietary deficiencies, and shortage of food could be the main reason for the existence of coca dependence. Given this, any campaign for suppressing this pernicious habit would have to be accompanied in the first place by improved nutrition in the coca-chewing population.[4]

Since 1947 there has been a coca monopoly in Bolivia which co-operates in its production and sale, seeking outlets and maintaining a balance between the landowner and the planter. It is also responsible for collecting the tax on coca, the revenue obtained having been used, in 1952, for building army barracks.

Export of dry leaves from South America started when the

importance of the plant from the medicinal point of view became appreciated. Factories were started in Peru in the 1890s to extract cocaine in crude form for export to save the cost of transporting the whole leaf, and thus the alkaloid replaced the leaf. Between 1890 and 1910 cocaine began to be fairly widely misused in the U.S.A. Among the adult population in particular the drug was used in the form of snuff, and ulceration of the septum of the nose (the membrane between the nostrils) was a not uncommon result. Knowledge of the striking toxic effect of cocaine gradually spread to Europe, India, and China. At the time it was thought that administering cocaine would help to break addiction in cases involving opium and morphine as well as in alcoholism. Unfortunately, instead of curing morphinism, it produced morphine-cocainism. During the First World War there was such an increase in the habitual use of cocaine in Europe that vigorous measures became essential.[5]

THE LEGAL POSITION

In the United Kingdom, cocaine products, including coca leaves, containing more than 0·1 per cent cocaine are controlled by the Dangerous Drugs Act 1965, to which the full restrictions under the Dangerous Drugs (No. 2) Regulations 1964 apply. That is, it may be supplied only to authorized persons or on prescription, must be specially labelled, stored under lock and key, and entered in a Dangerous Drugs register. They are also subject to the special restrictions applied to First Schedule poisons.

In the U.S.A. cocaine is similarly controlled by the Harrison Act 1914 under the regulatory control of the Bureau of Narcotics, known since 1968 as the Bureau of Narcotics and Dangerous Drugs, which regulates the manufacture and distribution of narcotics.

CONSUMPTION

In Peru and Bolivia the coca leaf is chewed, often mixed with ground limestone or the ashes of plants, to relieve sensations of cold, hunger, and fatigue. The leaf can also be used in the form of an elixir or liquid extract. An individual may consume up to

100 grains daily in doses of about 15 grains. Release of the alkaloid and its absorption are generally too slow, or quantitatively too small, to induce the abnormal behaviour which results from an intake of pure cocaine, which may be taken by either absorption through the mucous membranes – the sniffing of crystals – or intravenous injection. In India the drug is put in 'pan', the East's masticatory, also known as 'betel' (see pp. 156–7).

THE EFFECTS OF COCAINE

The most striking systemic action of cocaine is stimulation of the central nervous system, from the upper to the lower parts of the brain (see Fig. 1, page 8). Its first recognizable action is on the cortex, and results in garrulity, restlessness, and excitement, some increase in mental power, an increased capacity for work from lessened fatigue, and a general feeling of well-being. Following small amounts of cocaine, motor activity is perfectly co-ordinated, but with an increase in dose the lower centres are also affected, and tremors, an increase in cord reflexes, and eventually convulsions develop. From the action of cocaine on the medulla there is an increase in respiratory rate, stimulation of the vasomotor centre, and vomiting. After stimulation of the central nervous system, depression sets in, first on the higher parts of the brain, then the medullary region, and eventually death from respiratory failure can occur.

Small doses may slow the heart, but on increasing the dose the heart rate is increased. A large dose may have a direct toxic action on the heart muscle and result in immediate death from cardiac failure. Sometimes an increase in blood pressure followed by a fall may occur. The pyretic action of cocaine is attributed to three factors: increased muscular activity as a result of stimulation, a decrease in heat elimination, and direct action on the heat regulating centres.

Cocaine, is, of course, well known as a local anaesthetic. It has little effect on unbroken skin, but if injected subcutaneously or applied to mucous membranes it causes complete local anaesthesia by its ability to block terminal sensory nerve fibres. When applied to mucous membranes, surface anaesthesia develops in about five to ten minutes and can persist for twenty minutes or longer, depending on the concentration of cocaine and on the vascularity of the tissue. Its use is now restricted to surgery of the eyes, ears, nose, and throat. It has also served in the past to treat gastric pain and vomiting.

Its local action led first to its use in ophthalmic operations. The drawbacks to cocaine as a local anaesthetic in ophthalmology, however, were found to be the mydriasis (dilation of pupils) and corneal injury which it produced. Because of its toxicity and tendency to produce dependence, it is no longer used ordinarily as a local anaesthetic. It has been largely superseded by various synthetic substitutes, such as procaine and lignocaine, which do not induce dependence and are free of the stimulant and euphoric properties of the natural product.

In spite of marked differences between the coca-chewing habit and cocaine dependence, it has been considered[6] that they have certain points in common, since the common factor, cocaine, is responsible for the principal effects. The ease and intensity of drug dependence largely follows from the method of administration. The most effective method is intravenous injection, with sub-cutaneous and oral methods being progressively less effective. In the case of coca-leaf chewers, the startling toxic features are not as common, only developing over a long period, and when they do, being essentially chronic. The weaker symptoms of dependence enable the individual to give up the drug with ease, but difficulties occur with consumers of above 100 or 200 grains of coca leaves a day.

THE METABOLISM OF COCAINE

The coca-leaf chewer who has become dependent chews on average 50 grams of leaf daily.[7] This means he is ingesting approximately 350 milligrams of basic cocaine. Afterwards, constant hydrolysis occurs, partly with the alkali with which the leaf is mixed and partly with the various digestive juices. Thus, by the time it reaches a point of absorption, the amount of cocaine is considerably reduced and is further broken down in the liver. The blood, having passed through the liver, then contains only traces of cocaine and the amount circulating in the body is insignificant.

The renal (kidney) elimination of the cocaine metabolite begins six hours after ingestion and continues for about another twenty in the urine. It is probable that the hydrolysis and elimination of cocaine products is more intense and rapid in the case of the dependent, as against the non-drug-taker.

MISUSE AND PREVENTION

The oldest form of the misuse of cocaine is naturally the centuries-old custom of coca-leaf chewing in the Andean regions, where, as already described, the leaf is mixed with lime to enhance its biological effects. By partly neutralizing the hydrochloric acid in the stomach the alkali enables more cocaine to be absorbed by way of the intestinal tract.[4] In South America the habit affects several million people. However, dependence on coca is known to be mild,[8] and since the habit is known usually to disappear when users are given improved social conditions, as, for instance, with men who are enrolled into the army, there would be grounds for allowing the problem to remain unexamined were it not for the suspicion that it produces chronic brain damage. The areas where dependence mainly exists correspond with a high illiteracy rate (up to 90 per cent) and low social achievement. As with many other drugs of psychotropic activity or dependence, the effects appear to be connected closely with the personality of the user, the dose employed, and the degree of sensitization reached.

The physiological effect has been considered to be the most plausible justification for the use of coca.[9] Coca affects the sensory perceptive centres and blurs the sense of time, thus apparently increasing the efficiency of muscular work and disguising any feeling of fatigue. This artificial energy, however, has also been ascribed to metabolical changes which result in malnutrition. The idea that coca is in any way a food, despite reports of the presence of vitamins B_1, B_2, and C, can confidently be disposed of. The anorexia of addicts, anaesthesia of the mouth, disappearance of taste, lesions caused to the mucous membranes by alkalis leading to ulceration and subsequent scarring which dull the sensitivity, are factors which fully explain the suppressions of hunger and thirst and are not evidence of its nutritive value.

As we have said, despite its vasoconstrictive properties, cocaine is easily absorbed through the mucous membranes.[10] A favourite method used to be the absorption of cocaine solutions within oral and nasal cavities. This rather resembles the snuffing of cocaine crystals, which causes perforation of the nasal membrane. The powder, known as 'snow' from its appearance, frequently produces ulceration in the nasal cavity.

The general appearance of cocaine eaters in India has been described as acutely pitiable.[11] They are, as a rule, emaciated, sickly and flabby, with dull facial expressions, who have lost any regard for personal appearance or cleanliness of body or clothes. They are pale and anaemic, have sallow complexions, sunken eyes, dilated pupils, prominent cheekbones, and look as if they were suffering from severe toxaemia.

An extremely dangerous type of abuse, intravenous injection, has now developed with cocaine, despite the fact that illicit use of the drug has diminished, as a result of stringent world control and from its reduced medical use. The addict may use this method intermittently to gain a maximum euphoria. Injection of cocaine is a form of drug abuse that appeals to psychopathic personalities. It induces exaggerated feelings of mental and muscular power, the user becoming a dangerous anti-social individual as he develops hallucinations associated with paranoid delusions of being threatened. Imaginary insects may be seen or felt crawling over the skin as the ecstasy gives way to a black depression. He is capable of using a weapon without reason if one is to hand. It has, in fact, been suggested that the 'dope fiend' of the popular late Victorian and Edwardian imagination was in reality a cocainist, and not a heroin addict, as he is usually thought of having been.

When psychic dependence on cocaine has developed, sleeplessness is common and loss of appetite, with nausea and digestive disorders, leads to emaciation. Convulsions often occur and mental deterioration takes place. Most extreme cases end as wretchedly reduced grumbling and irritating occupants in mental institutions. In women it leads to increased erotic tension and possibly eventually to a state of nymphomania. In men the physical component is increased and sexual perversions are a concomitant phenomenon. Cocaine being a drug of dependence, its addicts acquire a kind of tolerance to the drug, some taking as much as 5 grams daily, compared with the normal single dose of 8 to 16 milligrams. Though there is a marked psychic dependence on the drug, physical dependence does not develop to the extent it does with the opiates (see Chapter Four) and does not provoke serious withdrawal symptoms. But psychic dependence can develop after a very short time, even after a few weeks. Dependants tend to be gregarious and try to induce friends to share their pleasures. A recent development is a heroin-cocaine mixture ('speedball', or 'H and C'), the depressant effect of the one compensating for the stimulation of the other. The high level of excitement produced by cocaine thus results in the user voluntarily seeking sedation.

TREATMENT AND CURE

Dependence on cocaine is treated by abrupt withdrawal since withdrawal symptoms are not severe. The individual is removed from the environment in which he indulges his habit, and from the associates in whose company he takes the drug, and is treated with psychotherapy. The gravity of continuing the cocaine habit is impressed on patients and the remainder of the treatment is simple and symptomatic.

Though little – if any – physical dependence on cocaine develops, severe depression may occur and delusions may persist for some time following withdrawal.[12] Since cocaine undergoes rapid destruction in the organism, large quantities can be taken during a twenty-four-hour period. However, it is thought that true tolerance does not develop, but rather that in some instances there is sensitization to the drug's effects.[13]

The symptoms of acute cocaine poisoning, as of poisoning by

any local anaesthetic, are mainly referable to the central nervous system. The course is very rapid, the usual accepted fatal dose being 1·2 grams, but death has occurred with doses as low as 20 milligrams. Some people have a cocaine idiosyncrasy and with them death from cardiovascular collapse can occur suddenly after quite small doses.

THE SOCIOLOGICAL ASPECTS OF COCAINE DEPENDENCE

Whereas coca leaves do have some natural nutritive properties, their use as a food cannot be justified, and their nutritive value is virtually insignificant when compared with the possible natural products which could be grown as an alternative. The deadening of the feeling of hunger caused by coca leads to a permanent condition of under-nourishment and thus establishes a vicious circle, while the physical, physiological, and mental alterations produced in people who chew it prevent them from attaining a higher social level.

The coca habit has a bad economic effect as, against the opinion of its apologists, it decreases work output and depresses standards of living. Its necessity and usefulness for adaptation to life at high altitudes has not been scientifically proved, and the theory that coca leaves act differently on the indigenous population of the High Andes may be discarded.

Better social conditions and educational facilities should be a major reason in any campaign against cocainism. Health standards should be raised; nutrition, housing, and economic levels improved. It would seem essential that the governments concerned should consider improvements in legislation and in the criminal law. Effective legislation and a joint policy is essential if this injurious habit is ever to be countered. Only by setting up special institutes and initiating long-term projects or standing commissions to study the agricultural, economic, commercial, and medical aspects will the problem ever be dealt with effectively. In the West, cocaine as a dangerous agent has somewhat declined in popularity, except perhaps in combination with opiates (see previous page).

Chapter Six

The Mental Stimulants:
Amphetamines
and Anti-Depressants

1. The Amphetamines

ORIGIN AND HISTORY

Coca is a drug of dependence which is both a stimulant and
a natural product. Khat is another drug which is a natural
product, which also happens to have amphetamine-like properties and which is described later in this chapter (see pp. 107–9).
We turn now, however, to a group of stimulatory drugs which
are the synthetic products of the manufacturing chemist and
belong to the family of so-called psychotropic drugs, which may
be divided into three classes:[1] (a) *psycholeptics*, (b) *psychoanaleptics*, and (c) *psychodysleptics*. The psychoanaleptics, or psychic
stimulants, are the subject of this chapter. They can be further
sub-divided into drugs of alertness and stimulants of mood (i.e.
mental vigour and buoyancy). The drugs which stimulate
buoyancy (anti-depressants) are not so notorious as those that
stimulate mental vigour (amphetamines), but their misuse also
often poses problems for the toxicologist.

The stimulators of mental vigour, or noo-analeptics,[1]

comprise most of the psychotropic amines. These facilitate intellectual effort but make it difficult to sleep. Their action is the
opposite to that of barbiturates (see Chapter Seven), which are
soporific drugs, and they abolish sensations of fatigue. In addition, they have a stimulating action on the cerebral cortex (see
Fig. 1, page 8). Their pharmacological effects seem to fall
between those of cocaine and caffeine, and before 1950 they were
generally reported in some pharmacological books as having the
advantage of not possessing the more dangerous habit-forming
properties of cocaine. However, these views have undergone considerable revision following the experience of the past few years.

Amphetamine, or Benzedrine, first prepared in 1887 by
Edelsno in Germany, was originally used to treat narcolepsy (a
nervous disease where the patient has fits of irresistible drowsiness). Its first non-medical use was in ships' survival packs
during the Spanish Civil War, when it was also issued to
German paratroops. Both sides used it during the Second World
War, supporting the theory that, in a mild way, it is a sort of
'superman' drug. It increases the physical capacity to carry out
strenuous tasks which require a great deal of mental concentration without distorting judgement.

In 1954 the World Health Organization Expert Committee
on Drugs Liable to Produce Addiction[2] (now known as the
Expert Committee on Dependence-Producing Drugs) recommended that governments should control amphetamines by
allowing them to be dispensed only on prescription, each prescription specifying the number of times it might be repeated and
a careful record being kept. At its 1955 session the Commission
on Narcotic Drugs discussed the possibility of including amphetamines among the drugs to be controlled under the proposed
Single Convention, but it felt that the control measures already
recommended would suffice for the moment, as it could not be
said that these drugs were addiction-producing in the sense of
morphine or cocaine.[3] This attitude may undergo some changes
in the future.[4]

At a later session, in 1956, however, the Commission[5] adopted
a resolution considering the widespread increase in cases of

amphetamine (Benzedrine) poisoning, the number of accidents, or even deaths, that could be put down to the abuse of amphetamine, often when used in proprietory medicines designed to control the appetite and hence used in slimming. The drug was also prescribed for depression, fatigue, and anxiety states, among others. They found, in fact, that the amines possessed properties making them analogous to addiction-producing substances. Since they were still being sold without control in some countries, the Commission went on to consider the dangers arising from their abuse and to recommend that all governments should introduce preventive measures.

In 1962 it was calculated that there were 500 amphetamine addicts in Newcastle-on-Tyne out of a population of 270,000.[6] From a survey contributed to by thirty-three prescribing doctors in north-east England, it was concluded that one in five women and one in four men who took amphetamine or related drugs were liable to become habituated. This represented about four habituated patients in a practice of 2,500. Several practitioners commented that the anorectic effect (loss of appetite) of the drug failed after prolonged use[7] and estimated the incidence of misuse was approaching 100 to 200 per 100,000 of the general population in 1966. After 1961 detecting forgeries of National Health prescriptions, particularly for further supplies of Drinamyl – or Dexamyl (U.S.A.) – and dexamphetamine or Dexedrine (see later), became a special problem for the police drug squad in Britain.[8]

The sympathomimetic base amphetamine acts like adrenaline and was originally introduced as an inhalant to relieve nasal catarrh and hay fever. In 1964 a number of patients with amphetamine psychoses were admitted to an observation ward in London,[9] some of whom had taken large amounts of amphetamines by ingesting the contents of inhalers.

Popular products in London, and later in the rest of England, were the 'purple hearts' of notorious reputation, a nickname for Drinamyl, which contains amphetamine and the barbiturate amylobarbitone; and 'black bombers', a capsule known pharmaceutically as Durophet. Drinamyl is used to treat mild temporary neuroses and Durophet to treat obesity. The retail value of Durophet capsules was about 16s. a 100, but the café and coffee bar price fluctuated between 1s. and 7s. 6d. each. Naturally these high profit margins brought in the drug-pusher.

A series of articles in the London *Evening Standard* in February 1964 drew attention to the abuse of amphetamines by adolescents in London's West End, and later that year the Drugs (Prevention of Misuse) Act 1964 was passed. While previously they were only available on prescription, the Act made it an offence for an unauthorized person to be in possession of them or to distribute them without a licence. Similar steps were taken in the United States by means of the Drug Abuse Control Amendments of 1965.[10] Amphetamines and related compounds were among the first drugs to be controlled in this way (as were barbiturates and other depressant and stimulant drugs).

The using of amphetamines by athletes and competitors in international sporting events has posed some special incidental problems in recent years and the tragic death of Tommy Simpson, the leading British competitor in the Tour de France in 1967, following the taking of stimulants, was an example of what can happen. Methods are now in use which can detect a doping agent in an athlete's urine for up to forty-eight hours after it has been taken (see Appendix A, page 180), and checks were a matter of routine during the 1968 Olympic Games in Mexico City.

CONSUMPTION

As already mentioned, one of the most popular means of taking amphetamines is in the form of 'purple hearts'. The original 'purple hearts' were triangular pale blue tablets containing 5 milligrams of dexamphetamine and 32 milligrams of amylobarbitone, or amytal, but the shape and marking of the tablets have since been changed because of the publicity they received. The other most popular preparation is Durophet, its black capsule having become well known as the 'black bomber'. Then there is Methedrine (methylamphetamine), which has the same action and uses as amphetamine, but is more rapid in effect and acts for a longer period. Its supplies are restricted in Britain to hospitals only and it is given by mouth for narcolepsy and Parkinson's Disease or it is injected to treat the effects of overdoses of barbiturates or other depressants.

The variety of amphetamine preparations available on the market are legion. The collection of one of the authors of this book, which is by no means complete, contains examples of over 100 preparations containing amphetamine-type drugs. Different manufacturers use special colours and examples from other countries sometimes have different shapes and colours. A collection of over twenty types is reputed to be manufactured to special order for a medical practitioner in London. Accurate identification of different tablets, capsules, and ampoules has now become an increasingly important and difficult problem for the laboratories of forensic scientists. The practice of dissolving amphetamines in water and using the solution for intravenous injections has already presented Sweden with a major health problem and seems to be coming into fashion among drug addicts in Britain and the U.S.A. This is an aspect which the authorities should watch very carefully.

THE EFFECTS OF AMPHETAMINE

It has been thought that while the amphetamines are related, both chemically and pharmacologically, to a large group of compounds generally known as pressor or sympathomimetic amines (which include the natural products adrenaline and ephedrine), the amphetamines have a stronger effect on the central nervous system, particularly on the cerebral cortex and the respiratory and vasomotor centres.[11] The peripheral effects of the amphetamines are typically those of the natural amines: briefly, an increase in blood pressure following an increase in the heart rate, dilation of the pupils, relaxation of the smooth muscle of the gastro-intestinal tract, and a secretion of sparse thick saliva. They produce local vascoconstriction, when applied to the mucous linings, which lead to their use as inhalers for the treatment of hay fever and the common cold; this, as we have seen, also lead to their misuse.

The relative intensities of the central and peripheral effects of the drugs vary, and the amphetamines are now used mainly for their central effects, the most marked being a state of wakefulness, probably from direct action on the mid-brain. This is accompanied by an increase in psychic and motor activity, and that is why amphetamines are used as an antidote in the treatment of barbiturate poisoning, though if they are used to excess, they bring on the opposite symptom, insomnia. The mechanism by which they cause loss of appetite is debatable, but it has led to their important medical use in the treatment of obesity, another use followed not infrequently by misuse.

The central stimulatory effects have made the drug therapeutically suitable for treatment of some types of depression, but they have also given it its basis for misuse by those seeking the 'kicks' which are followed by an unpleasant increase in tension and sometimes feelings of anxiety, or, in extreme cases, hallucinations and other mental disturbances ('the horrors'). On ceasing a dosage, depression sets in and is often intense and of long duration, which inevitably leads to the victim craving for more drugs. Thus amphetamine addiction or dependence raises a comparison with barbiturate addiction (see page 124) and is often even more dangerous because of the extremely powerful effect that amphetamines have on the central nervous system.[12]

Laurie[13] quotes Eysenck[14] as saying that stimulants move the personality towards the introversion end of the spectrum and decrease nervous inhibition. It may be called the drug of the bored teenager and tired housewife, groups of people who may turn to them, sometimes illicitly, as stimulators and as a relief from lack of energy and mental stimulation, later having to rely on barbiturates to procure sleep.

MISUSE AND PREVENTION

Among the minor toxic side-effects of amphetamines are dry mouth, restlessness, headaches, dizziness, tremor, and loss of appetite. Larger doses lead to fatigue, mental depression, increase in blood pressure, cardio-vascular reactions, cyanosis (a condition due to insufficient aeration of blood), and respiratory failure. The addict may also suffer the disorientation and hallucinations previously mentioned, as well as convulsions and coma. Continued use can cause insanity and severe brain damage.

The capacity of amphetamines and similar drugs to elevate mood is probably the basis for their value,[15] and their widespread use as stimulants and slimming agents leads to their ready availability on the illicit market. Since even their legal use usually involves continuous and prolonged administration, any user may develop varying degrees of psychic dependence. So, in turn, increases in quantity and frequency of administration become necessary for them.

Carried to an extreme, the psychotoxic effects of large amounts of amphetamine can produce a kind of 'physical dependence' and lead to aggressive and dangerous anti-social behaviour. Qualitatively, the psychological effects are in many ways similar to those produced by cocaine. A unique feature of the amphetamines is their capacity to induce tolerance, a quality possessed by few other stimulants of the central nervous system. While this does develop slowly, the tolerance requirements may multiply almost a hundredfold. The effects of the enlarged doses are unevenly distributed over the central nervous system, producing abnormal symptoms, including the hallucinations. These are made more dramatic where intravenous injection is used, a factor utilized by dependants to obtain bizarre imagery, often of a sexual nature and extending to sensations of orgasm.[16] Where it is used in this way, the dosage is also increased, dependence accelerated, and severe psychoses caused. In fact one World Health Organization expert on drugs has been quoted as saying that paranoid psychosis occurs in 65 per cent of users, in advanced cases the patient losing all contact with reality and becoming dominated by a sense of panic and confusion. As with heroin, the use of dirty needles can lead to infection, and since improvised filters are used to drain off the solution, insoluble material can be introduced into the blood stream and damage the lung tissue.

The use of amphetamines by alcoholics and/or barbiturate

addicts has also increased in recent years. These cases seem to involve personalities showing a high relapse rate and continuous dependence on drugs.

THE LEGAL POSITION

The recommendations of the World Health Organization and their inclusion in the Misuse of Drug Act 1964 in Great Britain have already been described. Similarly the U.S. placed amphetamines under the Drug Abuse Control Amendments 1965. Japan in particular was early in the field with amphetamine control. It has been estimated that by 1955 Japan had approximately half a million amphetamine addicts, though the number has decreased since that time.[17] The sudden upsurge could be put down to the state of social confusion which prevailed there following the war. Amphetamines became popular and were used regularly by people working night-shifts or irregular hours. This led to an escalation in addiction and intoxication through the habitual use of injections to produce rapid and intensified effects. The impact on groups of younger criminals brought about such an increase in delinquency and crime that severe measures to control the drug's manufacture, sale, import, and medical use became a priority.

In Japan, an Amphetamine Control Law was enacted in 1951 and revised in 1954 and 1955, mainly in its penal provisions.[18] Ephedrine, methylephedrine, phenylacetic acid, phenylacetone, which all represent intermediates in the manufacturing process of the amphetamines, are also under control as a safeguard against illicit preparation, which is technically not difficult.

More recently, Sweden has had its severe epidemic of amphetamine (being injected in massive doses) and it is estimated that there are between 5,000 and 10,000 addicts in the country. This has resulted in the Swedes bringing strong pressure to bear on the United Nations Commission on Narcotic Drugs to bring the drug under strict international control.

Up to 1966 amphetamines seemed to be a less severe problem in Canada and the United States;[19] there, following the Federal Food, Drug and Cosmetic Act of the early 1960s, it was illegal to dispense these drugs without a doctor's prescription, though it was reported that the Secretary of Health, Education and Welfare of the time did not consider the Act strong enough to deal with the problem as it stood at that moment. Since then amphetamine abuse has been on the increase.

A Bill on Psychotoxic Drugs was promoted in 1964 and passed the Senate, coming to rest in the house,[20] its promoter referring to their use as becoming prevalent among middle-class youths with clean records and replacing hard narcotics. In 1965 the same Congress and Senate passed the Bill known as the Drug Abuse Control Amendments,[21] which, as previously mentioned, took legal care of these and other problems, including the control of barbiturates.

2. Khat: an Amphetamine-like Drug

The fresh leaves of the bush which carries the botanical name *Catha edulis* (*Celastraceae*) are commonly known as 'khat'. They can be made into a kind of tea, but are usually chewed, like coca leaves in the Andean republics, as a social habit, mainly by the inhabitants of a number of countries in Arabia and East Africa, including Saudi Arabia, the Yemen and South Yemen on the Asian side, and Somalia, Eritrea, Ethiopia, and even Kenya on the African side. It has also been reported from as far north as Afghanistan. The plant seems to have originated either in Arabia or Ethiopia and grows locally in the countries where it is used. The fact that it is apparently more potent when fresh could explain why it has been largely confined to the areas in which it grows freely.

Khat-chewing is a ritual which takes place in social gatherings with smoking and the normal pastimes of drinking tea and other liquors, which may include soft as well as alcoholic drinks. The initial effects appear to be the disappearance of worries and all symptoms of hunger and fatigue. These then change to hypomania, with talkativeness and aggression domi-nating as thought processes are speeded up, the subject finding difficulty in concentrating. There is also sexual excitement which ends in spontaneous ejaculation without orgasm.[22] The pupils dilate, and the heart beats rapidly. As the stimulating effect passes, sensations of depression, wakefulness, loss of appetite, and thirst set in.*

Although it is normally consumed by chewing the young leaves, older leaves are sometimes dried, powdered, and made into a paste with sugar, spices, and water, which is chewed and swallowed. Alternatively, the powder may be made into a tea-like infusion. In certain parts of Arabia, khat is smoked like tobacco or cannabis.[23]

The habitual use of khat may have a number of medical and social consequences,[24] even though it does not create irresistible craving. Consumed habitually, it has adverse effects on the gastro-intestinal tract, causing constipation, gastritis, and loss of appetite and leading to a number of nutritional deficiencies. The cardio-vascular system is also severely involved. Psychiatric disturbances can occur, including insomnia, anxiety, irritability, and states of excitation which may lead to manic crises. Individuals who are highly intoxicated with khat suffer from confused delusions. Advancing intoxication produces convulsions, sometimes death,[25] and chronic use numbs the intellectual faculties, leading to complete stupor or madness.

Social problems arising from its habitual use affect a high percentage of the adult populations of the countries involved, its economic impact being considerable.[26] It is an open question of which is the greater misery for the drug chewer: his ordinary life or the horrifying end results of the initial pleasures.

The loss of potency in the fresh leaves three to four days after they have been gathered has helped to restrict the problem, but better means of communication have, conversely, led to a rapid extension in its misuse, which is still most prevalent among the Moslem nations. This has been interpreted as an indication that

* All these effects are caused in the main by the alkaloid cathine, and two other alkaloids, cathinine and cathidine. Although it is less potent, there is a similarity between the actions of cathine and the amphetamines. Other constituents include sugar, tannin, and a small quantity of a yellowish and essential oil, which is pleasant to smell and taste.

social and cultural factors rather than psychological vulnerability govern the identity and extent of use of a drug.[27] Partial or total prohibition of the drug and the imposition of high taxes have largely failed to curb abuse. The World Health Organization Expert Committee[28] recently underlined the similarity of the habit in the affected areas to the non-therapeutic misuses of amphetamines in the West, the main difference being that amphetamines are detrimental mainly to the user and his immediate associates and are not an accepted part of Western general culture, while khat is part of the normal way of life in the Middle East and damages the whole society.

3. The Anti-Depressants

ORIGINS AND DIVISIONS

At present anti-depressants do not show the same problems as those discussed in connexion with amphetamines (see pp. 100–6), but they are a potential danger and as drugs that have psychopharmacological properties they form close links with the amphetamines. Their main characteristic is their capacity advantageously to modify mood states and to correct depressive conditions. Though their history is brief, they have become highly valuable in medical practice.

Technically they can be broadly divided into two classes: (a) inhibitors of monoamine oxidase (the 'MAO inhibitors');* and (b) tricyclic (three ring) derivatives, including imipramine and amitryptyline. (Tofranil and Laroxyl are the respective proprietary names.)

A further sub-division of the MAO inhibitors occurs as follows: (i) derivatives of hydrazine which are the most common (e.g. phenalzine); (ii) phenylcyclopropylamine derivatives (e.g. tranylcypromine preparations, such as Parnate); (iii) compounds of methylpropynylbenzylamine (e.g. pargyline).

* MAO is the enzyme that oxidizes and degrades adrenaline and noradrenaline and which occurs in both animal and plant tissues.

The anti-depressant action of the hydrazine group was discovered quite by chance. Some members of it were first used therapeutically for the treatment of tuberculosis and their stimulating action emerged as a side-effect. As their consumption could lead to the use of other drugs, this is a possible danger that must be borne in mind together with the fact that taken over a long period they may produce dependence.

THE EFFECTS OF ANTI-DEPRESSANTS[29]

MAO inhibitors are used in the treatment of exogenous and reactive depressions, particularly when anxiety is prominent. If a therapeutic response is not prompted within three to four weeks, there is usually little point in continuing treatment.

The *hydrazine derivatives* act as indirect stimulants, while the *tranylcypramine* preparations have both a direct and indirect (bimodal) activity. They produce, as well as indirect stimulation, a fast, direct stimulation comparable to that of amphetamine, except that this action is sustained and the drug has little cumulative effect.

Pargyline, which is said to have a beneficial effect on a patient's mood, acts slowly, and its effect lasts for some time after the drug has been withdrawn. It is used mainly for treating benign hypertension and is sometimes grouped with derivatives of *Rauwolfia* (see page 114), but its side-effects can be rather unpleasant, including dizziness and abnormal liver functions.

Amitriptyline is a tricyclic anti-depressant and *imipramine* is used in the treatment of patients with endogenous depression, though it is generally less effective than the MAO inhibitors for treating neurotic or reactive depression. Amitryptyline and imipramine are anti-depressants which should not be given to patients being treated with MAO inhibitors until at least three weeks after the treatment has been discontinued. In the case of amitryptyline, there is also a danger of enhancing the effects of barbiturates and alcohol. Both these tricyclic preparations have to be taken for about two weeks before their anti-depressant effect becomes evident.

MISUSE AND PREVENTION

The only serious misuse of anti-depressants at the present time is a matter of omission rather than commission, and occurs where a patient is unaware of the consequences of taking alcohol or eating certain foods rich in certain amino acids (cheese, yeast extract, game birds, sliced broad beans are all examples) while under treatment with an MAO inhibitor.

They also must be advised against taking certain other drugs (amphetamines, barbiturates, morphine, and cocaine among others) within three weeks.[30] Severe, even fatal, reactions can occur if an MAO inhibitor is given with these foods and drugs.

It is obviously essential that general practitioners and teachers should make themselves fully aware of the main causes of acute and chronic toxicity and the consequences that may follow a false step. The only sure way of preventing such an incident is for them to pass on information to their patients and pupils in a prompt and adequate form.

LEGAL POSITION

In Britain nialamide and iproniazid are controlled by Part 2 of the Therapeutic Substances Act, and so may only be sold on prescription. All the others mentioned in this section are included in Part B of Schedule Four of the Poisons Act and also need a prescription.[31] There is an additional restriction on tranylcypramine, since it is scheduled under the Drugs (Prevention of Misuse) Act 1964 which makes possession by other than an authorized person an offence.

The use and sale of anti-depressants in the U.S.A. is covered by the Drug Abuse Control Amendments 1965, being linked there with the barbiturates as having a habit-forming and abuse potential and placed under labelling and record requirements.

Chapter Seven

The Sedatives: Tranquillizers and Barbiturates

1. Tranquillizers

HISTORY AND ORIGIN

With the exception of the barbiturates, which will be dealt with towards the end of this chapter, drugs for the mentally sick,[1] whether suffering from anxiety states, depression, or severe psychotic disease, are not often listed among the drugs of abuse. This does not mean that they never turn up among drug habituates. They have tended to do so increasingly in recent years, as addicts try to ring the changes on the groups of drugs they turn to. And since they are frequently prescribed by doctors there is no difficulty in obtaining them under proper medical supervision. No black market seems to exist at present, but this is a situation which can always change. Like the so-called stimulants of mood (see Chapter Six), some tranquillizers or anti-anxiety drugs, represent a potential danger, since they can induce both tolerance and withdrawal symptoms.

Although for centuries men have sought for products to palliate or cure mental disorders, little progress was made before the early 1950s, when what has rightly been called a major breakthrough occurred with the isolation from *Rauwolfia serpen-tina* of the crystalline alkaloid reserpine.

Rauwolfia is a shrub native to India, Ceylon, and Java which was named after Leonhard Rauwolf, a sixteenth-century German doctor who travelled widely in India collecting medicinal

FIG. 5. The leaves and a section of root of
Rauwolfia serpentina

plants. For centuries, possibly from as early as 1000 B.C., use of its roots had been made as a cure[2] for madness and snakebite and a whole host of tropical diseases. Other representatives of the species were known to the Indians of the Colombian and Guatemalan jungles as a treatment for malaria, among other ills. Ironically, while a group of eminent doctors in India pointed out its genuine virtues in treating nervous disorders and lowering high blood pressure, Western scientists continued to ignore it until 1947 – a reflection on the sometimes, if not invariably, misplaced scepticism of the medical profession for anything which may fall under the heading of 'folk remedy'.

In 1952, after five years of work by a team of chemists in Switzerland, pure white crystals of reserpine were isolated from a crude extract of *Rauwolfia* root. Reserpine has proved to be an extraordinary drug. Its use in treating high blood pressure by reducing the patient's mental tension was a beginning, and led directly to the treatment of mental illnesses, particularly the terrible disability of chronic schizophrenia. It seems, in fact, to have helped to fulfil Freud's well-known prophetic dictum that 'behind every psychoanalyst stands the man with the syringe'. But while, together with the synthetic compounds (the phenothiazines) that the skill of the pharmaceutical industry produced at about the same time, it has literally revolutionized the whole modern approach to psychiatric treatment, it has also precipitated a major controversy and created a new division of opinion.

At one extreme is the psychiatrist who feels that analysis and related techniques are an outmoded therapy, that mental illness should now be treated exclusively by drugs, and that the future lies entirely with the new methods. At the other is the psychiatrist or psychoanalyst who believes that at best these drugs are a stop-gap measure, that since so little is understood of the way in which they work on the personality they should be regarded with extreme caution, and that the only real way of tackling personality disorders is on a personal level, through analysis leading to self-discovery and reintegration. The answer in the end may be a synthesis of these two viewpoints. But while it is a matter of vital importance for medical practice,* it is not within the scope of this book to try to indicate a solution. The fact is that through the use of these new drugs thousands of patients who, twenty years ago would have become the tragic, incurable inmates of our mental hospitals, are able to live normal or near-normal lives in the outside world; that through their judicious use by the general practitioner, many patients suffering from anxiety or reactive depression now avoid having to be referred on for hospital treatment at all.

However, it seems probable that the claims of those who advocate exclusive treatment by drugs are sometimes exaggerated, while there is no doubt that little is understood of the psychosomatic processes involved and that there may be as yet unrecognized dangers.

From our point of view, it is certain that further research will lead to improved compounds, and that these eventually may help not only to control mental diseases and disabilities but possibly will also help in the fight against drug dependence itself.

EFFECTS AND THEORIES

This is not a book on psychopharmacology or the psychotropic drugs, but there are aspects of this field of research which have some relevance to our subject.

Testing drugs out on animals is by no means easy, especially when it comes to translating any experimental results into the effects or action which may be expected with human patients suffering from specific mental diseases.[3] Any lines of enquiry will have to take the following progression: (1) The continued use of promising methods of animal experimentation in the hope that new and effective drugs will emerge; (2) a real attempt to develop in experimental animals conditions that closely resemble human clinical states; (3) a search for compounds producing a

* In contrast, it appears to be a matter of officially under-rated importance, considering that it has been noted that while nearly half the hospital beds in Great Britain are occupied by mental patients, this branch of medicine qualified for no more than 6·6 per cent of the Medical Research Council's annual allocation in 1967–8 – figure quoted in the *Annual Report 1966–67* of the Mental Health Research Fund.

variety of interesting and significant behavioural changes in the animal; (4) reaching an empirical assessment of the predictive value of a wide variety of animal tests by taking as standards drugs known to be effective in various conditions.

The complexity, of course, is great. How can major clinical problems properly be related to ordinary animal reactions, behavioural changes, emotional and learning performance reactions, arousal and catatonic states, 'taming', and its opposite, 'aggressiveness'?

While the drugs themselves, we are told, do not at present have much connexion with the problems of dependence, this may be an appropriate place to refer to these biologically difficult approaches, not only because similar discrepancies between experimental and clinical results arise in other fields of drug research, but also for reasons indicated below.

Apart from their potentially useful action during withdrawal processes (including the ravages of alcohol), and even though some authorities have reported them to be rather unsatisfactory, tranquillizers should be of some help in preventing drug-taking by people suffering from unstable personalities. The same may also apply when former addicts are exposed to renewed temptations. But one question stands out: if certain disciples of drug 'sub-cultures' are in this condition because of anxiety, frustration, or depression, why do they not choose to turn to one of the medically approved anti-anxiety or anti-depressant drugs? Why should they, in fact, take specific refuge in the fashionable drugs of abuse? Do they really need such drastic protection from the dark clouds of their troubled psyches? The reason may partly be put down to these drugs' initial lack of euphoric effects; or, subject to psychiatric confirmation, that these remedies carry the stigma of mental disease, while the drugs of abuse have the fascination of their association with 'mystery', social rebellion, gregariousness (with cannabis), and a mode of life with its own rules and laws which has rejected the 'establishment' and the doctors and nurses who are seen as a part of it.

To begin with the *phenothiazines*, these apparently act on the central nervous system, like so many of the drugs described in this book, but also act on other organs in the body.[4] They produce in some patients a state known as a 'neuroleptic syndrome', which has been likened to hibernation. This is rather an over-simplification, but, together with narcotics and soporifics, like the barbiturates, to be treated in the next section, phenothiazines are responsible for symptoms that are reminiscent of a state of 'hibernation': depressing movement and change of movement, so that animals or man will adopt the kind of frozen posture called 'cataleptic'. A point that deserves re-emphasis is that they do not produce euphoria and seem to lack properties that could lead to a strong tolerance and physical dependence, although in psychiatric patients some of both can develop. This series of compounds also show acute toxicity and a mixed range of side-effects, the most serious of which are depression and Parkinsonism, while jaundice appears in a small number of patients.

The *Rauwolfia* alkaloids, especially reserpine, show activities similar to the phenothiazine series. On the other hand, the actions of certain others (the benzodiazepines and meprobamate) are more closely related to the barbiturates (see pp. 118–26), with whom they share central and peripheral effects, which might be called a special kind of calming effect. Toxicity can be more pronounced in elderly people, and chronic toxicity, in the form of a build-up of physical dependence, has been found with meprobamate and the benzodiazepines and again resembles that of barbiturates.

It would be extremely useful to know more about how these drugs act, since their effect alone on the central nervous system and the peripheral organs does not explain much. But as the causal pathophysiology of underlying mental disturbances is itself so little understood, we can hardly expect to know a great deal more than that about the drugs which have a favourable influence. Much has been achieved during recent decades, but the neurochemical causes of psychosis have not been pinned down with certainty, although, as with the area of narcotic drugs and pain, components circulating in the body, and particularly in the brain (noradrenaline or norepinephrine and serotonin) are thought to be closely implicated. These have chemical similarities with parts of the reserpine molecule and some of the hallucinogens (see Chapters Six and Eight).

It seems reasonable to suggest that the whole subject of drug research, including drugs of abuse, is like a jig-saw puzzle: small pieces are discovered and wherever possible joined to each other. Consequently, any advance in research into mental illnesses – whether it concerns patients, their psychology or metabolism, the drugs used for their treatment, the side-effects and their chronic toxicity – could at any time throw a bright light on addiction and the addict.

2. Barbiturates

HISTORY AND ORIGIN

The large family of barbiturates has been and continues to be a source of worry for those concerned with drug abuse. Not only are these purely synthetic compounds sometimes over-administered to the middle-aged and elderly, but their common use in cases of suicide, their potentiating effect on alcohol and narcotics (or vice versa), and the increasing misuse of them by the younger generation make them a doubly urgent problem.

In Chapter Six the amphetamine-like drugs were called drugs of wakefulness. They have, in many ways, opposite effects to those of the barbiturates, which show hypnotic and soporific (sleep-making) effects. (Thus individuals suffering from an overdose of amphetamine are treated with barbiturates because of the generally depressant action they have on the central nervous system.) Barbiturates, together with the tranquillizers, form two of the three groups of the psycholeptics, and, as such, belong to the sub-group of hypnotics (see table, Appendix D, pp. 190–4).

Barbituric acid, a nitrogen-containing ring system, was discovered accidentally by the great German chemist, von Baeyer, as early as 1863. However, a proper barbiturate, then named 'Veronal', now known as 'barbitone', was prepared and introduced into medicine by another German chemist, Fischer, at the beginning of this century. After barbitone there came, still before the First World War, phenobarbitone; the specific properties of this will be considered later.

Out of approximately 2,500 synthetic compounds, about thirty barbiturates are still in medical use at the present time, though apart from their therapeutic usefulness, because of their misuse, they have become a menace of major proportions. In America,* barbiturates are considered to be the most commonly abused drugs,[5] and, known as 'goofballs' by their dependants, they are, in Britain,[6] together with other sedatives, also the greatest problem in numerical terms in the drug field. Not confined to the middle-aged and elderly, they have penetrated the adolescent's drug market and have, worse still, become associated with the abuse of heroin. It is strange that it has taken between fifty and sixty years for this group to move from being therapeutics, gingerly used and prescribed, to drugs of dependence, eagerly sought by both grandson and grandmother.

CONSUMPTION

Barbiturates can be taken orally, as the free acid, or alternatively as the sodium salt. Owing to its easier solubility in water, the action is more rapid with the latter method. Because of a bitter taste, the salts usually come in gelatine capsules which can be swallowed whole. Colours of capsules may help to identify their contents. Soluble barbiturates, kept in ampoules and then dissolved in sterile water, are used for intravenous injections, especially for anaesthetic purposes.

THE EFFECTS OF BARBITURATES

The main pharmacological effect of barbiturates is a depressive one on the central nervous system. They differ, however, in dosage, the duration of their action, and the margin of safety between a therapeutic and a toxic dose. Most important is the duration of action, since this is the difference by which they can be classified into four approximate sub-divisions.

* Whereas the names of types of barbiturate end in '*one*' in Britain, in American usage they end in '*al*'.

Following the standard textbooks of pharmacology,[7] the classification stems from experimental studies in animals; the relevance of these laboratory results to man cannot be considered completely reliable because of the variability of response in individual patients. However, the results help a toxicologist to interpret the significance of concentrations of a drug found in cases of poisoning.

Long-acting barbiturates include phenobarbitone, or Luminal, and barbitone, or Veronal,* whose effects last for six to ten hours. Barbitone is used to treat insomnia, but its prolonged action may make the patient drowsy the next day – harmless enough, if he can sleep it off, but with potentially catastrophic consequences if he has to drive a car. Phenobarbitone is of value in the treatment of epilepsy, for which at one time it used to be mixed with belladonna, and in the long-term treatment of migraine. Both these barbiturates tend to accumulate in the body.

Among the *intermediate-acting* barbiturates are butobarbitone, or Soneryl, and amylobarbitone, or Amytal – which are widely used for insomnia. Their action is usually apparent within thirty minutes and lasts five to six hours. The sense of hangover the next day is less pronounced than that from the long-lasting drugs.

The *short-acting* barbiturates, quinalbarbitone or secobarbital (U.S.), or Seconal, and pentobarbitone, or Nembutal, generally act within fifteen minutes, and their effect, within therapeutic doses, lasts two to three hours. They are suitable for patients who find difficulty in falling asleep, but who, once asleep, manage to remain asleep. However, their short duration makes these drugs potentially dangerous to individuals who may wake up frequently during the night and half-consciously continue repeating the dose. Cases of 'sleep-walking' patients, driven by nightmares, have also been recorded.

The *ultra-short acting* barbiturates, such as hexabarbitone, the sodium salt of which is known as Cyclonal, and thiopentone, or

* Names approved by pharmacopoeia commissions are spelt with a small letter, proprietary or brand names with a capital.

Pentothal, are used mainly for intravenous injection as rapidly acting anaesthetics on their own or as forerunner to a major anaesthetic.

Among the physiological effects of the barbiturates are respiratory depression, a decrease of the muscular tone in the gastro-intestinal tract, and a diminution of gastric secretion. Moreover, the drugs also have a complex effect on the autonomic nervous system.

Long-acting barbiturates are metabolized mainly in the kidney, while short-acting ones are broken down in the liver. There is evidence that alcohol potentiates their action, and similar properties are claimed for anti-histamines and disulfiram (Antabuse), an alcohol antagonist. It therefore stands to reason that these actions will dangerously reduce the margin of safety between a therapeutic and toxic dose.

Even an over-dosage by barbiturates alone will produce serious symptoms of intoxication, including non-coordination of muscular functions (ataxia), involuntary movements of the eye balls (nystagmus), and slurring of speech. Large or small doses can both impair speed of reaction, visual perception, and power of concentration as long as fourteen hours after administration. On the other hand, barbiturates are bad analgesics (pain-killers) unless an amount sufficient to cloud consciousness is given.[8] Except in cases of marked hypersensitivity, acute poisoning from medically controlled doses is extremely rare,[9] but overdosage, either accidental or suicidal, is a frequent cause of acute poisoning and death. The symptoms include respiratory depression, feeble heart beat, and lowered body temperature, anuria (absence of urinary secretion), and prolonged coma. While death from the short-acting drugs occurs through paralysis of the breathing centre, with the long-acting ones death can be delayed and finally result from inflammation of the lungs or other complications.

While phenobarbitone can safely be taken over the course of many years under medical supervision,* misuse, particularly of long-acting barbiturates, can over prolonged periods cause

* Its use to treat epilepsy is one particular example.

chronic poisoning, the effects of which resemble those of chronic alcohol intoxication: headache, visual disturbances, depression, slurred speech, and blood pigment and albumin in the urine.

In Chapter Two the significance of alcohol concentration in the blood and its relevance to the average individual's condition was emphasized. With barbiturates, concentration in the blood also plays a highly important part in any forensic, clinical, or post-mortem assessment. Concentrations in stomach contents are of less significance, since they do not necessarily tally with the clinical condition of the patient as the drug may not have been absorbed or may have passed on to the intestines. This content, however, can help to identify a brand of drug, and the total amount found in the stomach may assist in assessing the total dose of barbiturate swallowed by a patient.

MISUSE AND DEPENDENCE

Barbiturate addiction is still in many respects the 'hidden' problem of drug abuse. It is a problem of staggering proportions (at least one authority has estimated that the U.K. alone has 80,000 barbiturate addicts, and there may be about a million in the U.S.A.), and it has been created directly by the use of these drugs in everyday medicine and the way the general practitioner has prescribed them over the years, in particular to middle-aged women patients for various forms of neurotic complaint. The fact that the great majority of addicts are highly respectable members of society, whom one would never dream of describing as belonging to a drug 'sub-culture', has no doubt had a great deal to do with the way that the problem has been ignored by or evaded in the public mind. To quote a psychiatric social worker from Birmingham, England:[10]

These women are so reluctant to admit they take pills. They just don't like being coupled with the image of the drug addict yet by the time they come forward we've just as difficult a problem on our hands as we have with the young heroin addict. . . . Some narcotic addicts mature out of it. These women don't.

A woman addict is a much harder therapeutic prospect than a man, and the higher class the family, the harder our job because of the social stigma attached.

On the whole, the literature shows that the popularity of barbiturates like Veronal at the beginning of the century, when it could be obtained freely and was proclaimed 'an excellent drug' at the 73rd Annual Meeting of the British Medical Association in 1913, was great and growing. At that time there were few references to adverse effects and few reports of fatalities. This situation began to change rapidly after 1913, and as a result barbiturates were placed in Part II of the British Poisons Schedule, and in 1918 in Part I. The first case of actual dependence was reported in 1926,[11] and from then on the controversy about the inherent danger of barbiturates developed into an acrimonious battle. Debates in the medical press and at the meetings of the Royal Society of Medicine were bitter and passionate. But the arguments for even more stringent control were based on sound evidence, and from 1935 purchase was restricted to Schedule 4 poisons, which means that they could only be obtained on a doctor's prescription with a full record of patient and doctor being kept.

Unlike the toxicologist, pathologist, or specialist in the field of drug dependence, who see the ill-effects that can result from the abuse of barbiturates, on the whole the general practitioner only sees the benefits which his patients gain from this group of drugs. Consequently he often tends to over-prescribe, possibly producing the argument that persons determined to commit suicide will, in the absence of barbiturates, select another, perhaps more horrible method. While some barbiturates could be replaced by tranquillizers in therapeutic use, this would possibly only amount to taking on a devil we don't know in place of the one we do.

It may be that the time has come when the inclusion of barbiturates in the British Drugs (Prevention of Misuse) Act 1964, and corresponding legislation in other countries, should seriously be considered. While Swiss experts have thought that barbiturates (although declining in their medical use) and tranquillizers would be difficult to control strictly, the American Legislature, with the Drug Abuse Control Amendments 1965, has included barbiturates in its list and has moved towards an open-ended legislation that can be extended to cover any drug that becomes a social menace. While their therapeutic use is diverse and valuable, it appears from the figures given on page 126, and taking other information into account, that barbiturates are being produced far in excess of therapeutic needs. Moreover, an American doctor has estimated that, in the U.S.A., where the President's (Kennedy) Advisory Commission on Narcotic and Drug Abuse[12] paid as much attention to non-narcotic drugs as to hard ones, at least a million people regularly take sleeping pills with 10 to 25 per cent of constant users being 'unsuspected' dependants. The death-rate for barbiturate poisoning has doubled within five years in the town of Newark, New Jersey.

In Israel,[13] a country with a usually abstemious population, the use of pentobarbital has become widespread.

Dependence on barbiturates,[14] when these are taken regularly in large quantities, shows some similarities to dependence of the opiate type (see pp. 74–7), although there are differences if one considers the details. Tolerance develops, but the limit is a characteristic of the individual patient, and following withdrawal the tolerance is rapidly lost. However, the 'abstinence syndrome' is the most serious feature of this group of drugs. While 0·6 grams daily for six weeks or more will produce such moderate symptoms as anxiety, tremor, and weakness on sudden withdrawal, 0·8 grams or more during a similar period will produce severe withdrawal symptoms, with about 75 per cent of dependent individuals developing convulsions and about 60 per cent delirium (resembling *delirium tremens*) or psychotic episodes. Unfortunately, and not infrequently, emotional problems and tension coupled with impaired judgement help to boost dependence,[15] and withdrawal is not then an easy process.

Apart from the real dangers of barbiturate dependence, the development period is fraught with dangers of its own. While tolerance can be produced within seven days in some circumstances, and the worst abstinence syndrome may appear after eight to sixteen hours, reaching a peak two to three days after the drug has been discontinued, the habituated barbiturate consumer is in constant peril from the risk of chronic intoxication. He will be in a state of mental confusion and instability, and more likely than not may suddenly and unintentionally take an overdose or mix his tablets with alcoholic drink.

This is how even famous, successful, and wealthy individuals can move on from sleeplessness and over-work to eternal sleep and an end of all work – we are all familiar with actual examples from our reading of the newspapers. If people of every kind would only realize that the tablets of these strange synthetic compounds are capable of producing states that could only be acquired by taking many bottles of liquor!

TREATMENT, CURE, AND THE LEGAL ASPECTS

For anyone who has taken a serious overdosage or who has reached a state of toxic psychosis, prompt hospital treatment is essential – if he or she is lucky enough to be found in time (thinking here of the tragic case of Marilyn Monroe).

With chronic intoxication, including that coupled with dependence, abrupt withdrawal is not advisable, in contrast to other drugs, especially the opiates. Patients may be stabilized for several days on one of the rapidly-acting barbiturates, sufficient to maintain a mild intoxication.[16] After a gradual withdrawal, the patient should begin a more difficult long-term treatment designed to prevent relapses.* As with other drug-dependent people emerging from a drug-taking period, a thorough process of psychological and social rehabilitation must be followed through and will merge with the usual methods of vocational training and social work service. It seems clear that the after-treatment of drug dependence, whether of the barbiturate type or for any other deep-set dependence, follows a similar pattern in different countries. The facilities may be limited, however, and their efficiency and availability does not always necessarily depend on the wealth of the country concerned.

As has been said, in Britain barbiturates are controlled under the Poisons Schedule.[17] Apart from other restrictions, records have to be kept and an entry made in the prescription book,

---

* The chronic underlying illness has been appropriately called 'barbiturism', a name analogous to 'alcoholism'.

with one disquieting exemption. This is if the prescription is issued by a doctor or a dentist on a form made available by a local authority or under the National Health Service Act 1946. So there seems to be one loophole here which could lead to leakages on to a black market.

Initial resistance from pharmaceutical manufacturers in the U.S.A. and from the American Medical Association to increased Federal control of the barbiturates[18] has diminished, and the Drug Abuse Control Amendments 1965 have subsequently been strongly endorsed by representatives of consumers and the American pharmaceutical industry.[19] The Amendments are based on the Federal Food, Drug and Cosmetic Act and deal generally with depressants and stimulants. Barbiturates appear under two counts: (a) being designated as habit forming and thus linked with the narcotics; and (b) being at the same time linked with anti-depressants, stimulants, and depressants as having a potential for abuse and habit formation. The regulations thus tend to be more severe than those at present in force in the U.K. (see above). Very often, however, individual states issue laws that vary from the federal ones.

Barbiturate consumption in the U.S.A. was 700,000 lb per annum between 1954 and 1961, but sales have dropped to 436,000 lb during 1966, though 977,000 lb were manufactured. This discrepancy is interesting, as it seems to indicate that over 500,000 lb was left on the shelves of the pharmaceutical manufacturers, unless exported, which is doubtful. Possibly it represents some evidence that the Amendments were already having a considerable effect on barbiturate consumption by 1966.

3. A Miscellaneous Selection

There are a number of drugs which do not fit easily into any other chapter, either because they have multiple pharmacological actions, mainly therapeutic, or, as effective hypnotics, sedatives, or tranquillizers, have been thought of over the years as being relatively harmless. However, some of these have on occasion put in an appearance on the drug-abuse scene. Since they possess variegated effects, they may, in some cases, even represent potential dangers which could be the greater for not always being well recognized.

A group of natural drugs which inevitably have a special fascination are those associated with traditions of magic and witchcraft. These come from several well-known members of the nightshade family (*Solanaceae*), outstanding among them being the deadly nightshade (*Atropa belladonna*), henbane (*Hyoscyamus niger*), and the European mandrake (*Mandragora officinarum*). (This family, of course, also includes some of the most commonly cultivated food plants – potatoes, tomatoes, and eggplants – as well as the tobacco plants.) A fourth member of the family, possibly the most poisonous of them all, is the thorn-apple (*Datura stramonium*, known in the United States as Jimson or Jamestown weed), which is usually thought to have been spread across Europe by gipsies, who brought it from a place of origin lying roughly between India and the Caspian Sea.

The active principles of deadly nightshade, henbane, and thorn-apple have been found to be atropine* and scopolamine (hyoscine), which can also be obtained from the European mandrake root. These all have stimulatory and depressant effects on the central nervous system as well as antagonistic effects on the body's acetylcholine, one of the 'chemical messengers' which help to carry instructions from the brain to a muscle, in particular acting on the heart and blood vessels. In clinical use atropine helps to enlarge the eye's pupil for specialist examination.† Scopolamine is injected in association with morphine before the first stage of anaesthesia is induced: it has also been inaccurately called a 'truth serum'. Mandrake has a long history in folklore, and extracts from it were used to dull pain in early surgery. It was known to the Ancient Greeks as a pain-reliever and soporific, and in the first century A.D.

---

* Atropos was one of the three Fates.

† In central and southern Europe women traditionally used to put a drop of belladonna in each eye in preparation for parties, the enlarging of the pupils making their eyes shine more attractively – though blurring of vision with potentially irreversible eye damage was the result.

Dioscorides claimed it to be a cure for tumours and snake-bite. Its anti-depressant effects lead to mental aberration in high doses in a similar way to hellebore (an extract of the roots of the Christmas rose, *Helleborus niger*).

The central effects of atropine and scopolamine are on the medulla or even higher in the brain, and can produce hallucination states, combined sometimes with uncomfortably depressed respiration.

The notorious and cruel 'bible' of Europe's fifteenth-century witchhunters, the *Malleus Maleficarum* (*The Hammer of Witchcraft*), written by two Dominican monks, Jacobus Sprenger and Heinrich Kramer, contains this account:

> Now the following is their method of being transported. They take the unguent which, as we have said, they make at the devil's instruction from the limbs of children, particularly of those they have killed before baptism, and anoint with it a chair or broomstick; whereupon they are immediately carried up into the air, either by day or by night, and either visibly or, if they wish, invisibly. . . .[20]

The authors went on to concede that the transportation could take place in the imagination as well as in the physical body, not that that made it a less serious business from their point of view. The unguent, anyway, was rubbed all over the body as well as on to the potential steed. An appendix in Margaret Murray's *The Witch-Cult in Western Europe*[21] analyses some standard recipes for the ointments that witches were said to rub into their bodies before they could fly. Leaving on one side such ingredients as bat's blood and the fat of young children, these preparations would have contained hemlock, aconite, and belladonna. It is probable that enough belladonna would have found its way into the bloodstream, perhaps coupled with other drugs or poisons, to produce the individual or collective illusion of gaining the power of flight which is such a consistent feature of historical witch-lore.

The dangers of such drugs in the present age, however, may be expected to arise only in highly eclectic circumstances. Dangers of abuse probably lie more with such manufactured compounds as synthetic surrogates of atropine and the drugs which have anti-histamine properties in addition to atropine-like effects.* Anti-histamines may well have serious side-effects on a driver's judgement and reactions – side-effects of which the people who obtain them regularly over a chemist's counter are often unaware.

A tablet known as Mandrax (a combination of diphenhydramine with methaqualone, a sedative and hypnotic) has been reported as being misused as a hallucinogen and hypnotic. And apart from sporadic incidents with one or another of the tranquillizers (see the beginning of this chapter), a number of old-fashioned sedatives and hypnotics are from time to time referred to the medical and legal authorities as being the media for mild to severe cases of dependence.[22] Paraldehyde, chloral hydrate, and, starting with the simple bromides (e.g. potassium bromide), a number of bromide-containing compounds, carbromal, bromvaletone, and so on, have become drugs of choice for some people, not normally always regarded as belonging to any drug sub-culture, who gain by its 'regular' consumption a sense of security and a guarantee of restful sleep. The potential danger lies more in the possibility of eventual chronic intoxication or an advance from such remedies to barbiturates and other drugs officially recognized as being among those of dependence.

This miscellaneous account does not claim to be comprehensive, but it should help to indicate that no medicinal preparation which has any effect on the central nervous system is safe from being transformed from a metaphysical walking-stick into an elaborate and enfeebling crutch.

---

* These include agents like benzhexol (Artane, with stimulating and depressant actions on the nervous system), and diphenhydramine (Benadryl), which, together with pyrilamine, promethazine, and others, form a bridge with the tranquillizers to represent the group known as anti-histamines; these are the drugs which counteract the ill-effects of the release of the body chemical known as histamine in response to a pollen allergy, for example, and which can result in vascoconstriction and bronchial spasms.

Chapter Eight

The Hallucinogens: LSD and the Products of the Sacred Cactus

ORIGIN AND HISTORY
Just before, during, and following the Second World War, chemists and biologists at Sandoz, the Swiss pharmaceutical firm, studied the chemistry and properties of certain alkaloids, including ergot, and their derivatives; in 1943 one of them, Albert Hofmann,[1] accidentally stumbled across some most peculiar properties in the semi-synthetic drug d-lysergic acid diethylamide (Delyside), later to become popularly known as 'LSD-25'. The biological effects were certainly very strange, and centred on the mind, in which they produced hallucinations. They recalled the properties of mescaline, the alkaloid derived from the sacred Mexican cactus, *Lophophora williamsii*. A long-term study of these and similar products had commenced, and qualities possessed by these drugs led in the 1950s and 1960s to experiment and abuse – mainly among groups of intelligent and artistic people – as well as to a prolific literature.

Strangely enough, knowledge of some of the active principles involved came through a quite different channel. During the Middle Ages, and as recently as 1951 in the little village of Pont-

Saint-Esprit in France,[2]* rye periodically suffered from a plant disease caused by the fungus ergot *Claviceps purpurea*.[3] This had grave consequences for a people living on staple foods like bread, and any cattle grazing near affected fields. The fungus would naturally be ground with the grain, and anything baked from the flour led to outbreaks of the disease called ergotism or 'St Anthony's fire', which produced, in man, gangrened limbs and hands, and in cattle, gangrened ears, tails, and hooves. Another effect consisted of convulsions and delirium with bizarre and terrifying visions lasting over a long period. We know now that

FIG. 6. The Mexican sacred cactus, *Lophophora williamsii*

* Insecticides have also come under suspicion in this incident.

ergot contains such highly active components as tyramine, histamine, and the ergot alkaloids,[4] which were responsible for the symptoms. During ergotism, pregnant women and animals frequently aborted, owing to uterine contractions, and it is not surprising therefore that primitive medicine utilized the natural product as an obstetric drug. But not before the 1930s was the principle of this 'oxytocic' activity chemically and pharmacologically defined as 'ergometrine' or 'ergonovine'.[5,6] However, the other alkaloids,[7] such as ergotamine and ergotoxine (a mixture of three alkaloids), also turned out to be useful for treating migraine or any complaint that involved an over-activity of adrenaline or other sympathetic over-stimulation.

The chemistry of this group of substances was extensively studied, principally by the research group in Switzerland, under Stoll, Hofmann, and their colleagues.[8] They found that all the ergot alkaloids and other derivatives consist of two main parts: one being a tetracyclic acid (lysergic acid), the other a chain attached to the acid group in the form of so-called amides or peptides. Ergotamine and the other ergot-alkaloids are lysergic acid derivatives of the latter, ergometrine of the former. LSD is closely related to this compound, but differs from it because of its hallucinogenic properties.

It gradually emerged that closely related drugs occur in nature and that the knowledge of their hallucinogenic activities went back into ancient times. The seeds of certain varieties of 'morning-glory' (e.g. *Ipomoea tricolor*), the convolvulus and bindweed family, were found to produce 'psychedelic' effects. Then links with the Central American climber, the bindweed *Rivea corymbosa*, were established, leading to a final conclusion that one of the main principles of the ancient and now newly discovered hallucinogenic phenomena could be identified chemically with lysergic acid amide, lysergamide, or ergine.[9] During the course of the 1950s and 1960s, with steadily increasing interest in the whole field of hallucinogenic drugs (or psychotomimetics or psychedelics, as they are also known), a whole crop of drugs was linked together, partly of natural and ancient and partly of synthetic origin.[10] (See pp. 183–5.)

The natural hallucinogens, especially in ancient Central and South America, show a long history of use in magic and religious ritual. In Mexico *peyote*, the top buttons of the sacred cactus, was known as 'the flesh of the gods', a bringer of visions. The Native American Church in America today, most of whose members are of Indian descent, has continued to use peyote in its ceremonies, and for the participants the rites are a matter for great seriousness.

[They] feel that peyote aids contemplation by increasing their powers of introspection, sensitizing their consciousness and producing visions of great meaning. Throughout the ceremony the participants conduct themselves with due solemnity.[11]

Hallucinogens as the means to religious or mystical experience is a subject on its own, and an often vexed one. The evidence which is available does not rule out the possibility that genuinely remarkable perceptions may sometimes be obtainable under the influence of LSD, but the idea of this providing an automatic short cut, or 'hot line', to divinity or central spiritual truth is a dangerous misconception. Under controlled conditions, genuine mystical perception does seem to occur in a certain percentage of subjects, but it is notable that these are people whose thinking has already been cultivated in that direction. In the case of the Native American Church, for instance, peyote taking is strictly within the context of established ritual.[12] Unfortunately, our fragmented modern society, with its many divisions in loyalties, cannot be expected to provide this kind of safety barrier in the ordinary way, and those who take to a compulsive use of drugs are likely to be far from stable personalities. No doubt the formation of various 'psychedelic' churches and cults in the United States in the 1960s represented attempts to construct some kind of controlled context within which to release these drugs. In spite of the colourful eulogies of Timothy Leary among other propagandists, however, there is no convincing evidence that they have succeeded.

To deny totally that mystical insight can occur under LSD might be to deny the actual validity of mystical experience, assuming that similar levels of consciousness are involved and considering what we know of the extent to which mental processes are controlled by natural chemical balances. It must be remembered also that when reading, for example, Havelock Ellis's or Aldous Huxley's accounts of their experiences under mescaline, we are seeing its effects on two highly trained, exceptionally sensitive and articulate intelligences. In *Heaven and Hell,* where he outlines his interesting idea that the visions of the early Christian saints and anchorites were due to vitamin deficiency and other metabolic changes, Huxley remarks that 'the Devil revealed himself in their visions and ecstasies a good deal more frequently than did God'.[13] There is no reason to think that this should be different for us today, and we are probably far less able to cope with 'devils' should we come across them than were the ancients. The mind contains many closed or half-closed doors, and these are as likely to open on to chambers of horrors as lost paradises. Should LSD be given under experimental or clinical conditions, the therapist remains present throughout the experience and has specially evolved techniques to guide the patient through any crises that may arise; but in the same circumstances the casual user or experimenter is on his own, and may experience 'hell'.

THE EFFECTS OF THE HALLUCINOGENS

In contrast to most of the other drugs described in this book, the hallucinogens have not acquired a general basis for therapeutic application. There are groups of specialists who continue to believe that LSD and some of its relatives have a considerable potential value in the treatment of psychiatric disorders, comparable with, if on a narrower front than, other psychotropic remedies. A series of investigations showing some interesting results has been made at Spring Grove State Hospital in Baltimore, Maryland, and these include the treatment of alcoholism and psychoses, as well as the administration of LSD to terminal cancer patients.[14] The cancer patients in particular are apparently able to attain a new sense of fulfilment and an expression of deep feelings which help them to face death consciously. As all these applications involve intensive, individual periods of psychological preparation and therapeutic control, it is hard to visualize a time in the near future when a heavily burdened medical profession and hospital service will turn to any advantages which they might have to offer or take them up on a wide scale. Meanwhile it is the more sensational connotations of the hallucinogens and their often lurid news value which unfortunately mostly attracts public attention.

In general, like most of the tranquillizers and related compounds, the hallucinogens proper act directly on the central nervous system and in a peripheral sense on the autonomic nervous system. Apart from their cardio-vascular effects, which increase heart rate and blood pressure, they sometimes dilate the eye pupils and affect the blood sugar level, a situation reminiscent of adrenaline-like stimulation, which means that nausea, heavy perspiration, and a heightened body temperature may also appear as near-toxic symptoms. Taking mescaline as a different type of chemical, it produces roughly the same effects, but larger doses lower the blood glucose and near-lethal doses produce convulsions, breathing arrest, and heart failure. LSD's most impressive characteristic pharmacological property[15] is its high toxicity and effectiveness in very small amounts, and most of its doses, especially those to gain psychic effects, are measured in micrograms.*

The first question to try to answer is what is a hallucinogenic effect? But here we have to distinguish between effects on normal and on neurotic or mentally diseased people. This means, in fact, that there is *no* comprehensively valid description to cover adequately the experience of everybody who has tried it out, for whatever motive. Some people, on a real journey, may have a splendid flight or crossing, while others on the same plane or boat feel terrible. In the same way regular users of LSD ('cube-heads' or 'acid heads') may find themselves 'turned on', while others have what they call a 'bum trip'.

The most vivid descriptions of experiences often come from such people as scientists or literary men who, we may assume, have a high level of cultural equipment and whose descriptions

* 1 microgram = 0·00015 grains = $\frac{1}{1000}$ milligram = μg.

of visions, colours, and thoughts are, they state, beyond anything they ever met with; there are equally those who may
finish in acute or psychotic states of anxiety and distress and
with nothing but shreds of nightmarish images to show for
it.

Hallucinogenic effects are certainly nothing factual, whatever
significances they may take on for some individual imagina-
tions. They are combinations of illusions, and their physiological causes lie with changes in mental function, dream-like
phantasies, true and quasi-hallucinations, and light phenomena.
Since hallucinations are images formed 'quite independent of
external stimuli',[16] we may understand to a limited extent the
claims of the prophets of the LSD cult that they live in a reality
different from that of daily life: hence the much-quoted hippie
motto, 'Turn on, tune in, and drop out'. Before taking an
objective look at this 'reality', we ought to consider the chronic
toxicity and after-effects.

The results of many studies on various aspects of this intriguing field are available, and include animal experimentation,[17]
which to some extent objectivize subjective tests in man. It is
therefore possible tentatively to assess the value of hallucinogens
in the advance of medical science. In chronic toxicity, there
seems to be no doubt that some of these drugs produce serious
after-effects. Weeks, in some cases months, after administration,
hallucinatory phenomena can reassert themselves, and so can
certain personality changes which are acute enough to correspond to mental derangement.[18]

Naturally, as with the narcotics, allowance must be made for
the possibility that the drug-taker who suffers from after-effects
already suffers from a latent form of mental disturbance. On the
other hand, while nothing certain is known about the action
mechanism of these compounds, biochemical alterations in the
brain may be causally connected. At the same time, enough
evidence has accumulated over recent years to put forward a
hypothesis that certain internally produced hallucinogenic compounds are the causative agents of psychoses like schizophrenia.
It is not for nothing that the original representatives of these

drugs were called 'psychotomimetics'; that is, imitating the symptoms of psychotic disease.

One fear that LSD in particular may damage the chromosomes, the genetic material which carries inheritable characteristics, has not been borne out by subsequent investigations, including one carried out with human male and female volunteers.[19] A recent letter in *Nature*[20] about research into the production of embryonic malformations which could be put down to LSD-25 in pregnant hamsters and mice reported no difference between the litters of those hamsters which had received LSD and those acting as controls. Research by two of the present authors with mice had a similar result, in contrast to other reports published in 1967, which used different strains. It is not therefore impossible that, among men, some persons may be more susceptible to chromosome damage, embryotoxicity, or even premature abortion than are others.

While all this may appear to be a highly specialized field, it helps graphically to illustrate the complexity of a situation which is certainly no less 'confused' than that surrounding any of the other drug groups, particularly the opiates. It may also help to underline the fact that most of the hallucinogenic agents are 'investigational drugs'. They remain, at our present state of knowledge, highly delicate instruments with which we may perhaps explore more and more deeply the intricate patterns of brain function, normality, abnormality, slight or severe deviation, emotion and thought processes, even the nature of the artist's vision. They should teach us increasingly about the human mind, at its best and its worst, and about the possibilities of finding new and better remedies with which to fight neurotic and psychotic illness; they may actually help us in the urgent quest of rediscovering our true selves in a world that often denies deep and genuine feelings. But their misuse by individuals or drug cult groups to achieve 'new realities' remains a misguided, dangerous ambition. This is to ignore the fact that the brain's evolutionary development has occurred under terrestrial conditions and adjusted to a terrestrial reality. By all means let us strive to develop and understand the brain, its intelligence and sense of vision. But this should be done within the science's tradition of humanity and authority. We can be sure that Aldous Huxley would have been horrified had he known that LSD changes the brain's RNA (ribonucleic acid) structure,[21] thought to be responsible for memory and the processes of association, quite apart from the effect it has on electrical impulses within the brain.

MISUSE AND THE SOCIAL AND LEGAL POSITION

No sane group or organization would construct a case for making the opiates a basis for a culture, a philosophy, or a belief. Yet, with astonishing frequency, the propagandists and prophets of the psychedelic ideal present us with public state-ments, couched in terms of evangelical fervour, that cannabis and the hallucinogens are a way of life that ushers in a new millennium.[22] These often discount the possibility of any danger being involved and make sweeping and unsubstantiated claims that such substances ought to be freely available. The effects of these drugs, however, are, as Dr Alex Comfort has put it, 'rather as if the entire human cerebral and emotional potential were to be dumped pell-mell in front of us without further instructions for use'.[23] As for its being harmless, Louria[24] describes 130 patients in Bellevue Hospital, New York, who came under his observation for LSD-induced psychoses or else for the worsening of an established mental disorder as a result of LSD.

We have already indicated that the mechanisms behind these agents' actions is not completely known. There are signs, how-ever, that excessive use may not only have serious consequences, but also develop into tolerance,[25] though withdrawal does not produce an abstinence syndrome. Because of its rapid distribu-tion in the body, the onset of symptoms is quick, a minimal effective dose of LSD being in the region of 20 to 30 μg, an opti-mum psychotomimetic or psychedelic dose being about 100 μg to 1 milligram.

Whatever conclusion one may reach about the desirability of an artificially induced form of 'happiness', taking these drugs means acting against contemporary laws, unless the event comes within a scientific investigation. The international anti-drug organizations frown heavily on the abuse of the hallucino-gens, and in Britain and the United States the legislators have issued the Acts or Amendments already explained (see page 14). Britain has its open-ended Drugs (Prevention of Misuse) Act 1964, which was modified in 1966 to cover LSD, or any alkyl derivative of it, tryptamines, which may be less or more effective than LSD, depending on their structure, as well as mescaline. The law-makers of the U.S.A. have done the same, control-ling importation and unauthorized possession and specifying penalties under the Drug Abuse Control Amendments of 1965.

There is not much information available yet on the situation in other countries, but we may assume that most of those who signed the Single Convention of 1961 will have made similar provisions.

The question of responsibility for any act performed under the influence of a drug is an interesting point, and in British and American law it is not an exonerating circumstance, anyone acting under the influence of LSD having the same legal liabili-ties as anyone who has taken drink.[26] An American who killed a girl in London in 1968 while both were on an LSD 'trip', had the charge reduced from one of murder to manslaughter, but was convicted on that count though the Court acknowledged that he would have had no knowledge of his action.[27] Cases of people jumping from roofs and windows after taking LSD under the delusion that they can fly have not been as common in Britain as in America, where it seems to have become almost the classic LSD syndrome. It is ironical that in one of the few reported British incidents the man who jumped survived, but killed someone else in the car he landed on.[28]

The illicit manufacture of LSD is likely to pose increasing problems, since the financial rewards are considerable and it is relatively easy to make within certain technical limits. A recent case in London, where a group conspired together to manufac-ture nearly £1,800,000 worth of LSD for the American black market, illustrated this point.[29] The drug being let loose on the market in impure form could possibly be an additional and incalculable hazard.

Whether or not chromosome damage by LSD is a fact,[30] at least one recent observation is deeply disturbing.[31] It has been found that in rats (though not yet confirmed in man) behaviour patterns can be influenced by an earlier experience with psycho-active drugs (amphetamines and barbiturates), this experience possibly staying with the organism 'for life'. Whatever drug one may take, and to whatever 'school' of drug abuse one may belong, this in itself is an indication that anyone should think twice about the implications, since the effects of drug-taking may in certain respects stay with the taker for a very long time indeed. The situation is reminiscent of young men attracted by tatooing when abroad, subsequently regretting it during the whole of their middle and old age. Unfortunately an altered psycho-chemistry of the brain can never be etched away like a heart from across the chest.[32]

Chapter Nine

Further Enjoyments and Hazards

It can come as a surprise to find that the longer a bad habit's history, the closer it has moved to being a good habit. Tradition alone seems to be able to brainwash whole societies, making their members ignorant of the fact that they have developed psychic dependences at least as deleterious as any arising from the officially recognized drugs of abuse. Western man, looking at the Orientals or the South American Indians, sees them (apart from their long-established addiction to opium, cannabis, or coca) chewing betel or spicing their food with red pepper or curry and filling their rooms and temples with clouds of incense, and forgets how he has acquired in his past history habits like tobacco smoking and the drinking of coffee and tea. He may ask what harm could there be in these habits? Don't these natural products, though they may often carry poisons, form an ideal complement to his staple diet by being exactly what the Germans call them: *Genussmittel*, or necessary means of enjoyment?

The answer lies largely in the question of whether they prolong or shorten life with all social implications. With the enormous upsurge over the past fifty to sixty years of smoking, the consumption of tea and coffee, the possibility of unnecessary deaths which originate with these 'harmless' pleasures, have created consternation and questioning. Heart ailments, chest diseases, stroke, and cancer which can be traced back actually or circumstantially to the excessive consumption of any one of these natural products, have forced medical men and scientists to take unheeded dangers into account. The following facts will, we hope, give the reader a sufficient basis on which to reach his own conclusions. This is not so much a question of trying to ruin people's pleasures as of at least giving them a chance to assess the risks accurately and realistically.

1. Tobacco

ORIGIN, HISTORY, AND CONSUMPTION

The Americas have provided the world with a great number of materials of natural origin which have become drugs of abuse or, at least, of habituation, as is the experience with tobacco. After being brought back from the journeys of discovery of the fifteenth century, tobacco, in its various forms, had made rapid progress – despite stringent laws and the deep displeasure of the church, as well as James I's famous pamphlet *Counterblast to Tobacco* – by the end of the seventeenth and early eighteenth century. Its inhalation in the form of smoke, or its mastication, and, as snuff, its administration up the nostrils, are still the main means to its enjoyment.

Its botanical origin lies in the West Indies and South America. The main species, still used today, is *Nicotiana tabacum* (after a certain Doctor Nicot), or *N. rusticana* of ancient origin. However, it is the former variety which is cultivated in the tobacco-producing countries: North America, Canada, India, Japan, Rhodesia and other African states, Greece, Turkey, and Bulgaria among others. Tobacco is consumed as cigarettes, cigars, pipe tobacco, snuff, and chewing tobacco. The most up-to-date method of curing tobacco is by 'flue-curing', which uses heated flues with the tobacco leaves fixed above them and takes about four to five days from the preliminary yellowing of the leaves to the final drying out of the stems. There is another method which uses wood fires and smoke, and also the oldest one, which takes over two months and exposes the leaves in a barn to air, or sun and air. The different types of curing and varieties of tobacco plant produce different kinds of tobacco.

Most of the tobacco used for cigarettes in the West, particularly in Britain, is flue-cured and grown in the U.S.A. (Virginia), Africa, India, and Brazil. Air-cured types, to which oriental tobacco belongs, are grown in Greece, Turkey, Macedonia, and Russia. Pipe and cigar tobacco belong to different varieties, the cigar leaf coming from North America, Cuba, Jamaica, or Indonesia. Similar qualities are used for the cheroot-type of cigar. Snuff and chewing tobacco also represent different mixtures of other derivations. We shall see later how these various types differ in their chemical make-up and biological effects.

Some countries, like Britain and the U.S.A., have left the production of all tobacco products in the hands of private industry. But other countries, such as Austria (as far back as the Austro-Hungarian Empire), have state monopolies, and as a result a relatively small choice of brands but very advanced manufacturing methods and imaginative research of a kind which did not develop in the British and American tobacco industry until much later on.

ANALYSIS AND PREVENTION

It is mainly the chemistry, biochemistry, and pharmacology of tobacco itself, and its aerosol condensate after burning, which has led to great advances in medical research into this socially accepted custom. Before medical interest into its potentially damaging effects was aroused, the most important compound in leaf and smoke was known to be nicotine, which occurs in tobacco in quantities of between 0·5 and 0·8 per cent. In cigarette tobacco the alkaloid content is at its most intensive, the smoke carrying 6 to 8 milligrams per cigarette. Of course, the combustion process does destroy some of the alkaloid, but appreciable amounts still find their way into the oral cavity and upper-respiratory system and become absorbed there. How much depends very much on the type of tobacco, its moisture, the speed of smoking, and a number of other factors.[1]

Nicotine is a liquid, basic material, occurring in the tobacco leaf in the form of salts with organic acids; these salts and the free base are water soluble, which means they are easily absorbed. Comparing the composition of the plant material with the smoke and its condensate is complicated by the effects of the 'pyrolytic processes'. It is not therefore surprising if the results of chemical analysis differ in what they show of the content of such plant bases as nicotine, pyridine, and so on, as well as acids, phenols, sugars, cellulose, hydrocarbons. This depends, as we have seen, on the various types of nicotiana leaf, or on how the smoke is condensed and at what temperature.

Anyone who has cleaned a pipe or cleared ashtrays is familiar with the pungent smell of the pyridine bases produced by the process of smoking. But the finer points of its chemistry can only be discovered through proper analytical methods. A considerable literature has grown up around these questions of composition, e.g. the research papers issued by the Tobacco Research Council.[2] Apart from nicotine and the bases already mentioned, there are annotations to the numerous organic acids and phenols as well as the so-called 'polycyclic hydrocarbons', which include those with cancer-producing properties, important, with other components, in any consideration of possible long-term effects.

As already mentioned, the toxicological properties of nicotine were, in former years, the main concern of investigators, who had been mainly interested in the acute effects of this rather poisonous alkaloid, which produces, with its related plant bases, the nicotine-stained fingers of the heavy smoker. Nicotine shares with other drugs an effect on the central nervous system, but also exerts a number of peripheral actions and obnoxious effects on the circulation of the blood. The rapidity with which nicotine acts is similar to that of cyanide (as can be seen from the cases of unfortunates who have poisoned themselves accidentally with those insecticide sprays in which nicotine is the main ingredient). But more serious than any acute intoxication is the chronic form of nicotine poisoning and smoking in general (seemingly cigarettes are the most damaging) that sometimes leads to irreparable changes of tissues of nose and bronchial tract and to a widespread deterioration of heart and blood vessels. In the case of respiratory organs like the throat, bronchial tissue, and the lungs themselves, the constant irritation may produce chronic bronchitis, emphysema, bronchiectasis, and, after heavy use, especially of cigarettes, malignant changes that lead to the so far almost incurable cancer of the lung.

The latter is certainly caused more frequently by the smoke of cigarette tobacco than by that from pipes and cigars. There is some difference between them in that that of certain cigarettes is acid, while the smoke inhaled from pipes, cigars, and cheroots is alkaline.

Arguments have been pursued over the last two or three decades as to whether there really is a causal connexion between smoking and lung cancer. This has now undoubtedly been settled in favour of the pessimists. As to the direct causation itself, the processes are not completely clear – as yet. There are certainly cancer-producing materials in the smoke and its condensate. Results from experiments in animals have shown that the presence of a virus infection (e.g. influenza) could lead to lung tumours whether or not the animals are exposed to benzpyrene or cigarette smoke.[3] There is one idea, originally put forward by Biffinger, an Austrian scientist, which blames the flue-cured tobaccos more than those which undergo slow fermentation, since the latter process destroys most of the plant sugars in the leaves. Others have produced evidence to show that tobacco with a high sugar content is more toxic to animals exposed to its smoke than is tobacco containing low levels of sugars.[4] There is no doubt that in the course of the next few years the whole problem of aetiology in these 'smoking' diseases will become clear. Meanwhile it is essential to warn both the young, middle-aged, and old that misuse of tobacco, especially in the form of cigarettes, will produce changes in the organism which can lead to death.

A number of health authorities take an extremely serious view of increasing deaths from lung cancer and allied diseases.* The only measures of prevention they can apply, however, are educational ones and on the limitation of advertising. Television advertisements for cigarettes are no longer permitted in Britain, and we are now spared those showing cigarettes being puffed happily by 'young people in glamorous surroundings'. In America, the Surgeon General's Committee in 1964 issued a report[5] which led to the Federal Labelling and Advertising Act 1964–5 which made it obligatory for a printed warning reading 'Caution: Cigarette smoking may be hazardous to your health' to be put on all packets sold (see Plate 7b), and there would seem to be no reason why a similar ruling should not be applied in Britain. In April 1969, however, the Surgeon General of the United States, Dr W. H. Stewart, laid a proposal before the Congress House Commerce Committee that the wording should be changed to 'Cigarette smoking is dangerous to health and may cause death from cancer and other diseases'. Needless to say, the big tobacco interests have vigorously opposed this proposal, as they have the declared intention of the Federal Communication Commission to ban cigarette commercials on television. It remains to be seen who will win this battle.

A leading article in *Science*[6] recently stated that increasing evidence[7] points to the fact that the impacts of tobacco smoking are even more serious than had up till now been thought. 'The most striking finding is that the "life expectancy" for a two-pack a day, or more, smoker at the age of 25 is 8·3 years less than that for the corresponding non-smoker.' Among American physicians, only 29 per cent have continued smoking, as against 52 per cent of the general adult male population. What may still not be completely appreciated, since the lung cancer phenomenon overshadows all other ills, is the close association of heavy smoking with blood vessel (cardio-vascular) diseases, the biggest killers of them all.

* 28,000 in the U.K. in 1967. The most recent U.S. figures available date from the end of 1966 and total 55,000, excluding bronchitis and similar diseases.

Despite the protests that might be anticipated from the tobacco industry, it can only be in the widest public interest for future legislation to concentrate on further restrictions in advertising or any other measures which will help to take the pseudo-glamour out of smoking and cut back on the numbers who develop the habit in the first place. Meanwhile the tobacco industry can point to the fact that it contributes enormous sums in revenue to governments* as well as spending a considerable amount on research. But the amount spent on research must be balanced against the far greater amounts available for advertising budgets in what is in the U.K. and U.S.A. a ruthlessly competitive sales field. Any move in the right direction in the battle for improved health and genuinely fuller life and towards a more common-sense attitude reflecting a better developed sense of social responsibility must inevitably involve sacrifices by both producer and consumer.

*

The so-called 'Indian' tobacco (the leaves were first seen being cured and smoked by Indians by the New England colonists), derived from the plant *Lobelia inflata*, should be mentioned briefly since its main principle, the alkaloid lobeline, has similar pharmacological properties to those of nicotine – for instance, stimulating the central nervous system. It has been recommended as an 'antagonist' to combat the tobacco smoking habit, but its other therapeutic uses, e.g. against asthma, have become unfashionable.

2. Tea, Coffee, and Cocoa

ORIGIN AND HISTORY

Tea originated in China and is mentioned in a Chinese dictionary of about A.D. 350. The name is derived from a Chinese Amoy dialect word, pronounced 'tay', but in Cantonese pronounced

* In the U.K., £1,024·6 million for 1966/7; in the U.S.A., $2,000 million going to the Federal Revenue, with another $1,500 million to $1,600 million to State treasuries and $2,000 million paid in Customs and Excise duty.

'chah'. Its cultivation was spread through China and Japan by Buddhist and Taoist priests, who are said to have thought it might combat the intemperance caused by rice wine.

During the eighteenth century, it was advertised in England as 'that excellent Chinese drink', and by 1870 more than 90 per cent of Britain's tea still came from China.[8] In the early eighteenth century it was an occasional luxury for the urban rich, but by the 1840s tea had graduated to occupying a place beside white bread in the poverty-line diets described by Engels among others. A flourishing tea industry meanwhile developed in India, and later in Ceylon, under the aegis mainly of the East India Company, and by 1900 India and Ceylon between them supplied nearly 90 per cent of British tea requirements, a mere 10 per cent coming from China. It was the East India Company which introduced China and India teas into Britain and America and was involved in the Tea Act of 1773, which gave rise to the Boston Tea Party, an important factor in bringing about the American War of Independence. Another result of the Boston Tea Party was to swing the American nation away from tea drinking to coffee drinking, while the reverse happened in Britain, where the influence of the East India Company persuaded the nation to change from coffee to tea. Politics and commerce were thus intimately involved in the change of whole populations from one means of enjoyment to another.

In modern times, the main tea-exporting countries are India and Ceylon, which account for approximately 80 per cent of the world's total. Of this, half is used in the U.K., with a consumption of approximately 9 lb per head annually, compared with rather less than $\frac{3}{4}$ lb in the U.S.A.

The tea plant, *Camellia sinensis* (*Theaceae*), is an evergreen shrub which grows in the wild to a height of fifteen to thirty feet, but under cultivation is never allowed to develop to more than three to five feet. For the final drink there are three kinds of starting material, depending partly on which manufacturing process has been applied to the leaf:

1. Green, or unfermented tea.

2. Black or fermented tea, which may be prepared from the same leaf as the former.

3. Oolong, or semi-fermented tea.

The principal chemical constituents of tea are caffeine, tannin, and essential oil; caffeine supplies the stimulating quality, tannin the strength of the beverage, and the essential oil the flavour and aroma. An average tea may contain 3·5 per cent caffeine, 15 per cent tannin, and a small percentage of theophylline.[9]

The average cup of tea contains rather less than 65 milligrams of caffeine, the recommended medicinal dose of which is 65 to 300 milligrams,* and 20 to 40 milligrams of tannin. Adding milk removes most of the astringency, since some of the tannin is fixed by the casein in the milk, the remainder being fixed by proteins during its passage through the alimentary tract. Sugar merely sweetens the tea. The ingestion of caffeine begins in the stomach, and its stimulating effect is felt about a quarter of an hour later. The ideal way of preparing tea extracts is one which obtains a solution containing the maximum amount of caffeine and the minimum of tannin. Such a beverage will also preserve the aroma and flavour.

Maté or Paraguayan tea (*Ilex paraguayensis*), first brought under cultivation by the Jesuit missionaries in Paraguay, contains 0·5 per cent caffeine. *Kola nut* from the tree *Cola acuminata*, used as a beverage in Africa or chewed in the Sudan, contains 3 per cent caffeine. Cola-flavoured soft drinks, popular in America and wherever advertising has persuaded people to join in the fashion, also contains caffeine, as does a well-known glucose drink on sale in the U.K.

Coffee was probably discovered in Africa, where it grew only in its wild state until about 1880, when it began to be developed chiefly through British interests. African coffee now accounts for about a sixth of the coffee on the world export market.

The earliest cultivation of coffee may be traced to Southern Arabia, and its name is probably derived from the Arabic through the Turkish, although one theory connects it with the

---

* This compares with 250 milligrams of caffeine in a cup of coffee.

town of Kaffia in Ethiopia. The physiological action of coffee, its stimulant action of counteracting drowsiness, led to its classification by conservative Mohammedans as an intoxicating beverage (the drinking of the brew is prohibited in the Koran). Despite the threat of severe penalties, coffee drinking became widespread among the Islamic population of Arabia. It was introduced into Europe during the seventeenth century and received much publicity as a religious, political, and medical potion. The *Kaffee Cantata* of Johann Sebastian Bach in 1732 portrayed the protest of the fair sex against the propaganda for abstinence from coffee by women on account of its alleged use for provoking sterility.

The most adventurous story connected with coffee is about a Pole, Koltschitzki, who, during the siege of Vienna by the Turks in 1683, had acted as a spy for the victorious allies, and as a reward – so the saga goes – founded the first coffee-house in Vienna, with the coffee beans left behind by the defeated Turks.[10] It also became popular in London in the middle of the eighteenth century and led to the founding of the coffee-houses so famous in the English literary tradition. An advertisement from a handbill in the British Museum claims that coffee 'quickens the spirits and makes the heart lightsome, is good against sore eyes, excellent to prevent and cure the dropsy, gout and scurvy and is neither laxative nor restringent'. Between 1801 and 1841, the per capita consumption of coffee rose from just over 1 oz to over $1\frac{1}{2}$ lb.[11] Coffee-houses also became popular in North America, and the Merchants' Coffee-house, established in New York in 1737, is claimed as the birthplace of the American Union. First supplies of the bean came from the Yemen, but as the beverage became more fashionable propagation of the plant spread throughout the tropical countries of the New World. The largest supplies of green coffee now come from South and Central America, with Brazil producing a high percentage of the world's total.

The bulk of the world's supplies comes from the variety *Caffea arabica*. The bushes are allowed to grow to a height of approximately fifteen feet, then topped so that harvesting will be easy.

The white, jasmine-like flowers last only a few days and give way to clusters of green cherries which turn to golden brown and red on ripening. Until roasted, coffee has none of the familiar aroma and flavour. During its roasting, 'green' coffee loses about 16 per cent of its weight and forms the aroma-carrying principles. Coffee is usually packaged as the bean, and ground immediately before use, or else vacuum packed, since it begins to lose its characteristics when exposed to the air after grinding from the evaporation and oxidation of the essential strength and flavour-giving components (which have also been synthesized).

Cocoa (Cacao) is the tropical tree from which cocoa powder and chocolate come. Cocoa trees belong to the family *Sterculiaceae*, the most common variety of which is *Theobroma cacao*. This is a native of Central and South America and may attain a height of forty feet in a natural habitat, but is usually pruned to a height of fifteen to twenty-five feet in cultivation.

Its small pink blossoms are borne directly on the trunk and on larger branches, and are followed by green pod-like fruits, which, when ripe, produce seeds that provide materials useful as food and drink. They were well known to the pre-Columbian Indians of tropical Central America, and in 1502 Columbus, on his fourth voyage, took cocoa beans back to Spain, the Spaniards finding the addition of sugar improved the beverage.

The Mayas and Aztecs used the beans as a medium of exchange since they had a standard value in the market-place, and the word chocolate itself is of Aztec derivation. For the Aztecs,[12] it was a drink of rich men or dignitaries, a luxury import from the slopes of the isthmus of Tehuantepec. They would drink it whipped up in hot water and sweetened with vanilla-scented honey or else mixed with green maize, *octli* (fermented Agave sap), or pimento. It also seems to have had some reputation as an aphrodisiac as Bernal Díaz, the veteran conquistador and chronicler who accompanied Cortés, recorded that Montezuma took it before visiting his wives. But this was one belief anyway which was totally without foundation.

After a hundred years its fame spread to the rest of Europe. A Frenchman opened a shop in London to sell solid chocolate, for making the beverage, at 10s. to 15s. a pound, a price which restricted the sale to the wealthy. A further improvement through the addition of milk was introduced in England in about 1700, though in his *Compleat History of Druggs* Pomet wrote with national pride that 'the best chocolate, and the finest, is what we make now at *Paris*'.[13] In the mid nineteenth century, with the reduction of duty to 1d. a pound, chocolate became more widely used. This was helped by the development of machinery to remove the shell, extract the fat, powder the cocoa, and mould the chocolate.[14] Cocoa imports, totalling four million lb in 1865, had risen to twenty million by 1890.

THE ANALYSIS OF TEA, COFFEE, AND CHOCOLATE

In Chapter Seven the relation between the hypnotic drugs, barbiturates, and their parent acid, barbituric acid, was indicated. The purine group, to which the active principles in tea, coffee, and chocolate belong, is structurally related to the barbituric series. One of the most important purine derivatives is uric acid, a common metabolite found in most carnivorous animals, including man. Reduction and methylation lead to compounds known as xanthines,* of which the following are found in nature:

Caffeine, a crystalline compound, is a feeble base, slightly soluble in water, but reasonably soluble in organic solvents.

Theophylline is a white crystalline powder with a bitter taste,[15] sparingly soluble in water, but readily soluble in alkali hydroxide solutions. *Theobromine* is also a white crystalline powder with similar chemical properties to those of theophylline.

Since the xanthines in tea, coffee, and cocoa are relatively insoluble in water, they are not often used medicinally in the free state. However, caffeine (citrate, hydrobromide, or iodide), as tablets or powder, shows better solubility and has its uses.

Caffeine first affects the cortex, then the medulla, and finally, in the presence of large amounts, the spinal cord. As a result of

---

* The main feature of the xanthines is their powerful stimulant action on the central nervous system. This progressively decreases from that of caffeine via theophylline to theobromine, which has virtually no stimulant action.

its action on the cortex, a person becomes less tired and more alert, his thinking appears to be more precise, and there is a reduction in his reaction time. This accounts for the stimulant action of coffee and tea,[16] especially when taken as strong brews. By its stimulant action on the centres of the medulla, caffeine may also be used to counteract the depressant effect of morphine and other drugs, and the value of a strong cup of coffee in an alcoholic hangover is well-attested to.

The effects of large doses of caffeine excite the lower motor centres to such an extent in experimental animals that convulsions and even death may be caused, but fatalities are rare in humans as the toxic dose is large (over 600 milligrams). There is evidence, however, that when large doses are taken the stimulation of the central nervous system is succeeded by depression, but it is doubtful whether this shows very significantly after a normal cup of tea or coffee.

Theophylline is medically the more important of the xanthines, as it has a better therapeutic effect on the cardio-vascular system (widening the coronary artery) than does caffeine and acts less powerfully on the central cortex.* Theophylline, in particular, is useful in the treatment of bronchial asthma, and this has been attributed[17] to 'its capacity to relax the smooth muscles of the bronchi'. The drug is also used for relieving biliary colic, again presumably owing to its action on smooth muscle tissue, and the diuretic action of the xanthines is valuable because they are less damaging than mercurials (mercury-containing diuretics) to the kidneys.

As we have said, human fatalities which can be put down to a misuse of caffeine are rare, except where strong coffee might be imbibed by someone with a weak heart, and anyone with a peptic ulcer may find it harmful and should take care even with de-caffeinized coffee. Theophylline is more toxic, weight for weight, than caffeine, and has caused fatalities.

The reader may have gathered that the xanthines in coffee,

* It is also a valuable drug in the emergency treatment of congestive heart failure. The relief of headache by the xanthines is thought to be from vasoconstriction caused by direct action on the musculature of the cerebral arterioles.

tea, and so on, have a variety of therapeutic uses: caffeine preparations being principally applied as central stimulants; theophylline and theobromine being used in cases of bladder troubles and in crises of the heart and circulation. Theophylline combinations, in particular aminophylline, are also prescribed for the treatment of asthma.

SOME ASPECTS OF XANTHINE MISUSE

Before the appearance of the amphetamines (see page 100), caffeine tablets were misused, for example, by students before their examinations; but an average cup, or number of cups, of tea or coffee may contain sufficient doses of caffeine to poison such intellectual night workers as Honoré de Balzac, the famous French author, and ruin their health. A doctor certainly has a problem on his hands in cases where stimulants of this nature have become contra-indicated and he may be obliged to advise strongly against their regular intake. Children are more suscep- tible to xanthines than are adults, and neither coffee nor tea can really be considered suitable for them, since their metabolism is already lively enough in most cases.

The significant amount of fluoride in tea[18] may at first seem to support arguments against the fluoridation of public water supplies, since it could be said that dietary fluoride deficiencies (and there are such things, whether the emotionally motivated protester, layman or doctor, cares to believe it or not), could be compensated by an increase in tea consumption in an attempt to combat dental caries in the young and osteoporosis in the elderly. But one must balance any hypothetical increase in tea consumption against the fact that children would certainly not benefit from a greater caffeine intake. Moreover, the fluoride in tea may not be nutritionally available since it could be there in a bound form, not doing the same job as free fluoride ions. Apart from this, tea, and even cocoa, contains a significant amount of tannin, which may cause constipation, and coffee contains certain essential oils which can cause gastro-intestinal irritation and diarrhoea.

The possibility of chronic poisoning (as was the case with

Balzac and has occurred in Scandinavian countries where coffee consumption is high) caused by over-indulgence in tea and coffee has been considered together with the fact that there may even be a degree of psychic dependence.[19] Such problems, however, are insignificant by comparison with those encountered with the other drugs in this book, and the feeling of agreeable well-being after a 'cup which cheers', whether it be tea or coffee, is such that it is unlikely to be relinquished, even if it should be obtained at the expense of mild depression or some slight inefficiency after the initial effects have worn off. The xanthines are not classed as poisons and may generally be purchased from chemists or druggists without restriction. Whether the former considerable trade in caffeine, obtained during the manufacture of caffeine-free coffee (Sanka, and so on) by the Chinese, has stopped since the Communist government came to power is difficult to ascertain. It was always rather a puzzle as to what exactly happened to such relatively vast quantities of the drug.

3. Spices, Scents, and Smells

DOMESTIC SPICES

It is common knowledge that one of the driving forces behind the voyages of adventure during the Age of Exploration was the search for gold, and, for some merchants, an even stronger urge to open up trade routes for the spices of the Orient. It is no fairytale coincidence that the Three Wise Men from the East offered the Christchild gold, frankincense, and myrrh. There is a strange link between the religious meaning of these gifts and the material greed, particularly during the Middle Ages and a little later, for the yellow metal and for spices and scents. The latter two helped to combat the foul taste of certain foods, sometimes badly prepared in large amounts, and the intolerable smells associated with habitations that lacked the most primitive hygienic arrangements.

In this final section, we will briefly look at some of the spices

still in use today, as well as at betel-chewing and a number of
volatile materials (scents), derived from oriental or tropical
plants, that mankind has used for various purposes. The reason
for covering them here is that some of them have found their
way into the catalogues of the drug cognoscenti, while others
have been used for centuries in the form of joss sticks or incense.
Here we will also consider the juvenile habit of 'glue-sniffing',
since this also usually involves a volatile principle. With all
these the medical profession and the public analyst come into
contact, though a case of a true addiction may only rarely be
involved.

One spice that has possibly become a substitute for other
drugs of habituation, such as cannabis or alcohol, is nutmeg (or
mace). The plant from which the seeds and their arils (appen-
dages) are derived is usually *Myristica fragrans*, a native of the
Malay Archipelago and known to the Arabic, Indian, and later
Western world as a kitchen spice and medical remedy (mainly
for the digestive tract). However, owing to its essential oil,
myristicin, which can, it seems, be transformed by a metabolic
process into a biologically active amphetamine derivative very
closely related to mescaline,[20] it might produce effects which
would attract drug-users who had become tired of other drugs of
dependence. Perhaps the nearest one can get to describing its
actions is to liken it to a mild MAO inhibitor (see page 110), but
this would depend very much on the psychological background
prevailing at the moment of misuse.

Whether black or white pepper (from *Piper nigrum*, or chilli),
red or cayenne pepper (from *Capsicum* varieties), have more
than digestive stimulant qualities or do any damage cannot be
said with certainty. The former contains an alkaloid, piperine,
which apart from its pungent taste has a biological activity not
up till now well investigated. The latter contains oleoresin, very
small quantities of which stimulate appetite, though larger
amounts irritate the lining membranes of the digestive tract.

BETEL-CHEWING

In the Orient betel nut (*Areca catechu*) is combined with betel leaves, derived from another tropical pepper plant (*Piper betle*), lime, nutmegs, clover, camphor, and other materials which carry essential oils. It may be the betel nut part which contains, among its other constituents, such alkaloids as arecoline, which produce in some people mild exhilaration and giddiness.[21] So far none of these side-effects appear serious enough to merit international interest or an inquiry into the widespread habit of betel-chewing. The only concrete result seems to be red discolouration of the mouth and blackening of the teeth. Whether it may lead in some instances to malignant mouth tumours cannot be answered authoritatively. On the whole, the essential oils may help a betel-chewing population to combat the effects of hot, humid climatic conditions, just as it is possible that a similar result is achieved to some extent by other spices like curry, peppers, and even ginger.

INCENSE

With the burning of joss sticks and the use of incense in religious ceremonies, the question arises whether anyone exposed for long periods to the smoke and vapours of these evaporating resins may suffer from any untoward consequences. The mysterious prevalence of tumours of the nose and throat among the South Chinese has been linked, though without any definite conclusion being reached, to their exposure to heavy clouds of incense.[22]

'GLUE-SNIFFING'

It is not only essential oils and combusted resins that can become sources of danger. Chemical solvents with low evaporation points, such as petrol (gasoline) and its higher fractions, may produce a habit which seeks sensations not unlike those engendered by the well-known drugs. Nurses or even anaesthetists may take to sniffing ether bottles or opening cylinders containing laughing gas (nitrous oxide) for the same purpose. Juveniles who have inhaled petroleum vapour may become breathless, flushed, hallucinated, and frightened, and, even worse, can finally become unconscious and die from liver and kidney damage following prolonged periods of habitual sniffing.[23] A report from Australia in 1968 indicated that this was also becoming a problem among the aborigines of the Northern Territories, where they were breaking open drums of high octane fuel on remote airfields.

The whole syndrome, which can also develop with other solvents such as toluene or esters,[24,25] the higher alcohols, dry-cleaning fluid, paint thinners, shoe-polish solvents, solvents used for plastic cement, cellulose paint, and glue is actually known as 'glue-sniffing'.[26] Most teenage cases are probably attributable more to 'mischief' than to vice, but it is an absolute educational priority for the pathological dangers to be made quite clear to parents and teachers, and especially the youngsters themselves. The dangers which arise with the benzene group of solvents in particular can produce severe anaemias and even leukaemias. Whether menthol and the related substances used in cold pastils should be counted in with this group is doubtful, though in concentrated form the compounds show toxic properties which can be fatal to infants.

It is hoped that this final section will draw the reader's attention to the potential dangers or even the actual habit-forming properties of a mixed bunch of materials, some of which one can hardly call drugs, or only in a peripheral sense, and some of which can be found in the best-run household or in the spick and span kitchen of the most conservative housewife.

Main Text References

Chapter One

1 Report by the Advisory Committee on Drug Dependence, *Cannabis* ('the Wootton Report'), H.M.S.O., London, 1968.

2 *J. Amer. Med. Assoc.*, *204*, 1181, 1187 (1968).

3 Thomas de Quincey, *Confessions of an English Opium Eater*, London, 1822.

4 C. P. Baudelaire, *Les Paradis artificiels, opium et hachich*, Paris, 1860.

5 Aldous Huxley, *The Doors of Perception*, Chatto & Windus, London, 1954; *Heaven and Hell*, Chatto & Windus, 1956.

6 James Hemming, *Individual Morality*, Nelson, London, 1969.

7 W. H. O. Expert Committee on Addiction-Producing Drugs, Third Report, Wld Hlth Org. techn. Rep. Ser., *57*, 9 (1952); W.H.O. Expert Committee on Addiction-Producing Drugs, Seventh Report, Wld Hlth Org. techn. Rep. Ser., *116*, 9 (1957).

8 N. B. Eddy, H. Halbach, H. Isbell, and M. H. Seevers, 'Drug Dependence: its Significance and Characteristics', *Bull. Wld Hlth Org.*, *32*, 721 (1965).

9 W.H.O. Expert Committee on Addiction-Producing Drugs, Thirteenth Report, Wld Hlth Org. techn. Rep. Ser., *273*, 9 (1964); W.H.O. Scientific Group on the Evaluation of Dependence-Producing Drugs, Wld Hlth Org. techn. Rep. Ser., *287* (1964).

10 See for this and Poisons Schedules, *Poisons and the T. S. Guide*, Pharmaceutical Press, London, 1968.

11 D. Traverne, *The Criminologist*, *7*, 100 (1968).

12 U.N. Commission on Narcotic Drugs, Report of the 16th Session. Econ. and Soc. Council 32nd Session, Suppl. 9, p. 29; see also the Single Convention on Narcotic Drugs (third draft), Mim. document E/CN7/AC. 3/9; and see also Expert Committee on Addiction-Producing Drugs, Tenth Report, Wld Hlth Org. techn. Rep. Ser., *188*, 12 (1960).

13 As 12 above.

14 R. Brain, Chairman, Report of the Interdepartmental Committee, *Drug Addiction*, H.M.S.O., London, 1961.

15 Lord Brain, Chairman, Second Report of the Interdepartmental Committee, *Drug Addiction*, H.M.S.O., London, 1967.

16 Dangerous Drugs Act 1965 (Chapter 15: 'Dangerous Drugs Regulations 1965'), H.M.S.O., London, 1965; Dangerous Drugs Act 1967 (Chapter 82), H.M.S.O., London, 1967.

17 Drugs (Prevention of Misuse) Act 1964; Drugs (Prevention of Misuse) Act Exemptions Regulations 1964; Drugs (Prevention of Misuse) Act 1964, Modification Order 1966, H.M.S.O., London, 1964, 1966.

18 Smith, Kline & French Laboratories, *Drug Abuse: Escape to Nowhere. A Guide for Educators*, Philadelphia, 1967; J. B. Landis, ed., *Drug Abuse. A Manual for Law Enforcement Officers*, Smith, Kline & French Laboratories, Philadelphia, 1965.

19 See 12 above

20 'French Narcotics Legislation', *Bull. Narcotics*, 7 (2), 1 (1955); see also Decree of 24 December 1953.

21 See 12 (first item) above.

22 M. Nagahama, 'A review of Drug Abuse and Counter-Measures in Japan since World War II', *Bull. Narcotics*, 20 (3), 19 1968).

23 N. Campanini, *Bull. Narcotics*, 19 (2), 13 (1967).

24 See, e.g. 'Thailand', *Bull. Narcotics*, 20 (3), 7 (1968); 'Sweden', ibid., 13 (4), 17; 'Israel', ibid., 14 (2), 11 (1962).

25 As 24 above. See also N. Lewis, 'Going to the Source of the Drug Problem', *Daily Telegraph Magazine*, 14 July 1967.

26 S. O'Callaghan, *Drug Traffic*, Blond, London, 1967.

27 See J. Larner and R. Tefferteller, *The Addict in the Street*, Penguin Books, Harmondsworth, 1966; William Burroughs, *Junkie*, Olympia Press: New English Library, London, 1957.

28 J. Harrington, *J. For. Sci. Soc.*, 13, 37 (1968).

29 See W. D. M. Paton, 'Drug Dependence', *Listener*, 14 November 1968.

30 M. M. Glatt, D. J. Pittman, D. G. Gillespie, and D. R. Hills, *The Drug Scene in Britain, Journey into Loneliness*, Edward Arnold, London, 1967.

31 H. R. George and M. M. Glatt, 'A Brief Survey of a Drug Dependence Unit in a Psychiatric Hospital', *Brit. J. Addic.*, 62, 147 (1967).

32 See 18 (first item) above.

33 See 29 above.

34 *Drug and Therap. Bull.*, Consumers' Ass., 5, 97 (1967).

35 An excellent, comprehensible account of the whole problem of drug addiction is contained in J. H. Willis, *Drug Dependence, a Study for Nurses and Social Workers*, Faber & Faber, London, 1969.

36 See 18 above. See also D. P. King, 'The U.S. Drug Problem', *The Criminologist*, 3, 111 (1968).

37 See 30 above. See also I. P. James, 'Suicide and Mortality among Heroin Addicts in Britain', *Brit. J. Addic.*, *62* (1967).
38 R. Blumenthal, *New York Times*, 18 May 1968.
39 Quoted in 30 above.

Chapter Two
1 W.H.O., Expert Committee on Mental Health, 15th Report, *Services for the Prevention and Treatment of Dependence on Alcohol and other Drugs*, Wld Hlth Org. techn. Rep. Ser., *363* (1967).
2 W.H.O., Expert Committee on Alcohol, Wld Hlth Org. techn. Rep. Ser., *84*, 10 (1954).
3 *Government Chemist*, Report for 1967, H.M.S.O., London, 1968, p. 7.
4 *Statistical Abstracts of the United States*, 89th edition, Bureau of the Census, U.S. Department of Commerce, 1968.
5 John Burnett, *Plenty and Want, a Social History of Diet in England from 1815 to the Present Day*, Nelson, London, 1966.
6 L. Goodman and A. Gillman, *The Pharmacological Basis of Therapeutics*, 1st, 2nd, and 3rd editions, Macmillan, New York, 1941, 1955, 1965; H. Kalant, *Quart. J. Stud. of Alcohol*, Suppl. No. 1 (1961).
7 E. J. Wayne, Chairman of Special Committee, Report on Recognition of Intoxication, Brit. Med. Assoc. (1958).
8 N. H. Raskin and L. Sokoloff, 'Brain Alcohol Dehydrogenase', *Science*, *162*, 131 (1968).
9 H. A. Krebs, 'Symposium on Enzyme Regulation in Mammalian Tissues', *Science*, *160*, 210 (1968).
10 M. Collins and G. Cohen: see note in *New Scientist*, *39*, 668 (1968).
11 G. C. Drew, W. P. Colquhoun, and H. A. Long, Med. Res. Council Memo No. 38, H.M.S.O., London, 1958; see also idem., *Brit. Med. J.* (ii), 993 (1958).
12 See 1 above.
13 *The Times*, 7 August 1968.
14 *Whitaker's Almanac*, Whitaker, London, 1967.
15 A. J. B. Plaut, 'Transference Phenomena in Alcoholism', *Brit. J. Med. Psychol.* (in press).
16 ibid.

Chapter Three
1 Quoted in *The Times*, 29 January 1969.
2 F. Bergel: see T. S. Work, F. Bergel, and A. R. Todd, 'The Active Principles of *Cannabis Indica* Resin', *I. Biochem. J.*, *33*, 123 (1939).

3 See Edith Simon, *The Piebald Standard, a Biography of the Knights Templars*, Cassell, London, 1959.

4 C. P. Baudelaire, *Les Paradis artificiels, opium et hachich*, Paris. 1860; T. Gauthier, *Le Club des hachichins*, Paris, 1946.

5 Baudelaire, op. cit.

6 Fitz Hugh Ludlow, *The Hasheesh Eater*, New York.

7 D. Solomon (ed.), *The Marihuana Papers*, New American Library, New York, 1966; K. M. Nadkarni, *Indian Materia Medica*, K. M. Nadkarni, Bombay, 1927; A. Herxheimer, ed., *Drug and Therapeutics Bull.*, Consumers' Assoc., *5*, 97 (1967); G. E. W. Wolstenholme and J. Knight, eds., 'Hashish: its Chemistry and Pharmacology', CIBA Foundation Study Group No. 21, J. & A. Churchill, London, 1965; *The Sciences*, N.Y. Acad. of Sciences, *8*, 22 (1968); N. Lewis, 'Going to the Source of the Drug Problem', *Weekend Telegraph*, *145*, 12 (1967); R. Cordeiro de Farias, 'Use of Maconha (*Cannabis sativa*) in Brazil', *Bull. Narcotics*, *7* (2), 5 (1955); Smith, Kline & French Laboratories, *Drug Abuse: Escape to Nowhere*, Philadelphia, 1967; M. M. Glatt, *et al.*, *The Drug Scene in Britain*, Edward Arnold, London, 1967.

8 W. Straub, *Naturwiss.*, *14*, 1091 (1926); idem., *Münch. Med. Wchnschrift.*, *75*, 49 (1928).

9 La Guardia Report. See 7 above (first item).

10 J. R. Valle, *et al.*, *J. Pharm. Pharmac.*, *20*, 798 (1968).

11 F. Korte and H. Sieper, *Bull. Narcotics*, *17* (1), 35 (1965); L. Grlič, *Bull. Narcotics*, *14* (3), 37 (1962).

12 See Nadkarni, op. cit., under 7 above.

13 A. T. Weil, N. E. Zinberg, and J. M. Nelson, *Science*, *162*, 1234 (1968). See also *Sunday Times*, 12 January 1969; A. T. Weil and N. E. Zinberg, *Nature*, *222*, 434 (1969); A. Crancer, Jr, *et al.*, *Science*, *164*, 851 (1969).

14 S. Loewe, 'Cannabiswirkstoffe und Pharmakologie der Cannabinole', *Arch. exper. Path. u. Pharmakol.*, *211*, 175 (1950).

15 See Wolstenholme and Knight, op. cit., under 7 above.

16 As 14 above.

17 N. B. Eddy, *et al.*, 'Drug Dependence: its Significance and Characteristics', *Bull. Wld Hlth Org.*, *32*, 721 (1965).

18 As 9 above.

19 See also W. D. M. Paton, British Assoc. f. Advanc. Scie., in press, reported *The Times*, 27 August 1968; idem., *Listener*, 14 November 1968; G. B. Wallace, Chairman, La Guardia Comm. (see 7 above (first item)).

20 I. C. Chopra and R. N. Chopra, 'The Use of Cannabis Drugs in India', *Bull. Narcotics*, *9* (1), 4 (1957).

21 G. Tayleur Stockings; see in 7 above; *Brit. Med. J.* (i), 325 (1947).

22 F. Wrigley and C. S. Parker, *Lancet* (ii), *223* (1947).
23 P. H. Abelson, 'LSD and Marihuana', *Science, 159*, 1189 (1968).
24 *Sunday Times* interview, 12 January 1969.
25 *The Times*, 24 July 1967.
26 *Observer*, 28 July 1968.
27 *The Sciences*, N.Y. Acad. Scie., *8*, 22 (1969).
28 Paton, art. cit., under 19 above.
29 See Chapter One, ref. 2.
30 Report by the Advisory Committee on Drug Dependence, *Cannabis* ('the Wootton Report'), H.M.S.O., London, 1968.
31 See parliamentary report, *The Times*, 28 January 1969.
32 See letter to *The Times* from Sir Edward Wayne and Lady Wootton of Abinger, 5 February 1969. See also *Hansard*, Vol. 300, No. 51, for the full text of the House of Lords debate.

Chapter Four
1 M. Pomet, *A Compleat History of Druggs*, 3rd edition (translated), London, 1737.
2 Thomas de Quincey, *Confessions of an English Opium Eater*, London, 1822.
3 Jean Cocteau, *Opium*, Allen & Unwin, London, 1933.
4 See Alethea Hayter, *Opium and the Romantic Imagination*, Faber & Faber, London, 1969.
5 Geoffrey Grigson, reviewing ibid., *Listener*, 12 December 1968.
6 De Quincey, op. cit., Preface revised, 1856.
7 W. Kussner, *Bull. Narcotics, 13* (2), 1 (1961).
8 See Chapter One, ref. 12.
9 E. L. May, 'Analgesics' in *Medicinal Chemistry*, 2nd edition, Interscience Publishers, New York and London, 1960.
10 Eisleb and Schaumann, *Deut. med. Wochschr., 65*, 967 (1939).
11 F. Bergel and A. L. Morrison, 'Synthetic Analgesics', *Quart. Rev., 2*, 349 (1948).
12 N. B. Eddy, 'Analgesic and Dependence-Producing Properties of Drugs', in *The Addictive States*, Research Publications, Association for Research in Nervous and Mental Disease, ed. A. Wikler, The Williams & Wilkins Coy., Baltimore, 1968.
13 William Burroughs, *Junkie*, Olympia Press: New English Library, London, 1966.
14 J. Larner and R. Tefferteller, *The Addict in the Street*, Penguin Books, Harmondsworth, 1966.
15 See W. D. M. Paton, *Listener*, 14 November 1968.
16 S. J. Hopkins, *Drugs and Pharmacology for Nurses*, E. & S. Livingstone, Edinburgh and London, 1968.
17 M. L. Harney, 'Current Provisions and Practices in the United

States of America relating to the Commitment of Opiate Addicts', *Bull. Narcotics*, *14* (3), 11 (1962).

18 P. M. Yap, 'Lessons from the Anti-narcotic Voluntary Treatment Programme in Hong Kong', ibid., *19* (2), 35 (1967).

19 Editorial in *New Scientist*, 24 October 1968.

20 L. Goodman and A. Gilman, *The Pharmacological Basis of Therapeutics*, 1st, 2nd, and 3rd editions, Macmillan, New York, 1941, 1955, and 1965.

21 See 9 above.

22 *The Addictive States*, op. cit., as 12 above.

23 M. Vogt, 'Concentration of Sympathin in Different Parts of the CNS under Normal Conditions and after Administration of Drugs', *J. Physiol.*, *123*, 451 (1954).

24 E. W. Maynert, Chapter 6 in *The Addictive States*, see 12 above.

25 Peter Laurie, *Drugs*, Penguin Books, Harmondsworth, 1967.

26 E. F. Domino, Chapter 9, in *The Addictive States*, see 12 above; F. R. Ervin, Chapter 10, ibid.

27 See 25 above.

28 J. Axelrod, Chapter 18 in *The Addictive States*, see 12 above.

29 R. J. Collins, and J. R. Weeks, *Arch. exp. Path. Pharmacol.*, *249*, 509 (1965); idem., *Psychopharmacologia*, *11*, 287 (1967); idem., Chapter 22, see 12 above; A. Wikler, W. R. Martin, F. T. Pescor, and C. G. Eades, *Psychopharmacologia*, *5*, 55 (1963); see also A. Wikler, Chapter 21, 12 above.

30 See 12 above; see also W.H.O. Expert Committee on Addiction-Producing Drugs, Tenth Report, Wld Hlth Org. techn. Rep. Ser., *188*, 15 (1960).

31 I. Chein, D. L. Gerard, R. S. Lee, and E. Rosenfeld, *The Road to H.*, Basic Books, New York, 1964; see also D. L. Gerard, Chapter 24, 12 above.

32 A. S. Meyer, ed., *Social and Psychological Factors in Opiate Addiction*, Bureau of Appl. Soc. Res., Columbia University Press, 1952.

33 A. M. Freedman, 'Drug Addiction, an Eclectic View', *J. Amer. Med. Assoc.*, *197*, 878 (1966); idem., Chapter 30, 12 above.

34 C. Winnick, 'The Narcotic Addiction Problem', *The Amer. Soc. Hlth. Assoc.*, New York.

35 See 25 above; H. Steinberg, ed., Inst. of Biol., Symp. on Scientific Basis of Drug Dependence, held in March 1968, J. & A. Churchill, London, 1969.

36 See report in *The Times*, 10 March 1969.

37 *Observer*, 16 March 1969.

38 See Commission on Narc. Drugs (U.N.), Econ. and Soc. Council, Summ. of Ann. Reps. of Gvmts, Geneva (1960).

39 Lord Brain, Chairman, Second Report of the Interdepartmental Committee, *Drug Addiction*, H.M.S.O., London, 1965.

40 Smith, Kline & French Laboratories, *Drug Abuse: Escape to Nowhere*, Philadelphia, 1967.

41 United States Narcotic Addict Rehabilitation Act, 1966; see also U.S. Senate, *Treatment and Rehabilitation of Narcotic Addicts*, U.S. Government Printing Office, Washington, D.C., 1965.

42 R. W. Rasor, 'The Role of the United States Public Health Service Hospitals in the Field of Drug Abuse', Chapter 31, 12 above.

43 S. J. Holmes, 'Opioid Addiction Problems in Canada', Chapter 27, ibid.; J. K. W. Ferguson, *et al.*, 'Good Medical Practice in the Care of the Narcotic Addict', *Can. Med. Assoc. J.*, *92*, 1040 (1965).

44 L. Goldberg and G. Lundgren, 'Drug Control in Sweden', *Bull. Narcotics*, *13* (4), 7 (1961); for Switzerland, see N. Campanini, ibid., *19* (2), 13 (1967); for France, see French Narcotics Legislation, ibid., *7* (2), 1 (1955).

45 M. Huvanandana, 'The Centre for Treatment and Rehabilitation of Opium Addicts, Rangsit, Thailand', ibid., *14* (2), 1 (1962); United Nation's Survey Team, 'The Hill Tribes in Thailand and the Place of Opium in their Socio-Economic Setting', ibid., *20* (3), 7 (1968).

46 M. Nagahama, 'A Review of Drug Abuse and Countermeasures in Japan since World War II', ibid., *20* (3), 19 (1968).

47 W.H.O. Expert Committee on Dependence-Producing Drugs, Fifteenth Report, Wld Hlth Org., *343*, 9 (1966).

48 See 14 above.

49 See J. M. Robson, F. Sullivan, and R. L. Smith, eds., *Symposium on Embryopathic Action of Drugs*, J. & A. Churchill, London, 1965; M. Erikson and K. S. Lasson, 'Premature Birth in Mice by Salicylate', *Nature*, *220*, 385 (1968); E. Leong Way, 'Distribution and Metabolism of Morphine and its Surrogates', Chapter 2 in *The Addictive States*, see 12 above.

Chapter Five

1 See Ernest Jones, *The Life and Work of Sigmund Freud*, abridged by Lionel Trilling and Steven Marcus, Basic Books, New York, 1961.

2 R. P. Alcala, *Bull. Narcotics*, *4* (2), 10 (1952).

3 L. A. Leon, ibid., *4* (2), 21 (1952).

4 V. Z. Ottiz, ibid., *4* (2), 26 (1952).

5 Advisory Committee of the League of Nations on Traffic in Opium and other Dangerous Drugs (1925).

6 See 4 above.

7 A. F. Montesinos, *Bull. Narcotics, 17* (2), 11 (1965).
8 J. C. Negrete and H. B. M. Murphy, ibid., *19* (4), 11 (1967).
9 J. Bejarano, ibid., *4* (3), 8 (1952).
10 See N. B. Eddy, *et al., Bull. Wld Hlth Org., 32,* 721 (1965).
11 I. C. Chopra and R. N. Chopra, *Bull. Narcotics, 10* (2), 12 (1958).
12 See 3 above.
13 See 10 above.

Chapter Six
1 See J. Delay, *La Presse med., 74,* 1151 (1966); idem., *Bull. Narcotics, 19* (1), 1 (1967).
2 W.H.O. Expert Committee on Drugs Liable to Produce Addiction, Fourth Report, Wld Hlth Org. techn. Rep. Ser., *76,* 11 (1954).
3 Anon., *Bull. Narcotics, 19* (1), 15 (1967).
4 As foreshadowed during a recent debate in the House of Lords, ref. *Hansard,* Vol. 300, No. 51.
5 United Nations, Commission on Narcotic Drugs, Report, 11th Session, Chapter 9 (1956).
6 L. G. Kiloh and S. Brandon, *Brit. Med. J.* (ii), 40 (1962).
7 S. Brandon and J. Smith, *J. Coll. gen. Practit.* (i), 603 (1962); *Pharm. J.* (i), 22 (1963); T. Bewley, *Bull. Narcotics, 18* (4), 9 (1966).
8 E. Cook, *J. For. Sci. Soc., 3,* 43 (1962).
9 P. H. Connell, *Brit. J. Addic., 60,* 9 (1964).
10 Drug Abuse Control Amendments (to the Federal Food, Drug and Cosmetic Act) 1965; U.S. Public Law 89–74, 89th Congress (15 July 1965).
11 O. J. Kalant, *The Amphetamines. Toxicity and Addiction,* University of Toronto Press, 1966.
12 N. Campanini, *Bull. Narcotics, 19* (2), 16 (1967).
13 Peter Laurie, *Drugs,* Penguin Books, Harmondsworth, 1967.
14 H. J. Eysenck, *Crime and Personality,* Routledge & Kegan Paul, London, 1964.
15 N. B. Eddy, *et al., Bull. Wld. Hlth. Org., 32,* 721 (1965).
16 W. D. M. Paton, 'Drug Dependence', *Listener,* 14 November 1968.
17 I. K. Morimoto, *Bull. Narcotics, 9* (3), 8 (1957).
18 ibid.
19 See 11 above.
20 *Science, 145,* 1418 (1964).
21 See 10 above.
22 See 11 above.
23 Anon., *Bull. Narcotics, 8* (4), 6 (1956); see also W.H.O. Expert Committee on Addiction-Producing Drugs, Twelfth Report, Wld Hlth Org. techn. Rep. Ser., *229,* 9 (1962).

24 J. M. Laurent, *Ann. Medico-psychol.*, *120*, 649 (1962).
25 See 23 above.
26 See 24 above.
27 ibid.
28 W.H.O. Expert Committee on Addiction-Producing Drugs, Thirteenth Report, Wld Hlth Org. techn. Rep. Ser., *273*, 10 (1964).
29 See *Martindale's Extra Pharmacopoeia*, 25th edition, ed. R. G. Todd, Pharmaceutical Press, London, 1967.
30 *Pharm. J.* (i), *187* (1964).
31 See Chapter Seven, ref. 17 below.

Chapter Seven
 1 S. Garattini and V. Ghetti, eds., *Psychotropic Drugs*, Elsevier, Amsterdam and London, 1957.
 2 J. Delay, 'Psychopharmacology and Psychiatry', *Bull. Narcotics*, *19* (1), 1 (1967). See also *La Press Med.*, *74*, 22 (1966).
 3 See H. Steinberg, A. V. S. de Reuck, and J. Knight, eds., 'Animal Behaviour and Drug Action', *Symposium Ciba and the Co-ordinating Committee for Symposia on Drug Action*, J. & A. Churchill, London, 1964; S. Irwin, 'Prediction of Drug Effects from Animal to Man', in ibid.; J. O. Cole and R. E. Edwards, 'Prediction of Clinical Effects of Psycho-tropic Drugs from Animal Data', in ibid.
 4 For an exceptionally clear account, see M. E. Jarvik in L. S, Goodman and A. Gilman, *The Pharmacological Basis of Therapy*, Macmillan, New York, 1965.
 5 Smith, Kline & French Laboratories, *Drug Abuse, Escape to Nowhere*, Philadelphia, 1967.
 6 Kenneth Leech, *Daily Telegraph*, 4 October 1968.
 7 See *Martindale's Extra Pharmacopoeia*, 25th edition, ed. R. G. Todd, Pharmaceutical Press, London, 1967.
 8 H. E. Hill, R. E. Bellville, and A. Wikler, *Arch. Neurol. Psych.*, *73*, 602 (1955); A. Wikler, *Brit. J. Addic.*, *57*, 73 (1961); idem., *Fed. Proc.*, *11*, 647 (1952).
 9 See 7 above.
10 *Nova*, August 1968.
11 E. Stolkind, *Lancet* (i), 391 (1926).
12 The President's Advisory Commission on Narcotic and Drug Abuse, Final Reports, U.S. Government Printing Office, Washington, D.C., 1963.
13 Jermulowicz and Turnau, *Bull. Narcotics*, *14* (2), 11 (1962).
14 N. B. Eddy, H. Halbach, H. Isbell, and M. H. Seevers, *Bull. Wld Hlth Org.*, *32*, 721 (1965); H. Isbell, 'Manifestations and Treatment of Addiction to Narcotic Drugs and Barbiturates',

Med. Clin., *34*, 425 (1950); H. Isbell, and H. F. Fraser, 'Addiction to Analgesics and Barbiturates', *J. Pharmacol. Exp. Therap.*, *99*, 355 (1950); H. Isbell, *et al.*, *Arch. Neurol. Psych.*, *64*, 1 (1950); H. G. Fraser, *et al.*, 'Chronic Barbiturate Intoxication. Further Studies', *Arch. Int. Med.*, *94*, 34 (1954); H. G. Fraser, M. R. Shaver, E. S. Maxwell, and H. Isbell, 'Death due to Withdrawal of Barbiturates', *Ann. Int. Med.*, *38*, 1319 (1953).

15 Eddy, *et al.*, art. cit., 14 above.

16 J. Fort, *Bull. Narcotics*, *16* (1), 17 (1964).

17 See *Poisons and T.S.A. Guide* for details of the British regulations and legal requirements for Part I and Part II Poisons, Fourth Schedule Poisons, Dangerous Drugs, etc. (1968).

18 U.S. Congress, House of Representatives, Drug Industry Act 1962, Interstate and Foreign Comm., 87th Congress (1962).

19 See 5 above.

20 Jacobus Sprenger and Heinrich Kramer, *Malleus Maleficarum* (*Hammer of Witchcraft*), translated by Montague Summers, Rodker, London, 1928.

21 Margaret Murray, *The Witch-Cult in Western Europe*, London, 1921, Appendix compiled by Professor H. S. Clark.

22 See 7 above for Chloralhydrate and some other hypnotics.

Chapter Eight

1 A. Stoll and A. Hofmann, *Helv. Chim. Acta.*, *26*, 944 (1943).

2 See J. G. Fuller, *The Day of St Anthony's Fire*, Hutchinson, London, 1969, for a readable account of this incident.

3 G. Barger, F. H. Carr, and H. Dale, 'An Alkaloid from Ergot', *Brit. Med. J.* (ii), 1792 (1906).

4 See also L. Goodman and A. Gilman, *The Pharmacological Basis of Therapeutics*, 1st, 2nd, and 3rd editions, Macmillan, New York, 1941, 1955, and 1965.

5 H. W. Dudley and C. Moir, 'Substance Responsible for Traditional Clinical Effect of Ergot', *Brit. Med. J.* (i), 520 (1935).

6 G. L. Brown and H. Dale, 'The Pharmacology of Ergomertrine', *Proc. Roy. Soc.*, *118*, 446 (1935).

7 G. Barger, *Ergot and Ergotism*, Guerney & Jackson, Edinburgh, 1931; idem., 'The Alkaloids of Ergot', *Handbuch der exper. Pharmakol.*, ed. A. Heffter, *Ergänzungswerk*, *6*, 84, J. Springer, Berlin, 1938.

8 See W. A. Jacobs and L. C. Craig, *J. Biol. Chem.*, *104*, 547 (1934); A. Stoll, A. Hofmann and F. Troxler, *Helv. Chim. Acta*,. *32*, 506 (1949), and also later publications; A. Stoll, *Chem. Rev.*, *47*, 197 (1950).

9 A. Hoffer and H. Osmond, *The Hallucinogens*, Academic Press, New York, 1967.

10 See also M. M. Cohen, M. Marinello, and N. Beck, *Science, 155,* 1417 (1967); M. M. Cohen, *et al., New Engl. J. Med., 277,* 1043 (1967); S. Erwin and J. Egozue, *Science, 157,* 313 (1967); R. S. Sparkes, J. Melnyk, and L. P. Bozzetti, *Science, 160,* 1344 (1968).

11 W. N. Pahnke, 'LSD and Religious Experience', in Richard C. DeBold and Russell C. Leaf, eds., *LSD, Man and Society,* Wesleyan University Press, 1967; Faber & Faber, London, 1969.

12 ibid.

13 Aldous Huxley, *Heaven and Hell,* Chatto & Windus, London, 1956.

14 See A. A. Kurland, 'The Therapeutic Potential of LSD in Medicine', in DeBold and Leaf, eds., op. cit.

15 E. Rothlin, *J. Pharm. Pharmacol., 9,* 569, and *Ann. N. Y. Acad. Sci., 66,* 668 (both 1957). See also *Psychotropic Drugs,* ed. Garattini and Ghetti, Elsevier, Amsterdam and London, 1957.

16 See 10 above.

17 See 15 above.

18 Parke-Davis & Co., 'Hallucinogenic Drugs', *Therapeutic Notes, 1,* 106 (1968).

19 W. D. Loughman, T. W. Sargent, and D. M. Israelstam, *Science, 158,* 508 (1967).

20 J. A. DiPaolo, H. M. Givelber, and H. Ervine, *Nature, 220,* 490 (1968).

21 V. Neuhoff, *New Scientist, 40,* 206 (1968).

22 R. Alpert, S. Cohen, and L. Schiller, *LSD,* New American Library, New York, 1966.

23 Alex Comfort, reviewing DeBold and Leaf, eds., op. cit., *Guardian,* 6 March 1969.

24 David B. Louria, 'The Abuse of LSD', in DeBold and Leaf, eds., op. cit.

25 See N. B. Eddy, *et al.,* 'Drug Dependence: Its Significance and Characteristics', *Bull. Wld Hlth Org., 32,* 731: *Drug Dependence of the Hallucinogen (LSD) Type* (1965).

26 See report in *The Times,* 22 March 1969.

27 *The Times,* 8 and 9 October 1968.

28 See *The Times,* 22 March 1969.

29 See *The Times,* 7 February, 18 and 22 March 1969.

30 L. S. Browning, *Science, 161,* 1022 (1968).

31 R. Rushton, H. Steinberg, and M. Tomkiewicz, *Nature, 220,* 885 (1968).

32 See 25 above.

Chapter Nine

1 See British Empire Cancer Campaign, Ann. Reps, between the 1940s and the beginning of the 1950s; also E. L. Kennaway and M. M. Kennaway, *Brit. J. Cancer*, 5, 153 (1957); also L. Goodman and A. Gilman, *The Pharmacological Basis of Therapeutics*, 1st edition, Macmillan, New York, 1941; R. L. Volle and G. B. Koelle, ibid., 3rd edition, 1965.

2 H. R. Bentley and G. N. Berry, *The Constituents of Tobacco Smoke, An Annotated Bibliography*, 1959; 1st Supplement, 1960; 2nd Supplement, 1963; Tobacco Research Council, London W.1. See also H. R. Bentley and J. Burgen, *Cigarette Condensates, Preparation and Routine Laboratory Estimations*, 2nd edition, Tobacco Research Council, London, 1961.

3 R. J. C. Harris and G. Negroni, 'Production of Lung Carcinomas in C57BL Mice Exposed to a Cigarette Smoke and Air Mixture', *Brit. Med. J.*, 4, 637–41 (1967).

4 R. D. Passey and D. Warbrick-Smith, 'Types of Tobacco and Lung Cancer', *Brit. Emp. Cancer Camp., Ann. Rep.*, 45, 26 (1967).

5 U.S. Public Health Service, 'The Health Consequences of Smoking', Supplement (1968) to Public Health Service Review (1967), U.S. Public Health Service Publications, Washington, D.C., 1968.

6 P. H. Abelson, 'Changing Attitudes towards Smoking', *Science*, 161, 319 (1968).

7 Referring to 4 above.

8 John Burnett, *Plenty and Want, a Social History of Diet in England from 1815 to the Present Day*, Nelson, London, 1966.

9 H. E. Cox, *The Chemical Analysis of Foods*, 3rd edition, J. & A. Churchill, London, 1937.

10 G. Gugitz, *Das Wiener Kaffeehaus*, Vienna, 1940, quoted in J. Stoye, *The Siege of Vienna*, Collins, London, 1964.

11 Burnett, op. cit.

12 See Jaques Soustelle, *Daily Life of the Aztecs*, Weidenfeld & Nicolson, London, 1961; G. C. Vaillant, *The Aztecs of Mexico*, Penguin Books, Harmondsworth, 1960.

13 M. Pomet, *A Compleat History of Druggs*, 3rd edition, translated, London, 1737.

14 Burnett, op. cit.

15 R. F. Smith, *Analyst*, 89, 146 (1964).

16 *Martindale's Extra Pharmacopoeia*, 23rd Edition, ed. R. G. Todd, Pharmaceutical Press, London, 1967.

17 See J. M. Ritchie, in *The Pharmacological Basis of Therapeutics*, 3rd edition, ed. L. S. Goodman and A. Gilman, Macmillan, New York, 1965; according to Feldberg, Rain, in Germany, thought

the effect of caffeine was indirect via the liver (personal communication).

18 L. Fowden, 'The Occurrence and Metabolism of Carbon-Halogen Compounds in a Discussion on Anomalous Aspects of Biochemistry of Possible Significance in Discussing the Origins and Distribution of Life', *Proc. Roy. Soc., B.*, *171*, 5 (1968); see also D. S. Bernstein, N. Sadowsky, D. N. Hegsted, C. D. Guri, and F. J. Stare, 'Prevalence of Osteoporosis in High and Low Fluoride Areas in North Dakota', *J. Amer. Med. Assoc.*, *198*, 499 (1966).

19 As 18 above.

20 A. Weil, 'The Use of Nutmeg as a Psychotropic Agent', *Bull. Narcotics*, *18* (4), 15 (1966).

21 K. M. Nadkarni, *The Indian Materia Medica* (entries for *Areca catechu* and *Piper betle*), K. M. Nadkarni, Bombay, 1927.

22 R. Schoental and S. Gibbard, 'The Carcinogenic Constituents of Incense in their Role in the Naso-Pharyngeal Tumours of the Chinese', lecture to Brit. Assoc. for Cancer Res. (September 1967).

23 M. F. Bethell, *Brit. Med. J.* (ii), 276 (1965); see also *Martindale's Extra Pharmacopoeia*, op. cit.

24 A. J. Wood, *Drug Dependence*, Corporation of Bristol and the Bristol Council of Social Services, 1967.

25 A. L. Piochioni, *Amer. J. Hosp. Pharm.*, *18*, 302 (1961); V. N. Dodson, *J. Med.*, *268*, 719 (1963); see also *Martindale's Extra Pharmacopoeia*, op. cit.

26 See 24 above.

Appendix A: Notes on Chemistry and Analysis

1. *Alcohol*

There is a whole family of the so-called aliphatic alcohols, which all derive from water, sometimes annotated as H-O-H. If one of the H's (standing as the symbol for hydrogen) is replaced by an alkyl group, a chain of carbon and hydrogen atoms with a hydrogen atom missing at one end, we arrive first at methyl, then ethyl, then propyl, butyl, and amyl alcohols: HO. Me; HO. Et; HO. prop; HO. but; HO. amyl. If the chains are branched, the syllable 'iso' is added

The boiling-points of this series of alcohols rise steadily, ethanol's boiling-point (b.p.) being 78·6°C, 21·5°C lower than that of water. Ethanol is, of course, the most important type of alcohol within our terms of reference but since higher alcohols are quite often present in certain spirits, albeit in small amounts, it is important to account for them in case they have contributed to toxic or pathological effects of a 'mixed drink'. Methanol, which can be produced by the destructive distillation of wood (wood spirit), or synthetically from carbon monoxide and hydrogen, is used for denaturing ethanol, and is misused by 'meths drinkers' in the form of methylated spirit, which contains this dangerous lower relation of ethanol to the extent of 5 per cent.

It was briefly mentioned in the text that most alcohol is produced by a fermentation process that transforms sugars into alcohol and carbon dioxide. The sugars may be present in the original fruit (e.g. grapes) or be formed from starch used in the brewing process. The catalysts which help these transformations are called enzymes (in this case zymase), and consist of complex proteins possessing a strong ability to initiate and guide these biochemical reactions. If methyl or other alcohols are mixed with ethanol, the most up-to-date method of analysis or estimation must be applied (see Appendix B on gas-liquid chromatography), which can even detect traces of the order of parts per million.

If iso-propyl alcohol is present in methyl or ethyl alcohol, it can easily be detected by a white or yellow precipate which forms on heating the sample liquid with a solution of mercuric sulphate. Ethanol itself can be assessed by a number of qualitative and quantitative tests; one traditional one made use of the inflammability of alcohol, a flame being applied to a piece of cloth (or gunpowder) soaked in spirit; when the mixture burned steadily, it was considered to be 'proof', but if burning was difficult or impossible, it was 'under proof', or 'over proof' if it took place with explosive violence. All three expressions gave rise to the term 'proof spirit' (P.S.). Of course, these methods were later found far too crude for accuracy and were replaced by determinations of specific gravity (weight per milliliter) with hydrometers.

In the U.S.A., no product containing less than 0.5 per cent alcohol by volume shall bear the name beer, lager, etc., and the upper and lower alcohol limits (%V/V) for wine are 7 and 24 per cent respectively. Fruit wines have an upper limit of 13 per cent, and fruit dessert wines contain between 14 and 24 per cent, while light table grape wines contain up to 14 per cent alcohol by volume and the dessert wines of the grape type are expected to contain at least 17 per cent and not more than 24 per cent of alcohol by volume. Since in the U.S.A. the alcoholic strength of spirits is quoted in terms of U.S. degrees proof, it is obligatory to give this figure on the label in the case of cordials, liqueurs, cocktails, gin fizzes, high balls, and bitters in addition to the well known distilled spirits. The latter, whisky, gin, vodka, brandy, and rum, must have an alcohol content of at least 80° U.S. proof when bottled, but there is a relaxation to a minimum of 71° in the case of brandy which has been aged for at least fifty years. The U.S. maximum strength for whisky is 125° and for vodka 110°.

Variations in units of measurements between different countries has made agreed standards difficult to rationalize. In Britain, the U.S.A., and Holland, alcoholometry is for revenue purposes based on proof standards. Thus in Britain, Proof Spirit was defined in the Spirits Act of 1816 (as a result of a suggestion by Sikes) as 'that which at a temperature of 51°F weighs exactly $\frac{12}{13}$th of an equal measure of distilled water'. While Dutch Proof is 'that mixture with water which at 15°C contains 50 per cent by volume of pure alcohol'. The latter works out at 87.6 per cent in terms of British P.S.

The American definition is equivalent to 87·5 per cent of British P.S. and implies that pure alcohol is 200° Proof (U.S.). Thus American P.S. contains 50 per cent of alcohol by volume at 60°F.

Most of the other European countries, including Belgium, France, Germany, Norway, Russia, Spain, and Sweden, for official purposes base their alcoholometry on pure alcohol, the standards being based on a percentage by volume in all except Germany where it is expressed by weight. There are indications that there will be more unity in the future when it is likely that a uniform system based on percentage by volume will be accepted by all.

2. *Cannabis*

It took much time and research before the active principles together with the related inactive compounds were isolated from various cannabis preparations and chemically and biologically characterized. This was probably due to the eventually established fact that these components were, even in a pure form, oily or low-melting compounds (mixtures of closely related chemicals very often refuse to crystallize), and in contrast to plant alkaloids like morphine and cocaine lacked nitrogen in their molecule. This made it difficult to prepare them as crystalline and thus solid simple derivatives or salts. Not until the chemist had applied new methods of distillation under greatly diminished pressure (evaporation and condensation at temperatures which did not heat-damage the products) could purified compounds be obtained. But even these advances were not subtle enough for the final separation of intricate mixtures of the so-called isomers (see Table 4).

TABLE 4

Component	Biological or physiological activity
Cannabinol	No activity
Tetrahydrocannabinols	The active principles, viscous oils
Cannabidiol	No activity, but can be transformed by heat into above, usually as a mixture
Cannabidiolic Acid	Antibacterial and sedative activity; can be transformed into active principle

There also exists a number of related components which have no direct bearing on our problem. The different forms of the *tetrahydrocannabinols* have, quantitatively speaking, different physiological and toxicological activities. Returning to the natural materials present in most drug preparations, it is important to remember that the resin, containing also whatever plant material may also be present, represents a mixture. The composition of the mixture depends on various circumstances (see page 48).

It is obvious that any differences in the composition of the original materials will affect the physiological activity of products reaching the consumer. They may consist of viscous resinous materials, only slightly contaminated with plant residues, or of considerable amounts of leaves, flowering tops, and stalks, with the resin intermingling. After separation, the solid or resinous residues are left behind, which then must be processed by the chemist into purer substances. These may consist of different chemical entities (see Table 4) such as cannabinol, tetrahydrocannabinols, etc., depending on the original ratio that existed in the raw material. When these fractions are heated to temperatures of *c.* 200°C., a considerable amount of cannabidiol and also of the corresponding acid is transformed into tetrahydrocannabinols, and thus gain physiological activity. (Such transformations may also take place during the smoking of cannabis in any of its consumable forms.) Thus the variable mixtures make the chemistry of the cannabinolic constituents a complicated affair. The chemist and analyst have consequently turned to more up-to-date methods of purification, such as chromatography, using a glass column filled with aluminium oxide, and counter-current distribution in a glittering Craig apparatus, which utilizes different solubilities and the distribution between two layers of immiscible solvents (say, water and benzene).

The tests described in the literature are not necessarily all reliable and relatively simple, but the following two are:

1. Material containing parts of the hemp plant is submitted to 'old-fashioned' pharmacognistic tests: the microscopic inspection of selected samples.

2. Over the years, a number of colour and U.V. light absorption tests have been developed. The best method of colour testing uses the dye 'Echtblausalz B Merck', which combines with all cannabinols to give orange, red, and blue azo-compounds, and can be combined with a variant of the chromatographic technique (so-called thin-layer chromatography) using an inorganic powder, silica gel or kieselguhr. By this method nearly all constituents of a resin can be identified.

Gas chromatography (Appendix B) can also be utilized, and has proved to be a reliable, relatively simple technique for identifying any type of sample after an extract has been prepared by the gentle use of solvents.

These analytical procedures are all capable of standing up to any legal examination and are thus valuable forensic tools, objectively reliable from the point of view of suspect, analyst, and the judiciary alike.

3. *Opium, the opiates, and the antalgics*

While the chemistry of alcohol is 'child's play' for anyone who has studied natural history in school, cannabis constituents are more complex, whereas the structure of the opiates has remained a real puzzle, even to the experts, ever since the isolation of the first one (morphine) in 1805, until 120 years later, when the true intricate structure of this alkaloid was established. It then took another thirty years for the third stage (the total synthesis of morphine) to be achieved.

Leaving aside less important members of the papaver alkaloids (see Table 5), the large family consists of two main types: the morphine (narcotic) group and the papaverine group.

TABLE 5

Direct derivatives	Alkaloid	Therapeutic usefulness	Content (Average % of opium)
Heroin Dilaudid, etc. ⟩ Morphine		Medicinally useful as analgesic	10·0
	Codeine	Medicinally useful as cough depressant	0·5
	Thebaine	Useful as starting material	0·2
	Papaverine	Has spasmolytic action	1·0
	Narcotine	No pronounced action	6·0
	Narceine	No pronounced action	0·2

There are nearly a hundred natural, semi-synthetic, fully synthetic, and intermediate opiate compounds specified as drugs under International Narcotics Control. To these must be added the morphine antagonists and related substances. Among the narcotics group is the first fully effective drug to be synthesized, pethidine, or meperidine, and the more recent semi-synthetic ones, such as etorphine (M 99) and acetorphine (M 183), which are prepared by intricate processes from thebaine and which in animal tests are 1,200 and 1,500 times more active than morphine. While pethidine is weaker than morphine, methadone, alpha and beta-prodine, levorphanol (a morphinan which has most of the morphine rings) are of equal or superior strength by comparison with the natural opiate. These synthetic drugs consist, at least, of those parts of the morphine structure which are essential to its pharmacological and toxicological properties (the pharmacodynamic groups).

While the total skeleton of morphine is present in synthetic morphine, the morphinans, benzomorphans, and endothene-thebaines have additional chemical features which introduce,

TABLE 6

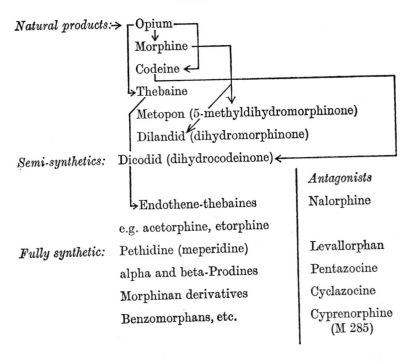

Natural products:→	Opium
	↓
	Morphine
	Codeine ←
	↳Thebaine
	Metopon (5-methyldihydromorphinone)
	Dilandid (dihydromorphinone)
Semi-synthetics:	Dicodid (dihydrocodeinone)←

		Antagonists
	↳Endothene-thebaines	Nalorphine
	e.g. acetorphine, etorphine	
Fully synthetic:	Pethidine (meperidine)	Levallorphan
	alpha and beta-Prodines	Pentazocine
	Morphinan derivatives	Cyclazocine
	Benzomorphans, etc.	Cyprenorphine (M 285)

under certain conditions, differences in biological effects. Thus in the semi-synthetic series a morphine with an allyl-group instead of a methyl group becomes an antagonist. Some other synthetic products carry similar properties (see Table 6 under Antagonists). In a few instances they even possess disphoric (unpleasant) as opposed to euphorigenic properties. As we saw in

Chapter 4 (p. 69), the first representative of an ideal syn-opiate may have been produced in pentazocine, which apparently has no dependence-producing effects. Before this and similar drugs can eventually replace the analgesics at present in medical use, however, it will have to undergo extensive clinical tests.

Compared with the opiates, the antalgics, represented by aspirin and salicylic acid (ortho-hydroxy-benzoic acid) and its derivatives are relatively simple aromatic compounds.

The analytical recognition of this series of weak pain-killers is also far less complicated than that of the opiates and syn-opiates. Whether the procedures are applied to the drug in more or less pure form, or to body-fluids or organs containing such drugs, whether the analyses are for forensic or identification reasons, the analyst has over the last few years adopted more sophisticated and reliable methods. These comprise, apart from the older types of technique (titrations, colour reactions, and isolation of crystals; and, of course, pharmacognosy as applied to natural products), a number of chromatographic methods (thin layer chromatography, gas chromatography, and spetrophotometric methods).

4. *Cocaine*

The most important alkaloid in *E. coca* leaves is cocaine (0·25–0·50 per cent), equivalent to about 70 to 80 per cent of the total alkaloid present. The total alkaloid content of the truxillo leaf is higher, but in this case only about half consists of cocaine.

Chemically, cocaine may be termed methyl-benzoyl-ecgonine. It is insoluble in water, but soluble in most organic solvents such as alcohol, ether, and chloroform.

The natural alkaloids found in the coca leaf are derivatives of the parent base, ecgonine, which differs from tropine, a product of the hydrolysis of atropine, in possessing a carboxyl group. As ecgonine contains an alcohol and an acid group, it can be esterfied by combination with acids and alcohols. Treatment with benzoic anhydride produces benzoyl-ecgonine; on methylation, methyl-benzoyl ecgonine or cocaine is formed by replacement of the hydrogen of the carboxyl group.

Coca leaves contain cocaine plus benzoyl-ecgonine and other esters. The alkaloids are extracted by using as solvent petroleum ether on leaves, digested with lime water. The organic solution is then treated with dilute hydrochloric acid to remove the mixed alkaloids. Impure cocaine hydrochloride crystals separate from the aqueous solution after concentration. The alkaloids remaining in the mother liquor are then hydrolyzed to form ecgonine, which is afterwards re-benzoylated and re-methylated.

The presence of cocaine in the blood can be determined after extraction with chloroform from the alkaline medium, and re-extraction from the chloroform solution with dilute hydrochloric acid. On spectrophotometric analysis, a characteristic absorption in the ultra-violet indicates the presence of cocaine.

5. *Amphetamines*

The Drugs (Prevention of Misuse) Act 1964 controls certain derivatives of beta-aminopropylbenzene and beta-aminoisopropyl benzene, including synthetic derivatives of these compounds but exempting ephedrine and a few related products. Chlorphentermine and pemoline, with actions similar to amphetamine, are included. The scheme of identification relies on paper and thin-layer chromatography, using a variety of locating reagents. In routine identification in a forensic laboratory, ultraviolet and infra-red spectrophotometers may also be very useful in identifying or eliminating the presence of these compounds.

Urine has been found to be the best medium of assays, as the blood levels of many of these drugs after normal doses remain extremely low, owing to considerable concentration of the drug outside blood vessels; it is possible to detect it in the urine as long as forty-eight hours after ingesting a normal dose.

The screening now adopted as routine in most forensic and Public Analyst's Laboratories is carried out on 2–5 ml urine.

6. *Tranquillizers and sedatives*

The chemical structure of the psychopharmacological drugs (we include here, for comparison's sake, the MAO inhibitors and the

dibenzazepines and related substances) is considerably variegated. With the exception of meprobamate and 'Oblivon', most
form multi-ring systems and have nitrogen in at least one of the
rings. The phenothiazines, as the name implies, also have sulphur as one of the hetero-atoms (as chemists call elements other
than carbon). The other exception is the group of MAO compounds, which usually consist of one benzene ring which carries a
hydrazine (two nitrogens, N–N) or one nitrogen.

The phenothiazines, which show throughout a basic system,
possess a side-chain, which in contrast to related compounds,
active as anti-histamine or anti-Parkinson drugs, with two
carbons, have three carbons between the ring nitrogen and a
second nitrogen in the chain.

The interesting point with the natural reserpine derivatives
is that part of their molecule shows great similarity to some of
the hallucinogens. This demonstrates some definite links between chemical structure and action on the central nervous
system.

Looking at this pot-pourri of chemicals, their analysis cannot
follow a simple recipe. As most of them are derived from legitimate preparations produced by the chemical manufacturer, their
classification and identification might start with the type of
tablet, capsule, or cachet in which they are sold. More elaborate
procedures would include modern methods of spectro-photo-
metry in the ultra-violet and infra-red regions of the spectrum,
chromatography, perhaps even mass spectrometry, or X-ray
diffraction. It depends, as in all other cases of drug analysis, on
the amount of the substance available. However, international
concern is felt about the medical and legal situation and recommendations aim at prohibiting the non-authorized possession of
drugs belonging to this group.

7. *Barbiturates*

Urea is the di-amide of carbonic acid and is formed as a metabolite in the body from carbon dioxide and ammonia, but is
really the end product of an intertwined series of reactions.
When one or both of its amide groups react with organic acids,

products called ureides or diureïdes are formed which possess sleep-producing properties. The diureïdes have the greater hypnotic activity. This effect is even more enhanced when urea is condensed with malonic acid ($=HO_2C. CH_2. CO_2H$), a dicarboxylic acid, in which the two hydrogens of the centre CH_2 can be replaced by the chemist by two identical or different alkyl, aryl, or aralkyl groups to form, with urea, after condensation, the series of compounds under discussion. If the hydrogen of the amide groups in urea is replaced, barbiturates carrying substituents on one or both nitrogen atoms can be prepared. If the oxygen of the urea moeity is exchanged for sulphur, so-called thiobarbiturates are produced. Aqueous solutions of the metal derivatives which barbituric acids, as weak acids, form with sodium or potassium metal or their hydroxides, react alkaline. They undergo the typical hydrolytic reactions of salts of one weak and one strong partner, as for instance their solubility depends on the acidity or alkalinity of their solution. Moreover, they are unstable in alkaline solution as sodium salts; it is therefore necessary, each time an aqueous solution is required, to prepare it freshly immediately before use.

A suitable method of assay for barbiturates is typified by that given in the *British Pharmacopoeia* (1963) for amylobarbitone. This is issued in tablets as barbituric acid, or in capsules as the sodium salt. (The contents of the latter are easily dissolved in water, while the former, if required as a solution, is made alkaline with sodium hydroxide.) After the solution has been saturated with sodium chloride (table salt), and made acid with aqueous hydrochloric acid, the mixture is repeatedly extracted with ether, which is then evaporated. This leaves a residue which is dried at a raised temperature to constant weight. Purity of the sample is checked by melting-points, or maybe by crystal form. Another check on purity is obtained by infra-red spectrophotometry. The curves of the spectrum are then compared with a standard set.

Nowadays it is customary to rely on paper chromatography or thin layer chromatography for identifying barbiturates present in viscera. Additional confirmation may be obtained from gas chromatography (see Appendix B), X-ray diffraction, and infra-red spectrophotometry.

8. *The hallucinogens*

The chemistry of the hallucinogens divides them into the following six main groups:

1. The so-called *poly-cyclic compounds*, such as lysergide or LSD-25, its closely related amide or oliluiqui, and ibogaine.

2. The *tryptamine family*, which like (1) contains a benzene ring fused to a pyrrolring, the two together called indole; the simplest is DMT or dimthyltryptamine, a natural and laboratory product; from time to time variations on the theme of tryptamine turn up, some originally tested as MAO inhibitors (see page 110) but later tried out as psychedelic drugs. The tryptamine family also has members that carry on the benzene ring OH-groups, like the animal substance of great importance called serotonin, which occurs in all animal tissues and evidently plays an essential part in brain functions. These members are bufotenine, produced by plants and toads, psilocybin, and psilocin, mushroom poisons, the second being a phosphoric acid derivative.

3. (1) and (2) link up neatly with the *harmine derivatives*, which, like the other compounds just mentioned, still carry the indole nucleus, but fused on to a third (pyridine) ring. Another chemical difference lies in the fact that the OH-substituent has changed into what the chemists call a methoxy group which has slipped further down the benzene ring of the tricyclic system.

4. While it is not obvious that a chemical relation exists between the indole derivatives and the series of so-called *phenylethylamines* (which include amphetamine), but this is in fact the case. The main difference is that the ethylamine chain is hooked on to the indole ring system in the family of hallucinogens, and directly on to the benzene ring in the stimulatory group. However, a number of phenylethylamines are known to share pronounced hallucinogenic properties with the indoles. The most well known is mescaline, a trimethoxylated phenylethylamine with a number of synthetic analogues such as the trimethoxy-amphetamine.

5. This brings us to related compounds of a purely synthetic nature, frequently produced in the laboratory for pharmacological and therapeutic purposes, but having hallucinogenic activities. One of these is a drug known as S.T.P. or D.O.M. which shows many features reminiscent of the mescaline-like compounds. Further removed from this series are compounds like phencyclidine, also known as 'Peace pill', which carries a benzene, piperidine, and cyclohexyl ring. Another benzene-piperidine combination is Ritalin or methylphenidate, which actually belongs to the drugs described in Chapter 6. But it has arrived among the drug abusers and joins, in that respect, a family of compounds known as benzylates. For example Benactycine, which also plays a part among psychopharmalogical drugs and has parasympatholytic (atropine-like) properties, and consists of benzene rings, forming what is known to the chemist as benzilic acid, linked with an ester bond to an alcohol, continued in the ever-present ethylamine chain. A large number of similar compounds have been made over the last few years and submitted for tests as remedies for mental diseases and against any over-activity of certain autonomic functions. Most members of the series also produce psychotomimetic effects.

6. *Adrenochrome* and its derivatives in a sense take us back to the indole compounds. But their derivation from the adrenaline, together with nor-adrenaline, the physiological chemical balancers of acetylcholine, makes it interesting, although it has so far been produced only in the laboratory and is only suspected to be formed in the body. Adrenaline and nor-adrenaline, or epinephrine and nor-epinephrine, it will be remembered, may play a part in the way opiates affect the C.N.S. (see page 75). Their role, or that of their oxidative transformation products, i.e. adrenochrome, etc., in mental diseases, rests at this moment mainly on a working hypothesis. These compounds are mentioned here because of the claims which are made for their psychotomimetic activities.

*

With a mixture of chemicals as diverse as all these, it is not easy to indicate simple analytical methods for their estimation or even for their qualitative detection. The whole question of identification is not made any easier by the high effectiveness of LSD in very small doses. The main techniques are roughly the same as those the analytical chemist has utilized, for example, in the case of opiates and syn-opiates: thin-layer chromatography, ultra-violet spectrophotometry, spectrofluorometry (using fluorescence as measuring property), gas chromatography (where applicable), densitometry, and, combined with chemical reactions, all the physical measurement methods available. Some laboratories may prefer other techniques, such as paper chromatography, and counter-current distribution, and (if normally used in the institute or department) infra-red spectrophotometry and, perhaps, N.M.R. (nuclear magnetic resonance).

Apart from the few representatives of this group used in research or clinical therapy, the drugs that are misused usually turn up in form of tablets or gelatine capsules with powder contents. However, with bufotenine its oral inactivity has produced samples for snuff and i.v. or i.m. injections, and the same applies to any of the drugs which are sufficiently water soluble, particularly if the compounds form salts. In some instances the drug is mixed with parsley leaves, tobacco (especially DMT) or, drop by drop, absorbed on sugar lumps.

See also Appendix E, pp. 194–5.

Appendix B: The Principles of Gas Chromatography

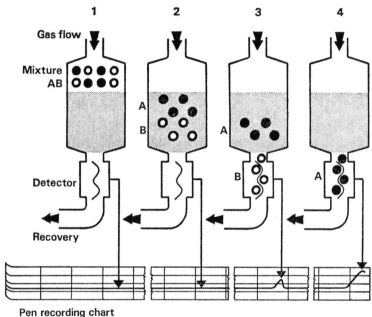

This diagram demonstrates how two substances which together make up a mixture are separated by gas chromatography so that they can be identified. In Stage 1 a sample of the mixture has been introduced into the head of the column. A suitable gas is already flowing through the column at a constant speed, and the column is heated and kept at a fixed temperature by some means such as a vapour jacket. The sample to be analysed is vaporized by the heat of the column and begins to move down, borne on the gas stream. The column is filled with a granulated solid substance which serves no other purpose than to support a suitable liquid on the outer surfaces of its granules. This liquid has a different affinity for each of the two substances in the mixture. Being more attractive to one, it will tend to delay its passage, whilst the other, being less hampered, moves on ahead (Stage 2).

Stage 3 of the diagram shows how the substance B, having become completely separated in this way from substance A, is passing a detector device on its way out of the column. The detector measures some physical characteristic of the substance and transmits this to a pen-recording chart on which is also automatically noted the time the passage through the column has taken.

In Stage 4 of the diagram is shown the moment when the second substance A, having completed its reluctant journey through the column, is passing the detector and causing the pen recorder to register the fact.

From the data thus produced, and from other known factors, the scientist conducting the experiment is subsequently able to identify some or all of the substances.

(The above notes and diagram have been reproduced here by kind permission of Lord Ritchie Calder and Messrs Unilever Ltd, and appeared first in *Progress*, the Unilever quarterly.)

Appendix C: Alcohol Limits in Selected Countries

	Level in *mg*/100 ml
U.K.	80
Belgium	150
West Germany	150 (130 for motor-cycles) (accepted in practice)
Iceland	120
Denmark	100 (accepted in practice)
Finland	100
Switzerland	100 (accepted in practice)
New York	100
Austria	80
Northern Ireland	80 (with a higher level offence above 125)
Norway	50
Poland	50
Sweden	50 (with a higher level offence above 150)
Bulgaria	30
Czechoslovakia	30

Information from other sources

Republic of Ireland	125
Italy	No prescribed level tests permissive
Netherlands	100–125 permissive
Israel	No prescribed level tests permissive
Yugoslavia	No prescribed level
Luxembourg	Tests permissive up to 150, evidence of being under influence; over 150 mg, evidence of intoxication

Australia	No prescribed level tests permissive if person consents
Victoria	Tests permissive over 50 mg evidence considered
W. Australia	As Victoria except that over 150 mg is evidence of being under influence
United States	As at 1 June 1968, in 42 states out of 50, prescribed levels were 100 or 150 mg, except in Rhode Island, Vermont, West Virginia, and Utah, where it is 80 mg

(With acknowledgements to the Home Office Forensic Science Adviser, London, through whose courtesy the first 15 levels were obtained.)

Appendix D: Table of Main Drugs

Drug or group of drugs	Chemistry	Main effects in therapy
Alcohol	Ethanol and higher alcohols; fermentation product from sugars	First-aid remedy in vascular collapse
Cannabis products	Tetrahydro-cannabinols (cannabidiolic compounds). Natural origin and synthetic products	None (some in India)
Opiates and synopiates (narcotics)	Morphine, heroin, etc., and synopiates. Natural, origin and synthetic products	Mainly as analgesics, anticough remedies
Coca	Cocaine	Replaced by synthetic local anaesthetics
Stimulators (of mental vigour)	Amphetamine and related compounds; Khat	CNS stimulants, capillary constrictors (cold, allergies slimming agents, antidote for barbiturates)
Stimulators (of mental buoyancy)	(a) MAO inhibitors (b) Tricyclic anti-depressants	Mainly as anti-depressant Anti-anxiety, mental energizers
Tranquillizers, psychopharmacological agents	Anti-depressants (see above); phenothiazines; Rauwolfia Alkaloids Benzodiazepine; Meprobamate; Methylpentynol	Neuroleptic, psychotic diseases Neurosis treatments Anxiety treatments

Main effects in misuse	Legal controls
(Kind of euphoria); chronic alcoholism; dipsomania	Restricted drinking hours; total prohibition in some countries; driving restrictions and traffic laws
(Euphoria); problem of triggering off drug abuse; long-term effects possible, main evidence from the East. La Guardia Report 1944 apparently no physical dependence, no tolerance	International Single Convention 1961, classed together with opiates and cocaine *U.K.*: Dangerous Drug Act 1965, 1967, 1968 *U.S.*: Marihuana Tax Act 1937
Physical dependence, tolerance, and abstinence syndrome; (euphoria)	International Single Convention 1961 *U.K.*: Dangerous Drug Act 1965, 1967, 1968 *U.S.A.*: Harrison Act 1914 and Amendments
(Euphoria); leaves chewed in S. America, chronic CNS damage; general deterioration	International Single Convention 1961 *U.K.*: Dangerous Drug Act 1965, 1967 *U.S.A.*: Harrison Act 1914
Psycho-analeptic effects: (kind of euphoria); tension; hallucinations; withdrawal symptoms; tolerance	Recommendations by U.N. committees *U.K.*: Drugs (Prevention of Misuse) Act 1964 *U.S.A.*: Drug Abuse Control Amendments 1965
(Kind of euphoria); could lead to mental upheavals; danger with alcohol and proteins	International recommendations incorporated *U.K.*: Pt 2, Therapeutic Substances Act; also Pt B, 4th Schedule; also Drugs (Prevention of Misuse) Act 1964; similar *U.S.A.*
Non-euphoric; some misuse and potential danger if over-indulgence develops	*U.K.*: Schedule 4B. *U.S.A.*: Proviso in Drug Control Amendment 1965: 'any drug which contains any quantity of a substance which the Secretary has found to have a potential for abuse. . .'

Drug or group of drugs	Chemistry	Main effects in therapy
Barbiturates	Diureides of di-substituted malonic acids and urea	Hypnotics, sedatives; coronary diseases
Hallucinogens (*indole group*)	LSD—25, morning glory seeds, ololuiqui, etc.; bufotenine, DMT, psilocine, psilocybin; harmine in caapi, etc.	Clinical research tools in psychotic diseases
Hallucinogens (*aromatic group*)	Mescaline; STP; PCP; benzylates, such as Benactycine	Research tools into behavioural problems; atropine-like; used in treatment of mental diseases
Tobacco	Nicotine and other bases, but, more important, a number of products of pyrolysis	None
Tea, coffee, and cocoa	Purine (xanthine) derivatives	Stimulants
Spices and scents	Nutmeg; incenses; solvents	Kitchen spice, industrial solvents, plastic diluents

Main effects in misuse	Legal controls
Over-indulgence; danger in combination with alcohol, opiates, amphetamines	*International*: warnings and discussions. *U.K.*; Poisons Schedule, 4A (see discussion and reference, pp. 125 and 168) *U.S.A.*: Drug Abuse Control Amendments 1965
Hallucinations, delusions, visions, etc.	*U.K.*: 4B Poisons Schedule. The Drugs (Prevention of Misuse) Act 1964. Modification Order 1966 *U.S.A.*: Drug Abuse Control Amendments 1965
Hallucinations, colour visions, etc.	*U.K.*: 4B Poisons Schedule and Drugs (Prevention of Misuse) Act 1964; Modification Order 1966 *U.S.A.*: see Drug Abuse Control Amendments 1965
Excess produces problems of respiratory diseases, etc.; lung cancer, chronic bronchitis	Certain restrictions in advertising, especially on television; taxes; otherwise legalized
Unfavourable effects on heart and circulation, if taken in excess	No regulations
Hallucinogenic; sniffing habit	No regulations

Appendix E: Table of Main Hallucinogens

Compound	Plant and plant part	Habitat	Effects
A. Plant products (indole derivatives)			
Bufotenine, 5-hydroxy-dimethyltryptamine (5-OH-DMT) mappin, cohoba, niopo; plus DMT and oxides plus muscarine etc.	*Piptadenia peregrina* (shrub, tree, pods, seeds, bark); *P. macrocarpa. Amanita mappa* and *muscaria* (fungi). *Acacia niopo* (a mimosa). Chinese toad, *Bufovulgaris* (skin and excretion). *Phalaris tuberosa* (grass)	South America, Haiti, and Siberia; known among Indian tribes	Sensory disorder, 'intoxication', cardiotoxic for man – not active orally but as snuff or i.v. injection
Psilocine, 4-hydroxy-DMT. Psilocybine 4-phosphatoxy-DMT	*Psilocibe mexicana; P. sempervirens cubensis. Cinocybe cyanopus. Stropharia.* (All mushrooms)	South and North America	Coloured vision, changes in perception, thought and mood in absence of changes in consciousness and disorientation. Similar to LSD but 100–150 times shorter in duration
Ololuiqui (Morning Glory seeds). Lysergamide; ergine	*Rivea corymbosa* (Mexican bindweed). *Ipomea tricolour* etc.	Mexico	
Lysergide, LSD-25. Dilyside, Lysergic acid diethylamide	From *Claviceps purpura* (ergot): lysergic acid, then semi-synthetic	Europe (Mediterranean area)	The hallucinogenic ('psychedelic') drug
Ibogaine (twelve alkaloids); complex indole derivatives	*Tabernantho iboga* (bark of roots, stems and leaves of shrub)	West Africa	Intoxication, excitement, and hallucination

Compound	Plant and plant part	Habitat	Effects
Harmine, 7-methoxy-N-methyl-9-pyrid (3–4b) indole banisterine *caapi* contains harmine, harmaline; ayahusca, *yage* contains harmine = yageine	*Perganum harmala. Banistercopsis caapi* (jungle vine). *B. inebriens. Haemadictyon amazonis*	South America, west Ama-zon. Ecuador, Peru, and Colombia	Hallucinogenic, euphoric, and MAO inhibitor

B. Aromatic derivatives (For Nutmeg, see p. 156)

Mescaline. Trimethoxy-phenyl ethylamine. (For Khat, *see* pp. 107–109)	*Lopophora william-sii. L. Levinii* (cactus): peyote, peyotle, anhalon-ium	North Mexico	Natural 'psyche-delic', produ-cing delusions, hallucinations
Asarone, 1:2:4-trime-thoxypropenylbenzene	Rat root	North Canada	

Name	Chemical structure	Effects
C. From the laboratory		
DMT	Dimethyl tryptamine	Hallucinogenic, 5 times mescaline, but faster and briefer (3–5 mins., lasts 1 hour)
DET	Diethyl tryptamine	Tremors, visual effects, distortions; short-acting (0·7–0·8 mg has mesca-line-like actions)
Methyltryptamine IT-290		Visions; MAO inhibition (20 mg equivalent to 50 mg LSD)
Tryptamine		Catalepsy and paralysis in mind; stupor in cats
Adrenochrome	An indole from adrenaline (epinephrine)	Mild psychotomimetic

Name	Chemical structure	Effects
STP, DOM	4-methyl-2, 5-dime-thoxyamphetamine.	Hallucinogenic, *c.* 100 times effects of mescaline
TMA	Trimethoxyamphetamine	
Phencyclidine: peace pill, PCP, Sernyl	Phenylpiperidine-cyclo-hexane	Hallucinogenic in man
Benzilates, e.g. Benactycine	Piperidine benzilate	Psychopharmacological, para sympatholytic, atropine-like psychotonimetric

Appendix F: Glossary of Drug Terms

Acid	LSD, LSD-25 (lysergic acid diethylamide)
Acidhead	Frequent user of LSD
Bag	Packet of drugs
Ball	Absorption of stimulants and cocaine via genitalia
Bang	Injection of drugs; the sensation when injecting drugs intravenously
Barbs	Barbiturates
Bennies	Benzedrine, amphetamine sulphate
Big O	Opium
Black beauty	Benzedrine, amphetamine sulphate
Black bomber	Benzedrine, amphetamine sulphate
Black stuff	Opium
Blank	Extremely low-grade narcotics
Blast	Strong effect from a drug
Blasted	Under the influence of drugs
Block	Ounce of hashish
Blow a stick (or joint)	Smoke marihuana
Blow lunch	To vomit from too much dope
Blue angels	Amytal, a barbiturate
Bomber	Benzedrine, amphetamine sulphate
Bombita	Amphetamine injection, sometimes taken with heroin
Bring down	Depressed
Brown	Benzedrine, amphetamine sulphate
Brown stuff	Opium
Bull	Federal Narcotic Agent
Bullet	Capsule
Bummer	Bad experience with psychedelics
Bum trip	Bad experience with psychedelics
Bundle	Packet of narcotics
Burned	Obtain badly diluted or nonactive drugs

Business	Equipment for injecting drug
Busted	Arrested
Buttons	Sections of the peyote cactus
Buzz	Elation produced by drug
C	Cocaine
California sunshine	LSD
Cap	Capsule
Carrier	Pusher's middleman
Charged up	Under the influence of drugs
Chipping	Taking narcotics occasionally
Chippy	Occasional drug user
Chuck	Eat excessively, especially candy after recovery from withdrawal
Coke	Cocaine
Cokie	Cocaine addict
Cold turkey	Sudden withdrawal of narcotics
Coming down	Recovering from a psychedelic trip; also recovering from a high
Connect	Obtain drugs
Connection	Drug supplier
Cook up a pill	Prepare opium for smoking
Cop	Obtain drugs
Co-pilots	Benzedrine, amphetamine sulphate
Cop out	Quit, take off, confess, defect, inform
Crash	Effects of stopping the use of amphetamines
Cubehead	Frequent user of LSD
Dealer	Drug supplier
Deck	Packet of narcotics
Dexies	Dexedrine, an amphetamine
Dime bag	$10 package of narcotics
Dirty	Possessing drugs, liable to arrest if searched

197

Dollies	Dolophine (also known as methadone), a synthetic narcotic	Head	Person dependent on drugs
		Hearts	Dexedrine tablets (from the shape)
Double blue	Amphetamine and barbiturate	Heat	Police
		High	Under the influence of drugs
Downers	Sedatives, alcohol, tranquilizers, and narcotics	Hit	Obtain drugs; also a drag of a marihuana cigarette
Down habit	Extreme addiction	Holding	Having drugs in one's possession
Drag	Smoke marihuana		
Dummy	Purchase which did not contain narcotics	Hooked	Addicted
		Hophead	Narcotics addict
Dynamite	High-grade heroin	Hopped up	Under the influence of drugs
Fix	Injection of narcotics	Horse	Heroin
Flaked out	Unconscious	Hot	Wanted by the police
Flash	Initial feeling after injecting	Hot shot	Fatal drug dose
		Hype	Narcotics addict
Flip	Become psychotic		
Floating	Under the influence of drugs	Joint	Marihuana cigarette
		Jolly beans	Pep pills
Freakout	Bad experience with psychedelics; also a chemical high	Junk	Narcotic
		Junkie	Narcotics addict
		Kick the habit	Stop using narcotics
Gimmicks	Equipment for injecting drug		
		Lame	Person who does not use drugs
Goods	Narcotic		
Good trip	Happy experience with psychedelics	Lit up	Under the influence of drugs
Goofballs	Sleeping pills	Load	Stock of illegal drugs
Goofed up	Under the influence of drugs	Loaded	Full of drugs
Grass	Marihuana	M	Morphine
Greenies	Dextro amphetamine sulphate with amobarbital	Mainline	Inject drugs into a vein
		Maintaining	Keeping at a certain level of drug effect
Guns	Equipment for injecting drug		
Guru	Promoter of LSD; a person who watches a drug user on a trip	Make a buy	Obtain drugs
		Man (The)	Police
		Mary Jane	Marihuana; hashish; cannabis resin
H	Heroin		
Habit	Under the influence of drugs	Mesc	Mescaline, the alkaloid in peyote
Half load	Packet of narcotics	Meth	Methamphetamine; also Methedrine
Hard narcotics	Opiates, such as heroin and morphine	Methhead	Habitual user of methamphetamine
Hard stuff	Heroin	Monkey	Drug addiction producing physical dependence
Hash	Hashish, the resin of cannabis		
Hawaiian sunshine	LSD	Narc	Narcotics detective
		Nickel bag	$5 packet of drugs

O	Opium
O. D.	Overdose of narcotics
Off	Not using drugs
On the nod	Sleepy from narcotics
Panic	Shortage of narcotics on the market
Pep pills	Benzedrine, amphetamine sulphate
Pillhead	Heavy user of pills, barbiturates or amphetamines, or both
Pop	Inject drugs
Pot	Marihuana
Pothead	Heavy marihuana user
Psychedelic	Mind manifesting
Purple haze	LSD
Purple hearts	Dexamyl, a combination of Dexedrine and Amytal
Pusher	Drug peddler
Quill	Matchbook cover for sniffing Methedrine, cocaine, or heroin
Red devils	Seconal, a barbiturate
Reefer	Marihuana cigarette
Roach	Marihuana butt
Roach holder	Device for holding the butt of a marihuana cigarette
Rolling dip	Making marihuana cigarette
Rope	Marihuana cigarette
Run	Amphetamine binge
Salt shot	Salt and water injected under the skin when a person takes an overdose of heroin
Scag	Heroin
Score	Make a purchase of drugs
Script	Drug prescription
Shmeck	Heroin
Shooting gallery	Place where addicts inject
Shoot up	Inject drugs
Shot	Injection of drugs; the sensation when injecting drugs intravenously
Sick	Withdrawal symptoms
Skin popping	Injecting drugs under the skin

Sleepers	Barbiturates
Smack	Heroin
Smoke	Marihuana cigarette; wood alcohol
Sniff	Inhaling heroin or cocaine through the nose
Snorting	Inhaling drugs
Snow	Cocaine
Speed	Methamphetamine
Speedfreak	Habitual user of speed
Square	Person who does not use drugs
Stash	Supply of drugs in a secure place
Stick	Marihuana cigarette
Stoned	Effects of marihuana
Stoolie	Informer
Strung out	Addicted; withdrawal symptoms
Stuff	Heroin; also any drug
Sugar	Powdered narcotics
Sweets	Benzedrine, amphetamine sulphate
Tea	Marihuana; hashish; cannabis resin
Tea head	Marihuana user
Tracks	Scars along veins after many injections
Trip	Psychedelic experience
Tripping out	High on psychedelics
Turkey	Capsule with non-narcotic powder
Turned on	Under the influence of drugs
Turned off	Off the influence of drugs
25	LSD (from its original designation, LSD-25)
Uppers	Stimulants, cocaine, and psychedelics
Wasted	Under the influence of drugs
Weed	Marihuana
Weed head	Marihuana user
Whites	Benzedrine, amphetamine sulphate
White stuff	Morphine
Works	Equipment for injecting drugs
Yellow jacket	Nembutal, a barbiturate

Index

Abortions, 137; due to ergotism. 132
Abstinence, *see* Withdrawal
Accidents, alcohol and, 34
Acetylcholine, 127
Acetyl-coenzyme A, 31
  -salicylic acid (aspirin), 85
Acts concerned with drugs or alcohol, 12–15, 18, 20, 25, 26, 27, 34–7, 82, 92
Addict, social relationships, 16, 17; opiate, 73; as a sick person, 12, 20
Addict in the Street, 70, 84
Addiction, 1, 10, 19, 20, 21; alcohol, 29–33; amphetamine, 104; barbiturate, 122; coca, 91; opiates, 77, 80
Addictive States, 74
Addicts, 5, 20, 69, 82, 103; famous, 65; numbers of, 13, 39, 73, 80, 101, 122
Adrenaline, 75, 132, 184
Advertising, limitation on tobacco, 146
Alcohol, 11, 22–40, 50, 116, 172–4, 188–9; barbiturates and, 31, 121, 125; motorist and, 34–7
Alcoholics, use of amphetamines by, 105; number of, 36, 39
Alcoholics Anonymous, 38

Alcoholism, 23, 30, 32, **33–4, 55**; treatment, 37–40, 135
Alkaloids, 67, 90, 113, 130, 132, 143, 152, 177
Amitryptyline (Laroxyl), 109, 110
Amphetamines, 17, 99–109, 180, 183; addicts, 101–2; athletes and, 102; effects, 103–5
Amytal (amylobarbitone), 102, 120
Anaesthesia, 7, 127
Anaesthetics, 121
Analgesia, 68, 73, 74–5
Analgesics, mild, 85–7
Analysis, cannabis, 48; main drugs, 172–85; tea, coffee, chocolate, 152–154; tobacco, 143–4
Anorectic effect of amphetamine, 101
'Antalgics', 85–6, 179
Anti-anxiety drugs, 112–18; depressants, 109–11; histamines, 129, and barbituates, 121; social behaviour, 105; tussive action of opiates, 72
Anxiety, 101, 110, 112, 115
Apathy, with cannabis, 51
Areca catechu (betel), 156–7
Aspirin, 85–7, 179
Assassins, 42–4

Asthmatics, aspirin and, 86
Ataxia, due to cannabis, 51
Atropa belladonna (deadly nightshade), 127
Atropine, 68, 127, 128
Australia, aborigines in, 158; analgesics in, 87
Austria, tobacco production in, 143
Autonomic nervous system, 7, 53, 121, 135

Bach, Johann Sebastian, 150
Balzac, Honoré, de, 154
Bangh, 45
Barbitone, 118, 120
Barbiturate addicts, 105; antidote, 104
Barbiturates, 1, 17, 100, 118–26, 181–182
Barbiturism, 125
Baudelaire, C. P., 4, 44–5, 52, 66
Beer, 24, 25, 26, 29, 46–7; *chicha*, from maize and corn, 90
Belladonna, 120, 127, 128
Benzedrine, 100
Betel chewing, 141, 156–7
Bhang, 46, 49
Bindweed (*Rivea corymbosa*), 132
Biochemical changes in brain, 136–7
Biological balance, destruction of, 76
Black bombers (Durophet), 101
Blindness, due to methanol, 33
Blood, alcohol in, 32, 35–6, 37; nicotine and circulation of, 144
Brain Report, 13
Brain, 117; changes in, 136–7; damage, 95; divisions, 7; function, 137–8; RNA, 138; psychochemistry, 140
Breath test, 32, 34–5, 37
British Drug Scene, 17
British Humanist Association, 58
British Medical Association, 123
Bromides, 129
Bureau of Narcotics and Dangerous Drugs, U.S.A., 14, 92
Burroughs, William, *Junkie*, 70
Butobarbitone (*Soneryl*), 120

Cactus, products of sacred, 130–40; peyote in Mexico, 133
Caffea arabica, coffee plant, 150
Caffeine, 85, 149, 152, 154

Camellia sinensis (Theaceae), tea plant, 148
Cancer of the lung, 145
Cancer-producing substances in tobacco, 144, 145
Cancer, terminal, heroin and, 69; LSD and, 135
Cannabidiol, 175
Cannabidiolic acid, 54, 175
Cannabis, 3, 10, 14, 17, 19, 41–62, 174–6; *C. indica, sativa* (hemp), 42, 45; Wootton Report on, 2, 59, 60
Cardio-vascular diseases, 146
Catha edulis (Celastraceae), 107
Central nervous system and alcohol, 29, 30; amphetamine, 103; atropine, 127; cannabis, 51, 53; cocaine, 93; drugs, 7, 129; drug receptors, 76; hallucinogens, 135; nicotine, 144; opiates, 72
Cerebral cortex, 29
Champagne, 24, 27, 28
Charas (cannabis resin), 45
Chica, 90
China, opium in, 67
Chlorodyne, 73
Chromatography, 180, 182; gas, 182, 186–7
Chromosome damage, possible, 137, 140
Cider, 24, 26, 29
Cirrhosis, of liver, 30, 31, 38
Claviceps purpurea, 131
Cocaine, 10, 17, 88–98, 179–80; dependence, 94–7; legal position, 92, 98
Coca leaf, 88–98, 179; economy, 91
Cocoa, 151–3; analysis, 152–3; plant (*Theobroma cacao*), 151
Codeine, 67, 72, 85, 177
Coffee, 141, 149–51, 152; *Kaffee Cantata*, 150; plant (*Caffea arabica*), 150
Cola acuminata, 149
Columbus, Christopher, 151
Comfort, Dr Alex, 138
Compleat History of Druggs (Pomet), 152
Control of drugs, 2, 12, 13; *see also* Legislation
Corneal areflexia test, 51
Cough mixtures, or linctuses, 72
Crime, cannabis and, 53
Crusaders, 43–4

INDEX   202

Dangerous Drugs Acts 1965, 1967, 13,
  58, 62, 92
Datuna stramonium (Thorn-apple,
  Jimson or Jamestown Weed), 127
Delirium tremens, 30, 38, 54
Delyside (LSD), 130
Dependence, 1, 7–8, 10, 75, 76, 115;
  alcohol, 22, 29–33; amphetamine,
  104; aspirin, 86; barbiturate, 119,
  122, 124; cocaine, 94; coca leaf, 91;
  opiates, 72, 73, 76, 77, 78, 81; seda-
  tives, 129; tea, coffee, 155
Depression, 7, 29, 72, 101, 104, 110,
  112, 115, 117
de Quincey, Thomas, 4, 65, 66
Dexamphetamine, 102
Dexedrine, 101
Diacetylmorphine (heroin), 67
Dihydromorphinone (Dilaudid), 67
Dioscorides, 63, 64, 85, 128
Diphenhydramine and Methaqualone
  (Melsedin), 129
Distillation of alcohol, 24, 27, 172–4;
  cannabis, 48
Doors of Perception (Huxley), 5
Drinamyl, 101
Drinking and Driving Laws 1968, U.S.,
  37
'Drug', definitions of, 5
Drug Abuse Control Amendments
  (1965), 14, 102, 111, 123, 126, 139
Drug Abuse: Escape to Nowhere, 17,
  82
Drug Addiction, 82
Drugs (Prevention of Misuse) Act
  1964, 13, 102, 111, 139, 180
Drugs, tables of main, 190–5
Durophet, 101, 102

East India Company, 148
Ecgonine, 179
Ecuador, 91
Education, 2, 19, 20, 29, 33, 79, 146,
  158
Effects, of alcohol, 29–33; amphetamines, 103, 104–5; anti-depressants,
  110; aspirin, 85; atropine, 127–8;
  barbiturates, 119–25; cannabis, 50-
  55; caffeine, 152–3; cocaine, 93;
  hallucinogens, 134–9; main drugs,
  Appendix D, 191–2; nicotine, 144;
  opiates, 71–7; tranquillizers, 115–18
Ellis, Havelock, 134

Embolism, 70
Embryotoxicity, 86, 137
Emphysema, 145
Engels, Friedrich, 148
Enzymes, 32, 76, 172
Ephadrine, 180
Epinephrine, 184
Ergot alkaloids, 132; fungus (*Clavi-
  ceps purpurea*), 131
Ergotism, 131, 132
Erythroxylaceae, 88
Ethanol, 33, 172–4
Ethyl alcohol (ethanol) 23; *see also*
  Alcohol
Euphoria, 1, 7, 96
Eysenck, H. J., 104

Fermentation, products of, 22–40, 172;
  second, 24
Flight, delusion of, with LSD, 139
Fluoride, in tea, 154
Food and Drugs Acts, 25, 126
France, alcoholism in, 33; legislation
  in, 14
Freedman, A. M., 78
Freud, Sigmund, 90, 114

Ganja, 45, 49
Gas chromatography, 174, 176, 186–7
Gauthier, Théophile, 44
Gayer Test, 51
Generation gap, 56
Geneva Single Convention 1961, U.N.,
  59, 67, 100, 139,
'Glue-sniffing', 17, 157–8
'Goofballs', 119
Government income, from alcohol, 24;
  from tobacco, 147

Habituation, 1, 10
Hachachins, Le Club des, 44
Hallucinogenic agents, 31; properties,
  183
Hallucinogens, 17, 118, 129, 130–40,
  182–5; effects, 134–9; law and, 139;
  misuse, 138; toxicity, 136
Hard drugs, 8, 10, 19, 20
Harrison Act (1914), 14, 92
Hashashi, 42–4
Hasheesh Eater, 45
Hashish, 11, 42–5, 46, 49
Heaven and Hell (Huxley), 5, 134
Hellebore (*Helleborus niger*), 128

Helleborus niger (Christmas rose), 128
Hemlock, 128
Hemming, James, 5
Hemp fibres, 47; plant, 49; resins, 41–62
Henbane (*Hyoscyamus niger*), 127
Heroin, 10, 16, 17, 18, 67, 69, 71, 177; addicts, 73, 80; barbiturates and, 119
Hexabarbitone, 120
Hofmann, Albert, 130, 132
Homeostasis (biological balance), destruction by opiate of, 76
Humulus lupulus (hop), 47
Huxley, Aldous, 5, 134, 138
Hydrazine derivatives, 109; effects of, 110
Hyoscine (Scopolamine), 127
Hyoscyamus niger (henbane), 127
Hypertension, pargyline and, 110
Hypnotics, 118, 129

Ilex paraguayensis (maté), 149
Imipramine (Tofranile), 109, 110
Incense, 157
India, cannabis in, 14
Inhalant, amphetamine as an, 101
Inhalation of cannabis, 49–50; tobacco, 142
Inhibitors of monoamine oxidase (MAO inhibitors), 109, 110
Injections, amphetamine, 103, 105; barbiturate, 121; cocaine, 93, 96; opiate, 69
Intoxication, 10, 30, 34, 37–8; barbiturate, 121, 124–5, bromide, 129; cannabis, 54; opiate, 75; tobacco, 145
Ipomoea tricolor (morning glory) seeds, 132
Israel, use of pentobarbital, 124

Japan, abuse of heroin, 84; addiction control in, 14; amphetamine control in, 106
Joss sticks, 156
Junkie (W. Burroughs), 70

Kefir, 24
Khat, 99, 107–9
Kif, 45–6
Kola nut, 149
Koller, Carl, 90

Kramer, Heinrich, 128
Krebs, 31
Kumiss, 24

Lager, 25, 29
La Guardia Committee report, 47, 51, 52
Laudanum, 64, 66, 67
Laurie, Peter, 39, 76, 79, 104
Law, 11; act committed under influence of drug in, 139
Laws controlling drugs and alcohol, 12–15, 18, 20, 25, 26, 27, 34–5, 82–84, 92, 102, 105–6, 111
Leary, Timothy, 134
Legal aspects, of barbiturates, 125–6; controls of main drugs, Appendix D, 191–2; position of hallucinogens, 139; amphetamine control, 106; cannabis, 48
Legislation, 2, 11–14, 34–7, 123–4, 146–7
Lignocaine, 94
Li-po (701–62), Chinese poet, 24
Liqueurs, 27–8
Liver damage, 70; disease (cirrhosis), 30, 31, 38
Lobelia inflata ('Indian' tobacco plant), 147
Lobeline, 147
Lophophora williamsii (Mexican cactus), 130
LSD–25 (d-lysergic acid diethylamide, delyside), 17, 139–40, 183, 184; effects, 134–9; psychoses, 138; syndrome, 139
Ludlow, Fitz Hugh, *The Hasheesh Eater*, 45
Luminal, 120
Lung cancer, cigarettes and, 145, 146
Lysergamide, 132
Lysergic acid diethylamide (LSD), 130–40
Lysergide, 183

Maconha, 46
Mafia, 13, 16
Magic, drugs in, 127, 133
Majoom or *majun* sweetmeats, 46, 49
Malleus Maleficarum (*Hammer of Witchcraft*), 128
Mandragora officinarum (European mandrake), 127

Manninger, Karl, 39
MAO (monoamine oxidase) inhibitors, 109, 110, 180, 183
Marco Polo, 44
Marijuana (marihuana), 3, 11, 42, 47, 49, 50, 55, 58; Tax Act 1937, 14
Maté, 149
Mead, 24
Medicine, uses of opium in, 66, 67–68
Medulla, 128
Mental disorder, 114, 115, 118, 138; stimulants, 99–111
Mentally sick, drugs for, 112–18
Mescaline, 130, 134, 135, 183
Methanol (methyl alcohol), 32–3, 172–174
Methedrine (methylamphetamine), 102
'Meths' drinkers, 32–3
Methyl alcohol, 32–3
Methylamphetamine (Methedrine), 102
Methyl-benzoyl-ecgonine (cocaine), 179
Methyldihydromorphinone (metopon) 67
Mexican cactus (*Lophophora williamsii*), 130, 133
Mexico, peyote in, 133
Misuse, alcohol, 33–7; amphetamine, 104–6; anti-depressant, 110–11; barbiturate, 121–2; cocaine, 95–7; of Drug Act 1964, 106; hallucinogen, 138; xanthine, 154
Moraceae, 25, 47
Morning glory (*Ipomoea tricolor*) seeds, 132
Morphine, 10, 67, 72, 74, 80, 177; addict, 80; morphine-cocainism, 92; substitute, 68
Motorist, and alcohol, 34–7
Murray, Margaret, 128
Myristica fragans (nutmeg or mace), 156
Myristicin, 156
Mystical experience, under LSD, 134

Nalorphine, 77
Narceine, 177
Narcolepsy, 100, 103
Narcotic Addict Rehabilitation Act 1966, US, 20, 82

Narcotics, 10, 12, 14, 73–4, 77, 177; Anonymous, 20, 84
Narcotine, 177
Nembutal, 120
Nervous system, 1, 53; *see also* Central and Autonomic nervous system
New York Academy of Sciences, 58
Nicotiana tabacum (tobacco), 142
Nicotine, 143, 144
Nightshade family (*Solonaceae*), 127
Noradrenaline, 7, 75, 117, 184
Norepinephrine, 184
Nutmeg, 156

Old Man of the Mountains, 43–4
Oleoresin, 156
Opiate antagonist, 77, 81; dependant, 78, 79
Opiates, 17, 20, 63–84, 176–9; effects, 71–7; legal aspect, 82–4, treatment, 79–84
Opium, 10, 63–84, 176–9; origin, 63–9; consumption, 69–71; import into China, 67
Orepinephrine, 117
Oxytocic activity, 132

Pain-killers, 63, 85–7
Pain-killing (analgesic) action of opiates, 67, 75
Papaverine, 68, 177
Papaver somniferum (poppy), 63
Paracelsus, 23, 64
Paradis artificiels (Baudelaire), 4
Paraguayan tea (maté), 149
Paraldehyde, 129
Paregoric, 67, 73
Pargyline, 109; effects of, 110
Paton, W. D. M., 59
Pentobarbital, 124
Pentobarbitone (Nembutal), 120
Pentothal, 121
Pepper (*Piper nigrum*), 156, 157
Personality, 77, 81, 114; of addict, 78; change in, 17, 136; drugs and, 53, 104
Pethidine, 68–9
Petroleum vapour, 157
Peyote, 133
Pharmacotherapeutic agents, 6
Phenacetin, 85, 87
Phencyclidine, 184
Phenobarbitone, 119, 120, 121

Phenothiazines, 114, 116–17
Phenylethylamines, 183
Piperidine derivatives, 68
Piperine, 156
Piper betle (pepper), 157; *P. nigrum*, 156
Poisons Schedule, 111, 125
Pomet, *Compleat History of Druggs*, 65, 152
Pregnancy, salicylates and, 86
Procaine, 94
Proof spirit, 25, 27, 28, 173
'Psychedelic' churches, 133; effects, 132
Psychoactive drugs, 140
Psychoanaleptics, 99
Psycho-chemistry, of the brain, 140
Psycholeptics, 118
Psychopharmacology, 115–16, 180–1
Psychosis, drug-induced, 54, 101, 105, 112, 117, 125, 135, 138
Psychotic episodes, due to barbiturates, 124
Psychotomimetics, 133, 137, 184; *see also* hallucinogens
Psychotropic drugs, 50, 99
Purine group, barbituric series and, 152
'Purple hearts', 17, 101, 102
Pushers, 15, 16, 61, 70, 71, 102

Quinalbarbitone (Seconal), 120

Rauwolf, Leonhard, 113
Rauwolfia, 110; alkaloids, 117; *R. serpentina*, 113–14
Receptors, drug, 76
'Reefers', 47
Rehabilitation, 20, 38, 81, 125
Relapse, rate of, 106
Renaissance group, 20
Reserpine, 113–14, 117, 118, 181
Resin, cannabis, 47, 48
Respiration, effect of opiates on, 72
Respiratory organs, smoking and, 145
Rivea corymbosa (bindweed), 132
RNA (ribonucleic acid) of brain, 138
Road Safety Act 1967, 34
Rollestone Report, 12
Royal Society of Medicine, 123
Rum, 24, 27, 28
Rye, 24, 131

St Anthony's fire (ergotism), 131–2
Sake, 24
Salicin, 85
Salicylic acid, 85
Scopolamine, 127, 128
Seconal, 120
Sedatives, 85–7, 112–29
Self-help, for addicts, 20; -injection by animals,77; -medication, 85
Sepsis, among opiate dependants, 70
Serotonin, 117, 183
Shen-nung, Emperor of China, on hemp, 42
Simpson, Tommy, 102
Single Convention 1961, Geneva, 12, 59, 67, 100, 139
Slimming, amphetamine and, 101, 105
Smoking cannabis mixture (marijuana), 46, 49; opium, 81; tobacco, 141–7
Snuff, 142
Snuffing, cocaine crystals, 92, 93–4
Solonaceae, 127
Solvents, leading to 'glue-sniffing', 157–8
Soneryl, 120
Spirits, 24, 27
Sprenger, Jacobus, 128
Spring Grove State Hospital, Baltimore, Maryland, 135
Sterculiaceae, 151
Stimulants, alcohol, 29; amphetamine, 105, 110; coffee and tea, 152–3
Stimulators of mental vigour (amphetamines), 99–102
Stoll, A., 132
Suicide, barbiturates and, 118; in compulsive drinkers, 39–40
Sympathomimetic amines, 101, 103
Symptomatic drugs, 6
Synhexyl, 54

Tannin, 149, 154
Tea, 141, 147–9, 152–3; plant (*Camellia sinensis*), 148–9
Tetrahydrocannabinols, 48, 175
Thailand, opium problems, 83
Thalamus and pain, 76
Thebaine, 177
Theobroma cacao (cocoa plant), 151
Theobromine, 152
Theophylline, 149, 152, 153–4

Therapeutic attitudes, 82–3; use of barbiturates, 123, cannabis, 54; Substances Act, 111

Thiopentone, 120

Thorn-apple (*Datuna stramonium*), 127

Times, The, 57

Tobacco, 52, 142–7; curing, 142–3

Tolerance, 8, 54, 75, 76, 77, 97, 105, 112, 124, 138; curve, 70; definition of, 10

Toxicity, 29, 73, 75, 76, 92, 104–5, 125

Traffickers, 3, 13, 79; *see also* Pushers

Trafficking, in cannabis, 61

Tranquillizers, 17, 112–18

Tranylcypramine, 109, 110, 111

Treatment, alcohol, 37–40; barbiturates, 125; cannabis, 55–6; cocaine, 97–8; dependants, 19; opiate, 79–84; enforced, 20; opiate antagonists, 77; by persuasion, 12

Treatment centres, 13, 20, 81, 82; by persuasion, 12

Truxillo leaf (*E. truxillense*), 88

Tryptamine family, 183

Tuanoco leaf (*E. coca*), 88

Tyramine, 132

United Nations in Bolivia, 91; on Narcotic Drugs, 106; Single Convention, 12, 59, 57, 100, 139; and Interpol 1969, 41

United States, alcoholism, 37–7;

Bureau of Narcotics and Dangerous Drugs, 14; Rehabilitation Act 1966, 20

Urine, alcohol in, 32, 35–6

Urticaceae (nettle family), 25, 47

Veronal (barbitone), 118, 120, 123

Viticulture, by Romans and British, 23

Vitis vinifera, 26

Voluntary treatment, 20

Well-being, sense of (euphoria), 7

Whisky, 24, 28

Willow, 85

Wine, 23, 26–7, 28

Witchcraft, drugs of, 127, 128

Withdrawal, 8, 12, 38, 54, 55, 70, 75, 76, 77, 97, 112, 116, 124, 138

Wootton Report on cannabis, 2, 3, 57, 59, 60, 163

World Health Organization, 10, 22, 38, 84, 100, 105, 106, 109

Xanthine derivatives, 152, 153, 154, 155

Yugoslavia, absence of addiction in, 14

Zinberg, N. E., 56

Zymase, 172